Strive for a 5: Preparing for the AP ®
Microeconomics Examination

Strive for a 5: Preparing for the AP® Microeconomics Examination

to accompany

KRUGMAN'S
ECONOMICS for AP® Second Edition

Margaret Ray and David Anderson

Melanie Fox
University of Louisville

Brian Heggood
Stanton College Preparatory School

BFW/WORTH PUBLISHERS

Strive for a 5: Preparing for the AP® Microeconomics Examination
By Melanie Fox and Brian Heggood to accompany
Krugman's Economics for AP®, Second Edition

AP® is a trademark registered by the College Board®, which was not involved in the production
of, and does not endorse, this product.

ISBN 10: 1-4641-5593-3
ISBN 13: 978-1-4641-5593-2

First Printing

Printed in the United States of America

BFW/Worth Publishers
41 Madison Avenue
New York, NY 10010
highschool.bfwpub.com

CONTENTS

Preface

This book, *Strive for a 5: Preparing for the AP® Microeconomics Examination*, is designed for use with a main textbook: ***Krugman's Economics for AP®*, Second Edition** by Margaret Ray and David Anderson. It is intended to help you evaluate your understanding of the material covered in the textbook, reinforce the key concepts you need to learn, and get you comfortable in applying these concepts to problems, all of which will prepare you to take the AP® Microeconomics exam. This guide is divided into two sections: a study guide section and a test preparation section.

The Study Guide Section

The study guide section is designed for you to use throughout your AP® course. As each module is covered in your class, you can use the study guide to help you identify and learn the economic models, concepts, and terms that are important for your course. After you read the modules in each section, this guide provides practice problems and review questions to help you master the material and verify your understanding before moving on to the next section.

Each **Section** is organized as follows:

Overview: An overview of the section content that provides an orientation to the material covered in the section and modular material.

Featured model/graph: Each section focuses on an important economic model. At the beginning of each section, the economic model developed within the section is identified and described.

Listing of modules: Each section is broken into 4 – 8 modules. This list identifies each of the modules within the section.

Module content: Each section includes a module-by-module presentation of the important content in that section. The module content serves as your guide before you read the corresponding module in the text, while you read the corresponding module in the text, and after you have read the corresponding module in the text.

Before You Tackle the Test: When you have completed all of the modules for a section, this feature allows you to apply your new knowledge.

- **Draw the Featured Graph**: For each section, a framework is provided to help you practice the featured graph.
- **Complete the Exercise**: Each section includes an exercise designed to illustrate how to apply the economic content developed in that section.
- **Problems**: A set of comprehensive practice problems help you learn to apply economic concepts.
- **Review Questions**: A set of multiple-choice questions focus on the key concepts from the text. These questions are designed for quick exam preparation.
- **Answer Key**: Your teacher has access to the answers to all questions within this text and may provide them to you upon request. Because some teachers like to assign portions of the Strive for a 5 guide for a grade, we chose to restrict answer access to instructors only. Answers to all questions and problems in the study guide include thorough explanations, including examples of common student errors. You might be tempted to read questions, and then read the answers to those questions in the Answer Key, or to simply use the Answer Key to check that you got a question correct without considering the explanations. To get the most value out of this, we caution you to pay more attention to the explanation. Knowing *why* an answer is correct is just as important as getting the answer correct. In economics, the reasoning used in coming to conclusions and correctly modeling the problems are as important as coming to an accurate answer, and will enable you to apply that reasoning to other questions.

Each **Module** is organized as follows:

Before You Read the Module – Use this section to gain a basic understanding of module content and learning objectives BEFORE you start to read.

- **Summary**: An opening paragraph provides a brief overview of the Module.
- **Objectives**: This list outlines and describes the material that you should have learned in the Module with a space to check as you master each one.

While You Read the Module – Use this section to actively engage with module content to ensure you understand and remember what you read.

- **Key Terms**: A list of key terms from the module includes room to write definitions.
- **Practice the Model** exercises allow you to get familiar with an important graph and diagram within each module.
- **Questions**: Note any questions that you have as you read the module.

After You Read the Module – Use this section to identify areas where you need to spend more time reading and studying the material in the module.

- **Fill-in-the-Blanks** and **Multiple-Choice Questions** help identify important topics in the module.
- **Helpful Tips** and **Modules Notes** discuss common difficulties with the module material and provide tips for mastering the module content.

The Test Preparation Section

Preparing for the AP® Microeconomics Exam, the test preparation section of this guide, is written by AP® Economics teachers and exam readers with a wealth of experience preparing students to successfully show their mastery of economic principles on the AP® Microeconomics exam. Use this part of this book to help you better understand how the AP® Microeconomics exam is constructed and scored, how best to study for the exam, and how to make sure you convey what you have learned when answering exam questions. It is a good idea to read through the test preparation section early in the course so that you have a solid understanding of what you are preparing for from the start and understand how to best communicate your understanding on the AP® Microeconomics exam.

The study of economics has the potential to alter the way you evaluate and understand the world. I hope that your use of *Strive for a 5: Preparing for the AP® Microeconomics Examination*, Second Edition, will help you in your study of basic microeconomics principles and will provide a jumping-off point for further study in economics.

Melanie Fox

Brian Heggood

Section ① Basic Economic Concepts

Overview

This section provides an introduction to the study of economics. It presents the definition of economics and the difference between the two main branches of the discipline, microeconomics and macroeconomics. In addition, it introduces the business cycle, a major focus of macroeconomics, and three important measures economists use when they study it: unemployment, inflation, and aggregate output. Finally, this section develops the production possibilities curve model and uses it to explain basic economic activity, including trade between countries. Because the study of economics relies heavily on graphical models, an appendix on the use of graphs follows this section.

Economics is a social science, and therefore, like history or geography, it is concerned with the study of people. However, learning the economic way of thinking can be different from learning about other social sciences. Often, how you study math or statistics will be the best approach to studying economics. As you begin your study of economics, keep in mind that you need to adapt your approach to fit the unique nature of the discipline. Blend your approach to learning other social sciences with your approach to learning math or statistics.

Featured Model/Graph: The Production Possibilities Curve

This section presents the first of many economic models in the course, the production possibilities curve, or *PPC*. The *PPC* is a basic macroeconomic model that illustrates the alternative production choices (i.e. possibilities) from which an economy can choose. The model is used to illustrate the basic economic concepts presented in this section, as well as to introduce the use of models in economics.

MODULES IN THIS SECTION

Module 1   **The Study of Economics**

Module 2   **Introduction to Macroeconomics***

Module 3   **The Production Possibilities Curve Model**

Module 4   **Comparative Advantage and Trade**

BEFORE YOU TACKLE THE TEST

Draw the Featured Model

Complete the Exercise

Problems

Review Questions

Note that Module 2 is not part of the required material for the AP® Microeconomics Exam.

MODULE 1 | THE STUDY OF ECONOMICS

BEFORE YOU READ THE MODULE

Summary

This module presents economics as the study of the production, distribution, and consumption of goods and services. It focuses on scarcity and the need to make choices about the production, distribution, and consumption of goods and services, and the resulting importance of opportunity costs. The distinction between positive and normative economics and the two main branches of economics, microeconomics and macroeconomics, are also explained.

Module Objectives

Review these objectives before you read the module. Place a "√" on the line when you can do each of the following:

_____ **Objective #1.** Explain how scarcity and choice are central to the study of economics

_____ **Objective #2.** Discuss the importance of opportunity cost in individual choice and decision making

_____ **Objective #3.** Explain the difference between positive economics and normative economics

_____ **Objective #4.** Identify areas of agreement and disagreement among economists

_____ **Objective #5.** Distinguish between microeconomic concepts and macroeconomic concepts

WHILE YOU READ THE MODULE

Key Terms

Define these key terms as you read the module:

Economics:

Individual choice:

Economy:

Market economy:

Command economy:

Incentives:

Property rights:

Marginal analysis:

Resource:

Land:

Labor:

Capital:

Entrepreneurship:

Scarce:

Opportunity cost:

Microeconomics:

Macroeconomics:

Economic aggregates:

Positive economics:

Normative economics:

Practice the Model

1) Indicate whether each of the following questions is addressed in Microeconomics or Macroeconomics.
   a. How many hours per week will Jack be willing to work at a wage of $12 per hour?

   b. How many workers will be unemployed when aggregate output is $500 billion?

   c. How much will a firm produce if the price of a good is $20?

   d. What will happen to aggregate output if the price level increases?

2) Indicate whether each of the following statements is normative or positive.
   a. Jack should work harder when his wage increases.

   b. Mary produces 20 cakes per week when she can sell them for $30 per cake.

List questions or difficulties from your initial reading of the module.

AFTER YOU READ THE MODULE

Fill-in-the-Blanks

Fill in the blanks to complete the following statements. If you find yourself having difficulties, please refer back to the appropriate section in the text.

- Economics is the study of scarcity and **1)**_____, and at its most basic level every

  economic issue involves decision-making.

- An **2)**_____ is a system that coordinates choices about production and choices

  about consumption. One type of system, called a **3)**_____ economy, places the

  production and consumption decisions into the hands of individual producers and consumers.

- Unlike that decentralized type of economy, a **4)**_____ economy is an alternative system in which industry is publicly owned and a centralized decision-making authority makes production and consumption decisions.

- A key part of these motivations and punishments in a market system are **5)**_____, which establish ownership and grant individuals the right to trade goods and services with each other. When individuals and firms are making decisions such as whether to provide one more hour of work, whether to make one more good to sell, or how to spend one more dollar, they are engaging in **6)**_____ analysis.

- When economists refer to **7)**_____, they mean anything that is used to produce something else, and divide them into four categories. **8)**_____ is the effort of workers used to produce goods, **9)**_____ are goods that are manufactured to make other goods, **10)**_____ are all resources that come from nature, and **11)**_____ refers to the risk taking, innovation, and organization of other resources used in production.

- Economics is divided into two main branches. Microeconomics studies the choices made by **12)**_____ while macroeconomics focuses on data that summarizes measures across many markets, called economic **13)**_____.

- When economic analysis is used to answer questions about the way the world works that have definite right and wrong answers, it is known as **14)**_____ economics. In contrast, economic analysis that involves saying how the world should work is known as **15)**_____economics.

Multiple-Choice Questions

Circle the best choice to answer or complete the following questions or incomplete statements. For additional practice, use the space provided to explain why one or more of the incorrect options do not work.

16. Which of the following is not an economic resource?
   a. land
   b. labor
   c. capital
   d. entrepreneurship
   e. money

17. Which of the following describes opportunity cost?
  a. the price, in dollars, of obtaining an item
  b. the total cost of all of the resources used to produce a good
  c. all monetary costs associated with obtaining a good
  d. all of the nonmonetary costs associated with obtaining a good
  e. all of the monetary and nonmonetary costs of what must be given up to obtain a good

Helpful Tips

- Some people mistakenly think that economics is about money or picking stocks. However, ultimately economics is about choices. The driving forces behind the study of economics are scarcity and choice: because resources are scarce, we must choose how to allocate those resources.

- Positive analysis is stating how things "are." Normative analysis is stating how things "should be." An easy way to keep these straight is to think about social norms, the way you should behave in a given context. Positive analysis is absent of value statements.

- The opportunity cost of one choice is not the cost of all foregone opportunities; it is the cost of the *next best* foregone opportunity. For instance, if I decide to spend an hour babysitting and make $20, when I could have spent the same hour mowing a lawn for $15 or wash windows for $10, the opportunity cost of babysitting is only the value of mowing lawns.

Module Notes

John Maynard Keynes, considered by many to be the father of modern macroeconomics, wrote that "[Economics] is a method rather than a doctrine, an apparatus of the mind, a technique of thinking which helps its possessor to draw correct conclusions." Similarly, the influential microeconomist Alfred Marshall described economics as a study of the "ordinary business of life" and wrote that "[Economics] is not a body of concrete truth, but an engine for the discovery of concrete truth." Each of these important economists was pointing out that economics is a valuable way of thinking about the world rather than just an established body of knowledge.

You will be expected to solve new and varied problems not by providing memorized definitions or explanations, but by using this "technique of thinking." Knowing the definitions and equations are a necessary first step, but this is not sufficient to demonstrate that you can use this "technique of thinking."

Use the Problems and Review Questions in your textbook to determine if you have learned what you need to know. At the beginning, try all of the sample questions, problems, and approaches that you and your instructor can find, and determine which ones work best to help you master the material. Keep the following in mind as you continue:

- The study of economics is cumulative. You should master each topic as it is presented since later topics build on earlier topics.

- Pay attention to new vocabulary and make sure you know, understand, and can apply these terms. You will be expected to do more than just define the terms: you must also be able to indicate through your work an ability to apply these terms in a meaningful manner.

- Plan to spend time every day studying economics. Review your lecture notes, review the vocabulary, work on the practice questions, and identify questions you have about the material. Once you identify your questions, seek out answers by returning to your text, your lecture notes, your classmates, or your teacher. If you find you have made a mistake, focus on discovering the error in reasoning that led to that mistake, rather than simply memorizing the correct answer.

MODULE ⟨2⟩ INTRODUCTION TO MACROECONOMICS*

BEFORE YOU READ THE MODULE

Summary

This module introduces the business cycle in an economy. It also presents three important related macroeconomic concepts: unemployment, inflation, and economic growth. Measures of employment, the price level, and aggregate output are used to evaluate the performance of the macroeconomy. These topics illustrate the major topics studied in macroeconomics, but they are not part of the AP® Microeconomics course outline.

Module Objectives

Review these objectives before you read the module. Place a "√" on the line when you can do each of the following:

_____Objective #1.   Explain what a business cycle is and why policy makers seek to diminish the severity of business cycles

_____Objective #2.   Describe how employment and unemployment are measured and how they change over the business cycle

_____Objective #3.   Define aggregate output and explain how it changes over the business cycle

_____Objective #4.   Define inflation and deflation and explain why price stability is preferred

_____Objective #5.   Explain how economic growth determines a country's standard of living

_____Objective #6.   Summarize the crucial role of models--simplified representations of reality--in economics

Note that Module 2 is not part of the required material for the AP® Microeceonomics Exam.

WHILE YOU READ THE MODULE

Key Terms

Define these key terms as you read the module:

Business cycle:

Depression:

Recessions:

Expansions:

Employment:

Unemployment:

Labor force:

Unemployment rate:

Output:

Aggregate output:

Inflation:

Deflation:

Price stability:

Economic growth:

Model:

Other things equal assumption (*ceteris paribus*):

Practice the Model

Figure 2.1 in the text shows the unemployment rate and the timing of business cycles between 1989 and 2013. For each of the time frames below, indicate what was happening to Unemployment and GDP. The first one has been done for you.

Time Period	Unemployment and GDP
1989 - 1992	Unemployment was increasing; therefore, GDP was decreasing.
1992 - 2000	
2001 - 2004	
2005 - 2007	
2008 - 2010	
2011 - 2013	

List questions or difficulties from your initial reading of the module:

AFTER YOU READ THE MODULE

Fill-in-the-Blanks

Fill in the blanks to complete the following statements. If you find yourself having difficulties, please refer back to the appropriate section in the text.

- The upturns and downturns in the macroeconomy are known as the **1)**_____.

  Economic downturns are known as **2)**_____, and economic upturns are known as

  3)_____. During an economic downturn, employment and aggregate output both

  4)_____, while unemployment **5)**_____.

Multiple-Choice Questions

Circle the best choice to answer or complete the following questions or incomplete statements. For additional practice, use the space provided to explain why one or more of the incorrect options do not work.

6. Unemployment is best described as
   a. a rise in the overall price level.
   b. the total number of people who are not currently employed.
   c. the total number of people who are not currently employed but are actively looking for work.
   d. the labor force plus the total number of people looking for pay.
   e. what is experienced by anyone who is looking for a job.

7. Economists believe that which of the following is a desirable goal for an economy?
   a. deflation
   b. inflation
   c. depressions
   d. price stability
   e. recessions

Helpful Tips

- Inflation is undesirable, but that does not mean that its opposite, deflation, is desirable either. Both have negative consequences for the economy.

- Not all economic downturns are recessions. The term recession is generally reserved for a downturn that lasts two quarters (or six months) or more.

- Not all economic expansions (or recoveries) are economic growth. Economic expansions may be temporary, but economic growth is a permanent increase in the amount of goods and services that can be produced. Economic growth can only occur when there is an increase in one or more of the four economic resources.

- Aggregation of data is at the heart of macroeconomics. This module briefly describes the meaning of aggregation and gives examples of aggregated measures like employment, real GDP, and the overall price level.

Module Notes

A model is a simplified representation of reality used to better understand the world. An important part of economics is working with models. Very often, economic models use graphs to simplify reality and facilitate understanding. Graphs can make it much easier to understand verbal descriptions, numerical information, or ideas. To understand economics, you must learn how to interpret and manipulate graphs. A picture may be worth a thousand words, but a graph is even more valuable. Graphs are used not just to depict something, but they can be used to predict what might happen as well.

As you study economics, make sure that you are able to not only read and understand the graphs that you see, but also that you are able to construct and explain graphs on your own. The ability to represent an economic idea using a graph is different than the ability to look at and understand an existing graph and you should be able to do both. The appendix to this section explains how graphs are constructed and interpreted and how they are used in economics. The appendix, and lots of practice drawing graphs, will help you to master the material.

Graphs are a way of describing the relationship between two variables (in other words, two things that might vary with each other). For instance, how does the quantity people buy vary with the price that they pay, how does aggregate output vary over time, etc.? Each of the variables being compared will be one of the two axes on a graph.

To get used to the idea of drawing graphs in economics, begin by drawing your own graph of the business cycle. You can use the one in this module as a guide to the labels and information you will need on your graph. Labeling your graph is critical: without labels, nobody else reading your graph can tell what you are trying to show.

Many of the models you will encounter in this course make the other things equal assumption (also known as *ceteris paribus*), which means that the model considers only one change at a time while holding everything else constant. Make sure you understand this basic assumption before working with the models introduced in the module.

MODULE 3 THE PRODUCTION POSSIBILITIES CURVE MODEL

BEFORE YOU READ THE MODULE

Summary

This module introduces the concept of model building by presenting the production possibility curve model. The *PPC* provides a simplified framework for discussing the concept of opportunity cost, trade-offs, scarcity, efficiency, and (in the next module) gains from trade.

Module Objectives

Review these objectives before you read the module. Place a "√" on the line when you can do each of the following:

_____**Objective #1.** Explain the importance of tradeoffs in economic analysis

_____**Objective #2.** Describe what a production possibilities curve model tells us about efficiency, opportunity cost, and economic growth

_____**Objective #3.** Explain why increases in the availability of resources and improvements in technology are the two sources of economic growth

WHILE YOU READ THE MODULE

Key Terms

Define these key terms as you read the module:

Trade-off:

Production possibilities curve:

Efficient:

Productive efficiency:

Allocative efficiency:

Technology:

Practice the Model

Consider an economy that can produce two goods, A and B. In the space below, sketch a correctly labeled graph of a bowed-out production possibilities curve with A on the vertical axis and B on the horizontal axis.

List questions or difficulties from your initial reading of the module:

AFTER YOU READ THE MODULE

Fill-in-the-Blanks

Fill in the blanks to complete the following statements. If you find yourself having difficulties, please refer back to the appropriate section in the text.

- A production possibilities curve (*PPC*) shows the **1)**_____ between the

    production of two goods. If a production point lies on this curve, it is feasible and

    2)_____. If a production point lies inside this curve, it is feasible, but

    3)_____, which means there are missed opportunities from producing at that

    point. If a production point lies **4)**_____ this curve, it is not feasible.

- Producing more of one good means less of the other good can be produced, which is why a

    PPC has a **5)**_____ slope. Therefore, a movement from one point on the *PPC* to

    another point on the same *PPC* illustrates the concept of **6)**_____cost.

Multiple-Choice Questions

Circle the best choice to answer or complete the following questions or incomplete statements. For additional practice, use the space provided to explain why one or more of the incorrect options do not work.

Questions 7 and 8 refer to the following graph:

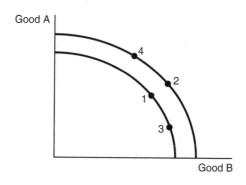

7. If an economy moves from ___ to ___ , it is experiencing economic growth.
   a. 1 to 3
   b. 1 to 4
   c. 4 to 2
   d. 1 to 3
   e. 2 to 4

8. Refer to the graph above. Which of the following could produce a movement from 1 to 3?
   a. an increase in the total amount of capital available
   b. moving some capital that was being used to produce good B to produce good A instead
   c. moving some capital that was being used to produce good A to produce good B instead
   d. an increase in the total amount of labor available
   e. an increase in the technology used to produce good B

Helpful Tips

- A movement along a production possibilities curve is not economic growth. Remember that economic growth occurs when there is more of any of the economic resources. A common error is to mistake being able to produce more of one good as growth. Economic growth means being able to produce more of one of the two goods, without reducing the amount of the other good available.

- Be careful when you calculate opportunity costs. Here is a useful method for calculating opportunity cost based on a linear *PPC*, which will be crucial when determining comparative advantage in the next module. First, construct the *PPC*. Since the *PPC* is linear, calculate the slope (any method to calculate the slope, such as "rise over run," will work to do this). You can then use the slope to find the opportunity cost for both goods. The opportunity cost of producing one more unit of the good on the *x*-axis is the slope. The opportunity cost of producing one more unit of the good on the *y*-axis is the reciprocal of the slope.

- Here is another useful method for calculating opportunity cost based on a linear *PPC*. Suppose Tom has a linear *PPC* and he can produce 30 coconuts (C) if he spends all of his time on coconuts, or 40 fish (F) if he spends all of his time on fish. We could represent these facts using equations:

  30 C = time
  40 F = time
  so, 30C = 40F

  To solve for the opportunity cost of something, solve for *that* letter. For instance, to find the opportunity cost of 1 coconut, solve for C:

  30C = 40 F
  C = 40/30 F
  C = 4/3 F

  Then solve for F to get the opportunity cost of a fish:

  30C = 40 F
  30/40 C = F
  3/4 C = F

  In other words, the opportunity cost of one fish is 3/4 of a coconut and the opportunity cost of one coconut is 4/3 of a fish. Note that this method only works when you have a linear *PPC*: a linear *PPC* implies that there is a constant trade-off (so 1 fish is always worth 3/4 of a coconut). A bowed out *PPC* implies that the trade-off will vary along the curve, so the slope, and therefore the opportunity cost, will be different at different points along the curve.

Module Notes

The production possibilities curve is the first model presented in this book. It is important that you identify what the *PPC* illustrates and how it is used to understand the choices facing any economy. The *PPC* model is a graphical representation of an economy that illustrates trade-offs, scarcity, opportunity cost, efficiency, and economic growth. Notice that each axis represents the *quantity* of a good being produced. For instance, the horizontal axis in the Crusoe example represented the *quantity* of fish, and the vertical axis represented the *quantity* of coconuts. Each point on the production possibility curve shows the amount of coconuts that could be produced when a given amount of fish was produced. For instance, with Crusoe's initial resources and technology, whenever he caught 20 fish, he could also pick 25 coconuts.

You will need to understand how these concepts are illustrated on a *PPC* graph (i.e. movements along the curve, points on the curve, and shifts of the curve). You also need to be able to draw a *PPC* graph and use it to illustrate and explain these concepts. Finally, you will need to understand how these concepts are illustrated on a *PPC* with enough depth to answer questions in examples and contexts that you have not seen before. Achieving this level of understanding requires practice with drawing and interpreting graphs and applying the *PPC* model to different real-world and hypothetical examples. The ability to use economic models to analyze situations and answer questions is an essential part of mastering introductory economics.

Economic models can be described verbally, but they can also be represented by graphs or equations. Another way to think about economic models is that they involve math and/or a graph to tell a story. You will want to be comfortable working with all three types of representations. You may find it helpful to be able to sketch graphs to illustrate the ideas you are analyzing. Even if you are just doing a quick sketch of a graph, it is important that you *always* take the time to correctly label both axes and any curves. Practice making precise graphs using any specific values given, but also practice graphs that sketch the general relationship between variables without numbers. For instance, when graphing a production possibilities curve for two goods that could be produced, include values of each good that can be produced if they are given. If they are not, be able to show a production possibilities curve that shows that there is an opportunity cost to producing more of one of those goods.

Opportunity cost can be measured using the production possibilities curve model. To do this calculation, pick a point on the *PPC* and identify how much of each good is being produced. Then pick a second point on the *PPC* and identify the new levels of production. The opportunity cost is measured as the number of units of the good you must give up to get more of the other good.

Make sure you understand how to interpret the shape of the curves in the *PPC* model. In particular, make sure you can draw and understand what is shown by both a linear and a "bowed out" *PPC*. Know the assumption that leads to a linear or bowed out *PPC*. Make sure you can identify and indicate feasible and infeasible points as well as efficient and inefficient points. Know what two factors can shift the *PPC* out in the future.

MODULE 4 COMPARATIVE ADVANTAGE AND TRADE

BEFORE YOU READ THE MODULE

Summary

This module introduces the concepts of comparative and absolute advantage, and explains the benefits of specialization and trade. It shows how the *PPC* model can be used to illustrate gains from trade based on comparative advantage, and presents the basic economic argument in favor of international trade by showing that total world output can increase when countries specialize and trade.

Module Objectives

Review these objectives before you read the module. Place a "√" on the line when you can do each of the following:

_____Objective #1. Explain how trade leads to gains for an individual or an economy

_____Objective #2. Explain the difference between absolute advantage and comparative advantage

_____Objective #3. Describe how comparative advantage leads to gains from trade in the global marketplace

WHILE YOU READ THE MODULE

Key Terms

Define these key terms as you read the module:

Trade:

Gains from trade:

Specialization:

Comparative advantage:

Absolute advantage:

Terms of trade:

Practice the Model

1) Use the data from the following table to construct correctly labeled side-by-side graphs showing the production possibilities curves for Theo and Marlee. Assume that both have constant opportunity costs.

	Bananas	Rice (in lbs)
Theo	20	30
Marlee	50	50

2) Suppose that Theo and Marlee each spent half of their day making each good; Theo makes 10 bananas and 15 pounds of rice and Marlee makes 25 bananas and 25 pounds of rice. Show this point on the production possibilities curve of each person, and label that point X on your graph above. What is the total production of each good?

3) Suppose that Theo and Marlee agree to exchange 4 bananas for 5 pounds of rice. Under this agreement, Theo sells 15 of his 30 pounds of rice to Marlee, in exchange for 12 of her 50 bananas. Show the new consumption points on the graph above for each person, and label these new consumption points Z.

List questions or difficulties from your initial reading of the module:

Fill-in-the-Blanks

Fill in the blanks to complete the following statements. If you find yourself having difficulties, please refer back to the appropriate section in the text.

- When people divide tasks among themselves and each person provides a good or service that other people want in return for different goods and services that he or she wants, it is called

  1)_____. This is a key to a much better standard of living for everyone because it allows a division of tasks based on what each person is better at producing, called

  2)_____.

- If the opportunity cost of production is lower for one person than it is for other people, then that person has a(n) 3)_____ advantage. If an individual can produce more output with a given amount of input than another person, then that person has a(n)

  4)_____ advantage.

- 5)_____ advantage is the basis for mutual gains from trade. In an example where two people can each produce the same two goods, it is possible for a person to have

  6)_____ advantage in both goods, but it is not possible for a person to have

  7)_____ advantage in both goods.

Multiple-Choice Questions

Circle the best choice to answer or complete the following questions or incomplete statements. For additional practice, use the space provided to explain why one or more of the incorrect options do not work.

Suppose that two countries, Texia and Urbania, produce food and clothing, and currently do not trade. Both countries have linear *PPC*s. If Texia devotes all of its resources to food production, it can produce 1,000 units of food this year and 0 units of clothing. If it devotes all of its resources to clothing production, it can produce 500 units of clothing and 0 units of food. Urbania can produce either 900 units of food and 0 units of clothing or 300 units of clothing and 0 units of food.

8. _____ has the absolute advantage in the production of clothing, and _____ has the absolute advantage in the production of food.
   a. Texia; Texia
   b. Texia; Urbania
   c. Urbania; Texia
   d. Urbania; Urbania
   e. Neither country, neither country

9. _____ has the comparative advantage in the production of clothing, and
   _____ has the comparative advantage in the production of food.
   a. Texia; Texia
   b. Texia; Urbania
   c. Urbania; Texia
   d. Urbania; Urbania
   e. Neither country, neither country

10. Specialization and trade benefit
    a. usually only one of the trading partners.
    b. the wealthier country more than the poorer country.
    c. the poorer country more than the wealthier country.
    d. both countries if they specialize according to their respective comparative advantages.
    e. neither country when one country is better at producing both goods.

Helpful Tips

- Gains from trade come from differences in opportunity cost (and therefore comparative advantage), not absolute advantage.

- It is not possible to have comparative advantage in more than one good.

- A common misperception is that trade will always make one trading partner worse off. Both will be better off with trade than they were without trade as long as there are differences in opportunity costs between the two. It is possible, however, that one country is made better off more than another country is made better off depending on the *terms of trade* (the trading prices), but they will still both be better off than they were before. The only possible other situation is that nobody is made better off, which would only occur when two countries have identical opportunity costs, in which case there would not be any point in trading.

- Gains from trade will occur when the terms of trade are between the opportunity costs for the traders. Recall from the text that Tom and Hank were made better off from trading 10 coconuts for 10 fish, which made the terms of trade 1C = 1F. Tom's opportunity cost for fish was 3/4 of a coconut and Hank's opportunity cost for a fish was 2 coconuts. One coconut is between ¾ coconut and 2 coconuts. *Any* price of fish between 3/4 of a coconut and 2 coconuts results in both Tom and Hank benefitting (for example, 1 F = 1 1/2 C or 1 F = 8/10 C).

Module Notes

Students do it, pundits do it, and politicians do it all the time: they confuse *comparative* advantage with *absolute* advantage. For example, back in the 1980s, when the U.S. economy seemed to be lagging behind that of Japan, commentators warned that if we didn't improve our productivity, we would soon have no comparative advantage in anything. What those commentators meant was that we would have no *absolute* advantage in anything—that there might come a time when the Japanese were better at producing everything than we were. And they had the idea that if that were to happen, Japan would no longer be able to benefit from trade with the United States. But just as Hank is able to benefit from trade with Tom (and vice versa) despite the fact that Tom is better at everything, nations can still gain from trade even if they are less productive in all industries than the countries they trade with.

Once you can calculate the opportunity cost of producing good X or good Y, as explained in the previous module, you can compare the opportunity costs faced by two countries. The model of comparative advantage illustrates that countries will benefit from trade when they specialize and produce the good that has the lowest opportunity cost of production relative to the other country. More simply: the country with the lower opportunity cost of a good has comparative advantage in that good.

BEFORE YOU TACKLE THE TEST: SECTION (1)

Draw The Featured Graph: Production Possibilities Curve

1) The following table gives the amount of two goods that a single person can produce in a single week. Graph the *PPC* corresponding to the data provided in the table.

Fish	Coconuts
0	8
2	6
4	4
6	2
8	0

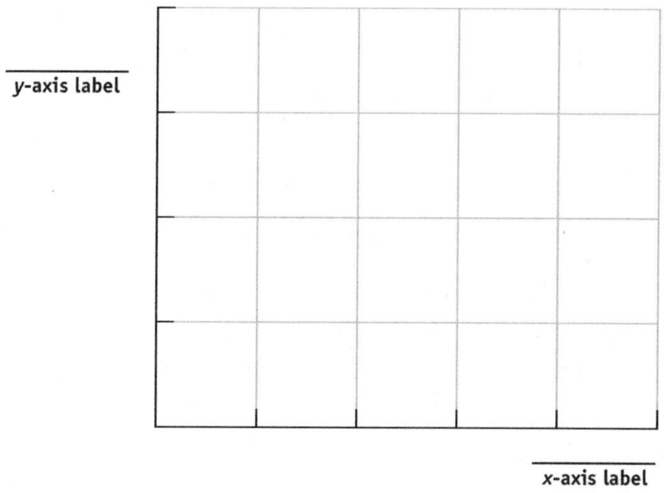

y-axis label
x-axis label

2) Using the graph you created above, give an equation that represents the amount of fish and coconuts that this person can produce in a single day, and then solve for the opportunity cost of each good.

3) Graph a *PPC* showing the trade-off between two goods, good A and good B. Draw your *PPC* so that it illustrates increasing opportunity costs.

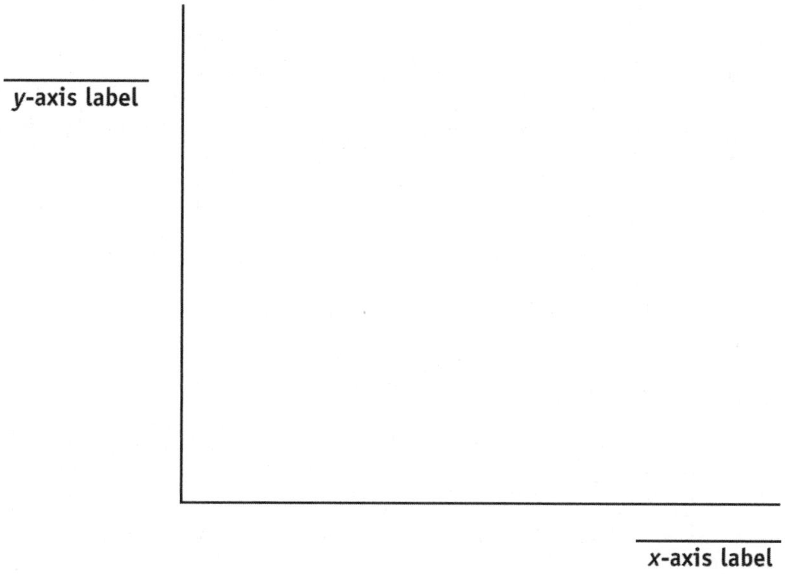

y-axis label
x-axis label

Complete the Exercise

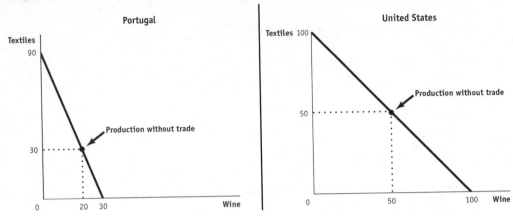

Use the information on the preceding graphs to fill in the blanks.

1) The opportunity cost of 1 unit of textiles in the United States is _____ and in

   Portugal is _____.

2) The opportunity cost of 1 unit of wine in the United States is _____ and in

   Portugal is _____.

3) Assuming the two countries have identical resources, the United States has an absolute

   advantage in_____. Portugal has an absolute advantage in _____.

4) The United States has a comparative advantage in _____. Portugal has a

   comparative advantage in _____.

Fill in the following table. Assume that with trade, each country specializes and exports ½ of its production.

	Without Trade		With Trade (Production)		With Trade (consumption)	
	Wine	Textiles	Wine	Textiles	Wine	Textiles
Portugal						
United States						
Total						

5) What is the trading price of 1 unit of wine when countries specialize and trade under these
   terms?

6) What happens to total world output when the countries specialize and trade?

7) What is this called?

8) Are both of the countries better off? Explain.

Problems

1. For each of the following situations, describe the opportunity cost of each decision.
   a. Sarah considers two options for Saturday night: she can attend a concert that costs $10 per ticket or she can see a free movie. She attends the concert.

   b. A new firm in town must decide between paying $20,000 for a prime location versus $12,000 for another less desirable location. The firm estimates that it will eventually serve the same number of customers in either location, but that it will take six months before the less desirable location provides the same number of customers as the prime location. The firm decides to purchase the $12,000 property.

   c. Jamie can either be an unpaid intern at a company or he can earn $2,000 working as a camp counselor. He takes the internship.

2. The following table presents the possible combinations of study time available to Roberto this week as he prepares for his two midterms: economics and chemistry. Assume Roberto has 20 hours to study and that he will use all 20 hours studying economics and chemistry. Roberto currently plans to study 10 hours for economics and 10 hours for chemistry.

Hours of study time spent on economics	Hours of study time spent on chemistry	Grade in economics	Grade in chemistry
0	20	60	90
5	15	70	85
10	10	80	75
15	5	86	73
20	0	90	70

   a. If he changes his plan and studies 15 hours for economics, what is his opportunity cost?

b. If he changes his plan and studies 15 hours for chemistry, what is his opportunity cost?

c. If he changes his plan and studies 20 hours for economics, what is his opportunity cost?

3. Decide whether each of the following statements is a normative statement or a positive statement. Explain.
   a. The gasoline tax is projected to yield $10 million in tax revenue next year.

   b. If the gasoline tax was raised by 10 cents per gallon, tax revenue would increase by 4%.

   c. The state should raise the gasoline tax for the coming year. An increase in the tax will reduce congestion and smog, which is more important than the cost to commuters if they shift from private car transportation to public transportation.

4. Economists sometimes disagree about positive economics, but more often they disagree about normative economics. Define each of these terms, and explain why economists do not always agree.

5. This section distinguishes between microeconomics and macroeconomics. What is the difference between microeconomics and macroeconomics?

6. Pam can produce a meal with one unit of labor or a load of laundry with two units of labor. Assume that Pam has constant opportunity costs.
   a. Sketch the *PPC* for Pam. (Hint: choose a relevant time period, e.g. 12 hours, as your labor constraint, and sketch your *PPC* based on this amount of time and labor.) Graph meals on the horizontal axis and laundry on the vertical axis.

   b. What is the slope of your *PPC*?

c. What is Pam's opportunity cost of producing an additional meal?

d. What is Pam's opportunity cost of producing an additional load of laundry?

7. The country of Jonesville produces two goods from its available resources and technology. The only resource that Jonesville has is labor. It takes 2 hours of labor to produce a gadget and 5 hours of labor to produce a widget. For this question assume that the *PPC* for Jonesville is linear.

    a. Suppose that you want to draw a *PPC* for Jonesville. What must you do first?

    b. Sketch the *PPC* for Jonesville assuming that it has 120 hours of labor available. Place gadgets on the *x*-axis and widgets on the *y*-axis.

    c. What is the slope of the *PPC*?

    d. What is the opportunity cost of producing an additional gadget?

    e. What is the opportunity cost of producing an additional widget?

    f. Suppose that Jonesville has 240 hours of labor instead of 120 hours of labor. Does this affect the opportunity cost of producing widgets or gadgets? Explain your answer.

8. The following table provides six possible production combinations that Smithtown can produce from its available resources and technology during this year. Assume that Smithtown only produces bicycles and tents from its available resources.

Combination	Bicycles	Tents
A	100	0
B	90	10
C	70	25
D	40	36
E	10	42
F	0	44

a. Sketch Smithtown's *PPC*. Measure bicycles along the *x*-axis and tents along the *y*-axis.

b. Suppose Smithtown is currently producing at combination *C*. If Smithtown chooses to produce at combination *B*, what is the opportunity cost of moving from combination *C* to *B*?

c. Suppose Smithtown is currently producing at combination *C*. If Smithtown chooses to produce at combination *D*, what is the opportunity cost of moving from combination *C* to *D*?

d. Smithtown's *PPC* is not linear. Explain why not.

10. There are two islands in the middle of the ocean, and these two islands produce fish and baskets. Big Island can produce either 100 fish and 0 baskets per day or 0 fish and 200 baskets per day. Big Island can also produce any combination of fish and baskets that lies on its linear *PPC*. Small Island can produce either 80 fish and 0 baskets per day or 0 fish and 80 baskets per day. Like Big Island, Small Island has a linear *PPC*.
a. Sketch two graphs. Sketch Big Island's *PPC* on the first graph and Small Island's *PPC* on the second graph. Place fish/day on the *y*-axis and baskets/day on the *x*-axis.

b. What is the slope of Big Island's *PPC*?

c. What is the slope of Small Island's *PPC*?

d. Express the production of Big Island as an equation. Solve for the opportunity cost of baskets, and then solve for the opportunity cost of fish. Then describe the opportunity cost for each.

e. Express the production of Small Island as an equation. Solve for the opportunity cost of baskets, and then solve for the opportunity cost of fish.

f. Which island can produce baskets at lower opportunity cost?

g. Which island can produce fish at lower opportunity cost?

h. What good should Big Island specialize in producing? Explain.

i. What good should Small Island specialize in producing?

Review Questions

Circle your answer to the following questions.

1. Scarcity of resources implies that
  a. people can do whatever they want and do not need to worry about making choices.
  b. life involves making choices about how to best use scarce resources.
  c. societies should invest time and money to discover more resources.
  d. only very wealthy individuals are not constrained by limited resources.
  e. only some resources are finite.

2. Jenny must choose between 4 different projects. Project 1 will earn her a profit of $20,000. Project 2 will earn her a profit of $30,000. Project 3 will earn her a profit of $40,000. And project 4 will earn her a profit of $55,000. What is her opportunity cost if Jenny chooses project 3?
  a. $55,000
  b. $40,000
  c. $30,000
  d. $50,000
  e. $105,000

3. Which of the following describes positive economics?
  a. It is descriptive.
  b. It is prescriptive.
  c. It is the way the world should work.
  d. It is subjective.
  e. It is value oriented.

4. Which of the following statements is an example of normative economics?
  a. United States should pass a value-added tax, since this is a tax that will work best.
  b. A value-added tax will add $10 billion to the administrative costs of the U.S. tax system.
  c. It can be demonstrated that value-added taxes increase the tax burden on less wealthy households.
  d. A value-added tax would generate $200 billion in revenue each year.
  e. Several other countries have value-added tax systems.

5. Microeconomics, unlike macroeconomics, focuses on
   a. the behavior of individual firms and markets.
   b. the production and consumption of all goods in an economy.
   c. the overall level of prices, rather than individual market prices.
   d. policies that will promote growth in the economy.
   e. the employment level in an economy.

6. Economic growth
   a. refers to increases in real GDP per capita over the long run.
   b. refers to short-term fluctuations in real GDP per capita.
   c. is best measured using the employment rate.
   d. is of little importance to economists.
   e. is best measured using inflation rates.

7. In a two country, two good model, which of the following statements is true?
   a. Two countries can have absolute advantage in the production of both goods.
   b. Two countries can have comparative advantage in the production of both goods.
   c. A country must have comparative advantage in one good and absolute advantage in the other.
   d. If a country has comparative advantage in a good, it must also have absolute advantage in that good.
   e. A country cannot have comparative advantage in both goods.

8. Inflation means that
   a. the aggregate level of output increases.
   b. the unemployment rate increases.
   c. the aggregate price level rises over time.
   d. consumers' purchasing power increases over time.
   e. workforce participation increases.

9. A recession is best described as
   a. a decrease in the price level.
   b. a decrease in unemployment.
   c. any decrease in output.
   d. a decrease in output that is at least 6 months long.
   e. an increase in output that is at least 1 year long.

10. Which of the following questions is answered with marginal analysis?
   a. What is the cost per unit for a firm to produce its good?
   b. How much profit will a firm earn?
   c. How much profit will a firm earn from selling one more unit of a good?
   d. How much does it cost a seller to produce its product?
   e. What is the cost per unit for a firm to produce its good?

11. Suppose Mike has a linear *PPC* in the production of potatoes and tomatoes. If Mike devotes all his time to the production of potatoes, he can produce 1,000 pounds of potatoes a year; if he devotes all his time to the production of tomatoes, he can produce 2,000 pounds of tomatoes a year. Which of the following combinations of potatoes and tomatoes are feasible for Mike in a year?
   a. 1,000 pounds of potatoes and 2,000 pounds of tomatoes
   b. 1,000 pounds of potatoes and 0 pounds of tomatoes
   c. 0 pounds of potatoes and 2,000 pounds of tomatoes
   d. 500 pounds of potatoes and 1,200 pounds of tomatoes
   e. 500 pounds of potatoes and 1,000 pounds of tomatoes

12. Utopia has a linear *PPC* in the production of widgets and gadgets. It can produce three gadgets per hour of labor time or four widgets per hour of labor time. What is the opportunity cost of producing one widget in Utopia?
  a. 3 gadgets
  b. 4 widgets
  c. 0.75 gadget
  d. 1.33 gadgets
  e. 1 gadget

Refer to the following scenario to answer questions 13 through 16:

Jonesville produces widgets and gadgets, and its *PPC* is linear. It takes 5 hours of labor to produce a gadget and 10 hours of labor to produce a widget.

13. Suppose that Jonesville has 100 hours of labor. What is the maximum number of widgets it can produce?
  a. 10 widgets
  b. 20 widgets
  c. 1 widget
  d. 100 widgets
  e. 50 widgets

14. How many widgets and gadgets can Jonesville produce if it devotes half of its labor time to the production of gadgets and half of its labor time to the production of widgets?
  a. 20 gadgets and 5 widgets
  b. 10 gadgets and 5 widgets
  c. 5 gadgets and 20 widgets
  d. 5 gadgets and 10 widgets
  e. 5 widgets and 10 gadgets

15. What happens to the opportunity cost of producing widgets and gadgets if Jonesville's labor resource increases to 200 hours?

Widgets	*Gadgets*
a. decreases	increases
b. increases	decreases
c. does not change	does not change
d. depends on the number produced	depends on the number produced
e. increase	does not change

16. If Jonesville has 100 units of labor, which of the following combinations of gadgets and widgets is both feasible and efficient for Jonesville?
  a. 4 gadgets and 18 widgets
  b. 7 gadgets and 0 widgets
  c. 8 gadgets and 6 widgets
  d. 2 gadgets and 10 widgets
  e. 8 gadgets and 1 widget

Refer to the following scenario to answer questions 17 and 18:

Suburbia has a *PPC* bowed out from the origin for two goods, guns and butter, that Suburbia produces from its available resources and technology. The following table describes six points that lie on Suburbia's *PPC*:

Combination	Number of guns	Pounds of butter
A	0	80
B	10	75
C	20	65
D	30	50
E	40	30
F	50	0

17. Suppose Suburbia initially produces at point *D*. What is the opportunity cost of moving to point *E*?

    a. 10 guns
    b. 40 guns
    c. 20 pounds of butter
    d. 30 pounds of butter
    e. 70 pounds of butter

18. Suppose Suburbia initially produces at point *D*. What is the opportunity cost of moving to point *B*?

    a. 25 pounds of butter
    b. 20 guns
    c. 10 guns
    d. 75 pounds of butter
    e. 50 pounds of butter

19. Specialization and trade benefit

    a. usually only one of the trading partners.
    b. the wealthier country more than the poorer country.
    c. the poorer country more than the wealthier country.
    d. both countries if they specialize according to their comparative advantage.
    e. neither country unless the countries are very different.

20. Assume there are two countries, country A and country B, that produce two goods, slosh and glem. Country A can produce 20 units of slosh in a day or 40 units of glem in a day. Country B can produce 30 units of slosh in a day or 60 units of glem in a day. Which of the following is true?

    a. Neither country has an absolute advantage in either good.
    b. Both Country A and country B should specialize in slosh.
    c. Country A should specialize in slosh and Country B should specialize in glem.
    d. There is no potential for gains from trade in this situation.
    e. Country A should specialize in slosh, but country B should not specialize in glem.

Section ② Supply and Demand

Overview

This section first presents the two sides of the market, demand and supply, individually. Once the supply and demand sides of the market have been presented, it puts them together to show how the supply and demand model can be used to understand markets. Variations on the supply and demand model, such as the market for loanable funds, aggregate supply and aggregate demand, and the money market will appear throughout the remainder of the course.

Featured Model/Graph: Supply and Demand

This section presents the supply and demand model, which is probably the best known and perhaps the most important economic model. The basic supply and demand model provides the framework for the macroeconomic models presented in later sections. There are five key elements in this model: the demand curve, the supply curve, the set of factors that cause the demand curve to shift, the set of factors that cause the supply curve to shift, and the market equilibrium (the price and quantity associated with a market clearing).The supply and demand model is used to determine the change in the market equilibrium when supply and/or demand changes.

MODULES IN THIS SECTION

Module 5   **Supply and Demand: Introduction and Demand**

Module 6   **Supply and Demand: Supply**

Module 7   **Supply and Demand: Equilibrium**

Module 8   **Supply and Demand: Price Controls (Ceilings and Floors)**

Module 9   **Supply and Demand: Quantity Controls**

BEFORE YOU TACKLE THE TEST

Draw the Featured Model

Complete the Exercise

Problems

Review Questions

MODULE 5 SUPPLY AND DEMAND: INTRODUCTION AND DEMAND

BEFORE YOU READ THE MODULE

Summary

This module introduces the supply and demand model and presents the demand side of the model. It develops the concept of demand and presents demand schedules (tables) and curves. The module explains the difference between a change in demand and a change in quantity demanded and presents the factors that will shift a demand curve (i.e. increase or decrease demand).

Module Objectives

Review these objectives before you read the module. Place a "√" on the line when you can do each of the following:

_____**Objective #1.** Explain what a competitive market is and how it is described by the supply and demand model

_____**Objective #2.** Draw a demand curve and interpret its meaning

_____**Objective #3.** Discuss the difference between movements along the demand curve and changes in demand

_____**Objective #4.** List the factors that shift the demand curve

WHILE YOU READ THE MODULE

Key Terms

Define these key terms as you read the module:

Competitive market:

Supply and demand model:

Demand schedule:

Quantity demanded:

Demand curve:

Law of demand:

Change in demand:

Movement along the demand curve:

Substitutes:

Complements:

Normal good:

Inferior good:

Individual demand curve:

Practice the Model

In the space below, sketch a correctly labeled graph of demand showing the effect of an increase in the number of buyers. Be sure to fully label your graph including all axes and curves. Label the demand curve before the change D_1 and the demand curve after the change D_2. Your graph should resemble the graphs in Table 5.1 in your textbook that show a decrease in demand.

List questions or difficulties from your initial reading of the module:

Fill-in-the-Blanks

Fill in the blanks to complete the following statements. If you find yourself having difficulties, please refer back to the appropriate section in the text.

- A competitive market is one in which there are **1)**_____ sellers each selling a(n)

  2)_____ good or service and individual buyers and sellers **3)** (do/do not)

  _____ have an effect on market price.

- Demand is the relationship between the amount of a good consumers want to purchase and its

  4)_____ . According to the law of demand, people purchase more of a good or

  service when the price is **5)**_____. As the price of a good or service increases, we

  say that there is an increase in the **6)**_____ of a good. However, whenever

  something changes that causes consumers to want less at any price, we say that there has been a

  decrease in the **7)**_____ for the good.

- An increase in demand will shift the demand curve to the **8)**_____. The 5 factors

  that will cause the demand curve to shift are; **9)**_____, _____,

  _____, _____, and _____.

Multiple-Choice Questions

Circle the best choice to answer or complete the following questions or incomplete statements. For additional practice, use the space provided to explain why one or more of the incorrect options do not work.

10. Ham and turkey are substitutes for many people. Holding everything else constant, if the price of ham decreases, the demand for
    a. turkey will shift to the left.
    b. turkey will shift to the right.
    c. ham will shift to the left.
    d. ham will shift to the right.
    e. turkey will not change.

11. For an inferior good, an increase in consumer income will
   a. shift the demand curve to the right.
   b. cause a movement to the right along the demand curve.
   c. shift the demand curve to the left.
   d. cause a movement to the left along the demand curve.
   e. not affect demand.

Helpful Tips

- It is easy to confuse a change in demand and a change in quantity demanded. A good's own price is *not* a determinant of demand. It is a determinant of quantity demanded. Because price is on one of the axes (the vertical axis), a change in price moves along a demand curve to a new quantity demanded. A change of the entire demand curve occurs when one of the determinants of demand (which are not on either axis) changes.

- When a demand curve shifts, think of the shift as a shift to the right (an increase in demand), or to the left (a decrease in demand). Avoid thinking of demand curve shifts as shifts "up" or "down," as this can lead to errors when working with supply curves.

- When the price of a good changes, the quantity demanded of *that* good changes, but the demand for its *complement or substitute* also changes. A change in a good's own price causes a movement along the demand curve, because its own price is on the vertical axis. The price of a related good is a determinant of demand and therefore shifts the entire demand curve.

Module Notes

When economists say "an increase in demand," they mean a rightward shift of the demand curve, and when they say "a decrease in demand," they mean a leftward shift of the demand curve—that is, when they're being careful. In ordinary speech, most people, including professional economists, use the word *demand* casually. For example, someone might say "the demand for air travel has doubled over the past 15 years, because of falling air fares" when he or she really means that the *quantity demanded* has doubled.

It is bad enough to be a bit sloppy in ordinary conversation, but when you're doing economic analysis, it's very important to make the distinction between changes in the quantity demanded, which involve movements along a demand curve, and shifts of the demand curve. Sometimes students end up writing something like this: "If demand increases, the price will go up, but that will lead to a fall in demand, which pushes the price down . . ." and then go around in circles. If you make a clear distinction between changes in *demand*, which mean shifts of the demand curve, and changes in *quantity demanded*, you can avoid a lot of confusion.

A full understanding of this section is critical for your study of economics. The model of supply and demand is used repeatedly in a variety of settings throughout this course.

A demand curve illustrates the relationship between the price of the good and the quantity demanded at each specific price. In drawing the demand curve, the other determinants of demand are held constant; this constancy is referred to as the other things equal (or *ceteris paribus*) assumption. In the examples throughout the remainder of the course, we typically consider a single change in a situation while holding the other variables constant. Any time you think, "But what if…", be careful, you may be violating this assumption!

The demand for a good is affected by changes in these factors: income, tastes, expectations, the price of related goods, and the number of consumers. You will need to remember these factors, recognize them in examples, and know how they affect the demand curve.

It can be easier to understand the concepts of substitutes and complements using examples. When the price of a good changes, the quantity demanded of that good will change, but the demand for its substitute will also change. For instance, if the price of hot dogs decreases, people will buy more hot dogs. However, people will need to buy more hot dog buns to go with those hot dogs regardless of the current price of buns, so the demand for buns will increase. Since the quantity demanded of hot dogs increased and the demand for buns also increased, hot dogs and buns are complements.

Whether two goods are substitutes or complements (or are unrelated) depends on individual preferences. When considering whether a good is a complement or substitute, focus on how each responds to changes in the price of the other, rather than making an assumption about the relationship between the goods. For example, you may think apples and peanut butter are complements because you will only eat apples with peanut butter on them, while someone else thinks they are substitutes because they will eat an apple OR have peanut butter as their snack. If you are told that in response to an increase in the price of apples, the demand for peanut butter increased, you know that apples and peanut butter are substitutes.

It can also be easier to understand questions about normal and inferior goods if you think of specific examples. But don't let the terms "normal" and "inferior" mislead you. In economics, the opposite of normal is inferior (not "abnormal") and the opposite of inferior is normal (not "superior"). Whether a good is normal or inferior for a particular individual depends on his or her preferences. A good that is normal for me might be inferior for you! A normal good is a good that you will choose to buy more of as your income increases (demand shifts to the right as income increases). For example, as your income increases you may take more vacations. An inferior good is a good that you will buy less of as your income increases (demand shifts to the left as income increases). For example, as your income increases you may buy fewer fast-food restaurant meals.

MODULE 6   SUPPLY AND DEMAND: SUPPLY

BEFORE YOU READ THE MODULE

Summary

This module presents the supply side of the market. It develops the concept of supply and presents supply schedules (tables) and curves. The module explains the difference between a change in supply and a change in quantity supplied and presents the factors that will shift a supply curve (i.e. increase or decrease supply)

Module Objectives

Review these objectives before you read the module. Place a "√" on the line when you can do each of the following:

_____**Objective #1.**   Draw a supply curve and interpret its meaning

_____**Objective #2.**   Discuss the difference between movements along the supply curve and changes in supply

_____**Objective #3.**   List the factors that shift the supply curve

WHILE YOU READ THE MODULE

Key Terms

Define these key terms as you read the module:

Quantity supplied:

Supply schedule:

Supply curve:

Law of supply:

A change in supply:

Movement along the supply curve:

Input:

Individual supply curve:

Practice the Model

In the space below, sketch a correctly labeled graph of the supply of gasoline today and show the effect if producers today start expecting that the price of gasoline tomorrow will increase. Be sure to label your axes and curves. Your graph should resemble the graphs in Table 6.1 in your textbook.

List questions or difficulties from your initial reading of the module:

AFTER YOU READ THE MODULE

Fill-in-the-Blanks

Fill in the blanks to complete the following statements. If you find yourself having difficulties, please refer back to the appropriate section in the text.

- Supply is the relationship between the amount of a good producers are willing to sell and its

  1)_____. As the price of a good or service increases, we say that there is an

  increase in **2)**_____. However, whenever something changes that causes producers

  to sell less at any price, we say that there has been a decrease in **3)** _____.

- An increase in supply will shift the supply curve to the **4)**_____. The 5 factors that

  will cause the supply curve to shift are **5)**_____, _____,

  _____, _____, and _____.

Multiple-Choice Questions

Circle the best choice to answer or complete the following questions or incomplete statements. For additional practice, use the space provided to explain why one or more of the incorrect options do not work.

6. Assume that research and development result in the discovery of a new technology for electricity generation. This discovery will
   a. increase the supply of electricity.
   b. increase the quantity supplied of electricity.
   c. decrease the supply of electricity.
   d. decrease the quantity supplied of electricity.
   e. have no effect on the supply of electricity.

7. An increase in supply causes which of the following?
   a. the supply curve to shift up
   b. the supply curve to shift to the right
   c. a movement to the right along the curve
   d. the supply curve to shift to the left
   e. a movement to the left along the curve

Helpful Tips

- Be careful when you shift the supply curve. Since quantities are higher as you move to the right along the horizontal axis, shifting a supply curve to the right represents an increase in supply. And since quantities are lower as you move to the left along the horizontal axis, shifting a supply curve to the left is a decrease in supply. Always think of increases and decreases as shifts to the right and left (rather than up or down).

Module Notes

We have been talking about the price at which a good or service is bought *and* sold, as if the two were the same. But shouldn't we make a distinction between the price received by sellers and the price paid by buyers? In principle, yes; but it is helpful at this point to sacrifice a bit of realism in the interest of simplicity—by assuming away the difference between the prices received by sellers and those paid by buyers. In reality, there is often a middleman—someone who brings buyers and sellers together—who buys from suppliers, then sells to consumers at a markup. However, the difference between the buying and selling price is quite small. So it's not a bad approximation to think of the price paid by buyers as being the *same* as the price received by sellers.

A supply curve illustrates the relationship between the price of the good and the quantity supplied at each specific price. In drawing the supply curve, the other determinants of supply are held constant; this constancy is referred to as the other things equal (or *ceteris paribus*) assumption. In the examples throughout the remainder of the course, we typically consider a single change in a situation while holding the other variables constant. Any time you think "But what if…", be careful, you may be violating this assumption!

The supply of a good is affected by changes in each of the following factors: input prices, the price of related goods, technology, expectations, and the number of producers. You will need to remember these factors, recognize them in examples, and know how they affect the supply curve.

MODULE 7 SUPPLY AND DEMAND: EQUILIBRIUM

BEFORE YOU READ THE MODULE

Summary

This module defines equilibrium, shows how to find equilibrium in a supply and demand model, and explains the forces that bring a market into equilibrium. Then, it uses the supply and demand model to determine how changes in a determinant of demand or supply will cause a change in the equilibrium price and quantity. The module presents how to use the supply and demand model to analyze real-world and hypothetical changes.

Module Objectives

Review these objectives before you read the module. Place a "√" on the line when you can do each of the following:

_____**Objective #1.** Explain how supply and demand curves determine a market's equilibrium price and equilibrium quantity

_____**Objective #2.** Describe how price moves the market back to an equilibrium in the case of a shortage or surplus

_____**Objective #3.** Explain how equilibrium price and quantity are affected when there is a change in either supply or demand

_____**Objective #4.** Explain how equilibrium price and quantity are affected when there is a simultaneous change in both supply and demand

WHILE YOU READ THE MODULE

Key Terms

Define these key terms as you read the module:

Equilibrium:

Equilibrium price:

Equilibrium quantity:

Market-clearing price:

Surplus:

Shortage:

Practice the Model

Sketch a correctly labeled graph showing each of the eight situations described below. Use the following steps to complete each graph.
1) Draw a supply and demand graph and label price on the vertical axis and quantity on the horizontal axis. Label the initial demand curve D_1 and the initial supply curve S_1.
2) Show the initial equilibrium price, labeled P_1 on the vertical axis and the initial equilibrium quantity, labeled Q_1 on the horizontal axis.
3) Draw the new supply and/or demand curve, labeling the new curve(s) D_2 or S_2.
4) Show the new equilibrium price labeled P_2 on the vertical axis and the equilibrium quantity labeled Q_2 on the horizontal axis.

In the first two graphs, some of these steps have been done for you to get you started.

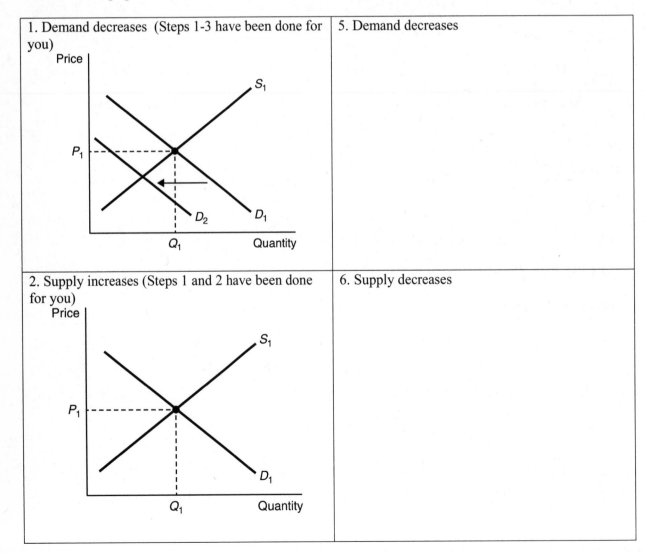

1. Demand decreases (Steps 1-3 have been done for you)

5. Demand decreases

2. Supply increases (Steps 1 and 2 have been done for you)

6. Supply decreases

3. Demand increases and supply increases	7. Demand increases and supply decreases
4. Demand decreases and supply increases	8. Demand decreases and supply decreases

List questions or difficulties from your initial reading of the module:

AFTER YOU READ THE MODULE

Fill-in-the-Blanks

Fill in the blanks to complete the following statements. If you find yourself having difficulties, please refer back to the appropriate section in the text.

- When demand increases, equilibrium price will **1)**_____ and equilibrium quantity

  will **2)**_____. When supply increases, equilibrium price will

  3)_____ and equilibrium quantity will **4)**_____. If there is a

  simultaneous increase in demand and supply, it is certain that equilibrium **5)**_____

  will increase but it is impossible to determine the effect on equilibrium **6)**_____.

Multiple-Choice Questions

Circle the best choice to answer or complete the following questions or incomplete statements. For additional practice, use the space provided to explain why one or more of the incorrect options do not work.

7. On a supply and demand graph, equilibrium price is shown
   a. where supply and demand intersect.
   b. where supply equals demand.
   c. on the horizontal axis below where supply and demand intersect.
   d. on the vertical axis to the left of where supply and demand intersect.
   e. where quantity supplied and quantity demanded are equal.

8. At the current price of peaches, the quantity demanded is less than the quantity supplied. There is a
   _____ of peaches and price will _____.
   a. shortage, increase
   b. surplus, decrease
   c. shortage, decrease
   d. surplus, increase
   e. shortage, remain the same

Helpful Tips

- Equilibrium is a price and quantity pair. When you are asked to label equilibrium price and quantity, make sure you label the equilibrium price on the vertical axis and the equilibrium quantity on the horizontal axis. For example, Graph 1 below does not correctly label the equilibrium price and quantity on the axes. Graph 2 shows the correct way to identify equilibrium price and quantity.

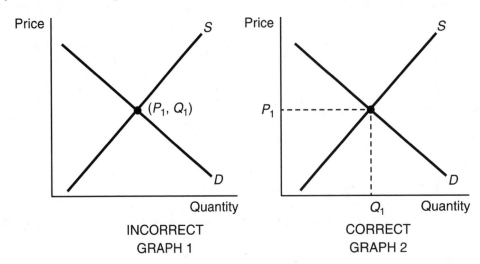

- When supply and demand both shift, without knowing the size of those shifts you will not be able to determine both the new equilibrium price and the new equilibrium quantity: one will be indeterminate. For instance, suppose supply and demand both increase. Both Graph A and Graph B on the following page show this. However, the impact on equilibrium price is different in each graph! Unless we know that one curve shifted by a greater amount, we cannot tell the effect on price; it is indeterminate.

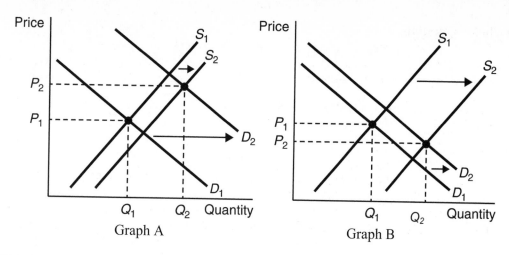

Graph A   Graph B

Module Notes

When the price of a good or service changes, in general, we can say that this reflects a change in either supply or demand. But it is easy to get confused about which one. A helpful clue is the direction of change in quantity. If the quantity sold changes in the *same* direction as the price—for example, if both the price and the quantity rise—this suggests that the demand curve has shifted. If the price and the quantity move in *opposite* directions, the likely cause is a shift of the supply curve.

The main goal of this section is to learn how to use the supply and demand model to answer questions and solve problems. Memorizing definitions, rules, or lists won't get you very far; you need to learn and practice using the supply and demand model. Use the model to help you find answers to questions rather than guessing the answer and trying to make the model fit your preconceived notion.

Often a quick sketch of a demand and supply curve is all that you need to answer questions about the effect of a change in the market on the equilibrium price or equilibrium quantity. Practice drawing a quick representation of the demand and supply curves as you do problems, recognizing that you do not always need a formal graph to find a solution. Use these sketches during your exams!

MODULE 8 SUPPLY AND DEMAND: PRICE CONTROLS

BEFORE YOU READ THE MODULE

Summary

This module looks at government intervention to affect the price in a market. Buyers would like to pay less, and sometimes they can make a strong moral or political case that they should pay lower prices. Sellers would like to receive a higher price, and sometimes they can make a strong moral or political case that they should receive higher prices. Buyers and sellers make strong appeals for governments to intervene in markets. When a government intervenes to regulate prices, we say that it imposes *price controls*. These controls take the form either of *a price ceiling* or a *price floor*. When a government tries to legislate prices, there are predictable side effects, which are presented in this module.

Module Objectives

Review these objectives before you read the module. Place a "√" on the line when you can do each of the following:

_____Objective #1. Explain the workings of price controls, one way government intervenes in markets

_____Objective #2. Describe how price controls can create problems and make a market inefficient

_____Objective #3. Explain why economists are often deeply skeptical of attempts to intervene in markets

_____Objective #4. Identify who benefits and who loses from price controls

WHILE YOU READ THE MODULE

Key Terms

Define these key terms as you read the module:

Price controls:

Price ceiling:

Price floor:

Inefficient allocation to consumers:

Wasted resources:

Inefficiently low quality:

Black markets:

Minimum wage:

Inefficient allocation of sales among sellers:

Inefficiently high quality:

Practice the Model

1) In the space below, sketch a correctly labeled graph showing an effective price ceiling on a market. Be sure to correctly label the quantity supplied, quantity demanded, equilibrium price, price ceiling, and any surplus or shortage that exists. Refer to Figure 8.2 in your textbook as a guide.

2) In the space below, sketch a correctly labeled graph showing an effective price floor on a market. Be sure to correctly label the quantity supplied, quantity demanded, equilibrium price, price floor, and any surplus or shortage. Refer to Figure 8.4 as a guide.

List questions or difficulties from your initial reading of the module:

AFTER YOU READ THE MODULE

Fill-in-the-Blanks

Fill in the blanks to complete the following statements. If you find yourself having difficulties, please refer back to the appropriate section in the text.

- One way the government may try to affect markets is to use price controls to set either a minimum or

  maximum legal price in a market. A maximum legal price is called a price **1)**_____

  and a minimum legal price is called a price **2)**_____.

- To be effective, a price ceiling would have to be set **3)**_____ the equilibrium price.

  To be effective, the price floor would have to be set **4)**_____ the equilibrium price.

- When an effective price ceiling is imposed on a market, the result will be a

  5)_____; when an effective price floor is imposed on a market, the result will be a

  6)_____.

Multiple-Choice Questions

Circle the best choice to answer or complete the following questions or incomplete statements. For additional practice, use the space provided to explain why one or more of the incorrect options do not work.

7. If an effective price floor is imposed on a market, the market price can't adjust
   a. upward, resulting in a surplus.
   b. downward, resulting in a surplus.
   c. upward, resulting in a shortage.
   d. downward, resulting in a shortage.
   e. upward, resulting in a new equilibrium.

8. Which of the following is NOT an inefficiency caused by a price ceiling?
   a. inefficient allocation to consumers
   b. inefficient allocation to producers
   c. wasted resources
   d. inefficiently low quantity
   e. black markets

Helpful Tips

- Both price floors and price ceilings result in inefficiencies and both sellers and buyers are hurt by them. For example, buyers are hurt by a price floor because some buyers who were willing and able to pay the equilibrium price may not be willing or able to pay the higher price floor and therefore will no longer purchase the good. Because there are fewer buyers, sellers are also hurt because some sellers who were actually willing and able to sell the good at the lower equilibrium price may be unable to sell that good at the higher price. Similarly, when there is a price ceiling, sellers are hurt because not all of the sellers who were able to sell their good at the equilibrium price can still participate in this market. As a result, buyers who had previously been willing to pay a higher price might find themselves unable to purchase the good at a lower price because of the lower quantity supplied.

Module Notes

A price ceiling below the equilibrium price pushes the price of a good *down*. A price floor above the equilibrium price pushes the price of a good *up*. So it's easy to assume that the effects of a price floor are the opposite of the effects of a price ceiling. In particular, if a price ceiling reduces the quantity of a good bought and sold, doesn't a price floor increase the quantity? No, it doesn't. In fact, both floors and ceilings reduce the quantity bought and sold. Why? When the quantity of a good supplied isn't equal to the quantity demanded, the quantity sold is determined by the "short side" of the market—whichever quantity is less. If sellers don't want to sell as much as buyers want to buy, it's the sellers who determine the actual quantity sold, because buyers can't force unwilling sellers to sell. If buyers don't want to buy as much as sellers want to sell, it's the buyers who determine the actual quantity sold, because sellers can't force unwilling buyers to buy.

A floor is a surface that you stand on and that is solid. Use this vision of a floor to remember that a price floor is the *lowest* price that can be charged for a good. To be effective, a price floor must be set at a price that is greater than the equilibrium price. Otherwise, the floor will not prevent the market from going to equilibrium. An effective price floor results in a surplus of the good, because at high prices, producers want to sell more but consumers want to buy less.

A ceiling is a surface that you hope is solid and stays above your head. Use this visual to remember that a price ceiling is the *highest* price that can be charged for a good. To be effective, a price ceiling must be set at a price that is less than the equilibrium price. Otherwise, the ceiling will not prevent the market from going to equilibrium. An effective price ceiling results in a shortage of the good because at low prices consumers want to buy more but producers don't want to sell as much.

MODULE 9   SUPPLY AND DEMAND: QUANTITY CONTROLS

BEFORE YOU READ THE MODULE

Summary

This module continues the discussion of government intervention in markets by looking at *quantity controls*, or *quotas*. The total amount of the good that can be transacted under the quantity control is called the *quota limit*. Typically, the government limits quantity in a market by issuing *licenses*.

Module Objectives

Review these objectives before you read the module. Place a "√" on the line when you can do each of the following:

_____ **Objective #1.** Explain the workings of quantity controls, another way government intervenes in markets

_____ **Objective #2.** Describe how quantity controls create problems and can make a market inefficient

_____ **Objective #3.** Explain who benefits and who loses from quantity controls

WHILE YOU READ THE MODULE

Key Terms

Define these key terms as you read the module:

Quantity control (Quota):

License:

Demand price:

Supply price:

Wedge:

Quota rent:

Deadweight loss:

Practice the Model

Suppose the equilibrium price in the market for salmon is $4 per pound, the equilibrium quantity is 20 pounds of salmon, and a quota of 10 pounds of salmon is imposed on the market. Draw a correctly labeled graph of the salmon market showing the effect of the quota. Be sure to label the demand price (P_d), the supply price (P_s), and the deadweight loss (DWL).

List questions or difficulties from your initial reading of the module:

AFTER YOU READ THE MODULE

Fill-in-the-Blanks

Fill in the blanks to complete the following statements. If you find yourself having difficulties, please refer back to the appropriate section in the text.

- Whenever the government imposes a limit on the amount that can be sold, it is called a

  1)_____. A government can limit the number of goods supplied in the market by

  requiring a **2)**_____ which grants the right to sell a good; it affects not only the

  amount of the good sold in the market, but also the price.

- When the government imposes a quantity control, it drives a **3)**_____ between the

  price that consumers are willing to pay for the quantity allowed of the good and the price at which

  producers are willing to offer that quantity. The price consumers are willing to pay for the legal

  market quantity is called the **4)**_____ price and the price at which producers are

  willing to offer the legal market quantity is called the **5)**_____ price.

- The price that consumers are willing to pay for a quota is higher than the price at which producers are

  willing to offer it. This difference is known as the quota **6)**_____.

Multiple-Choice Questions

Circle the best choice to answer or complete the following questions or incomplete statements. For additional practice, use the space provided to explain why one or more of the incorrect options do not work.

7. Quantity controls lead to which of the following?
   a. a market surplus
   b. a market shortage
   c. increased efficiency
   d. deadweight loss
   e. inefficiently low quality

8. An effective quantity control will have what effect on the market?
   a. It limits the price that suppliers can charge.
   b. It limits the price that consumers must pay.
   c. It limits the amount of the good or service available.
   d. It increases the quantity of the good sold.
   e. It has no impact on the market.

Helpful Tips

- Price controls and quantity controls are represented differently on a supply and demand graph. A price control is a horizontal line at the controlled price, and a quantity control is a vertical line at the controlled quantity.

Module Notes

In this module, we examine what happens when government intervention directly restricts the quantity of a good or service available in the market. There are similarities between this analysis of quantity controls and our previous analysis of price controls. When price is restricted through a price control, we draw a *horizontal* line on our supply and demand graph, at the level of the price ceiling or floor. When quantity is restricted, we draw a *vertical* line on our supply and demand graph at the maximum quantity permitted under the restriction—the quota limit. Note that we focus on maximum quantities (quotas) and do not talk about *minimum* quantities. In the case of a price control, the restricted price creates a difference between the quantity demanded and the quantity supplied. This leads to shortages or surpluses. In the case of a quantity control, the restriction creates a difference between the supply price and the demand price. This creates a wedge, or quota rent. While the terminology used to analyze quotas may be less familiar, the similarities with price controls can help you understand quantity controls. In each case, government intervention leads to market inefficiencies.

A quota, or quantity control, is a policy implemented by the government to set a maximum amount of the good or service that can be sold in a market. A quota has no effect if it is set at a level greater than the equilibrium quantity; to be effective, a quota must be set at a level lower than the equilibrium quantity.

With an effective quantity restriction, consumers are willing to pay more for each unit of the good, while suppliers are willing to supply the good for less. This difference is referred to as a wedge. This wedge corresponds to the quota rent the license holder of the good receives when the quantity control is imposed in a market.

Draw the Featured Graph: Supply and Demand

Graphing using data

Graph the supply and demand curves using the data in the table. Show equilibrium price and quantity on the axes.

P	Q_d	Q_s
0	8	0
2	6	6
4	4	12

Graphing relationships without numbers

Graph supply and demand curves and show equilibrium price and quantity on the axes.

Graphs like the ones you drew above serve as the starting point when using supply and demand analysis to determine the effects on price and quantity when a determinant of supply or demand changes. Always start your analysis with one of these "starting point" graphs. Then follow these steps:

1) Determine which side of the market is affected – supply or demand – using the lists of factors that affect supply and demand in previous modules. Any single change will affect supply *or* demand – not both.
2) Determine whether supply or demand increases or decreases.
3) Shift the supply or demand curve to the left for a decrease or to the right for an increase. Draw the new equilibrium using the new curve to find your answer. Remember, the equilibrium is the new price (on the vertical axis) and the new quantity (on the horizontal axis) using the new curve. Be sure to clearly label the new price and the new quantity.

Complete the Exercise

Draw a correctly labeled graph showing the effect on equilibrium price and equilibrium quantity in the market for oranges when each of the following (*ceteris paribus*) changes occurs. Use the steps shown in Draw the Featured Graph above.

a. There is a freeze in Florida that kills many of the orange groves.

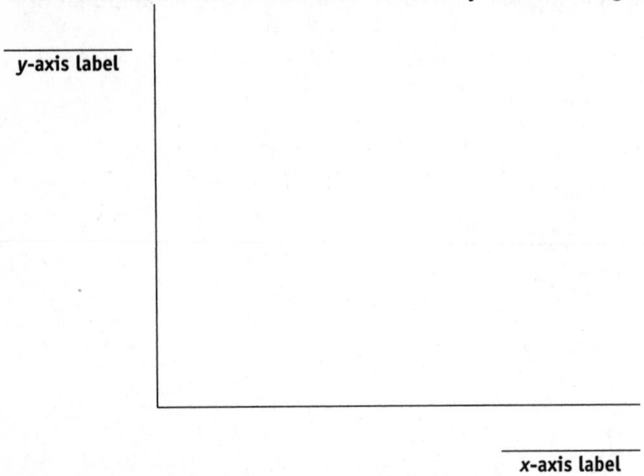

y-axis label

x-axis label

b. The wages of orange workers decrease.

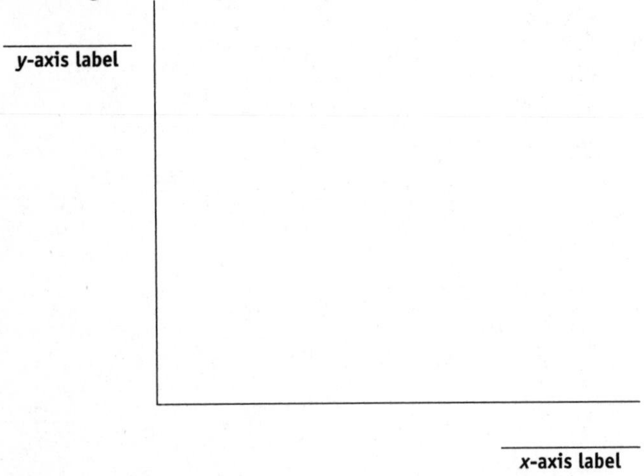

y-axis label

x-axis label

c. Research finds that oranges have additional health benefits.

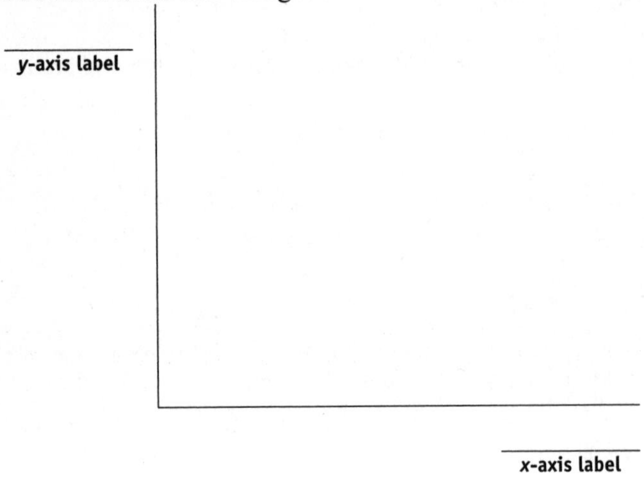

y-axis label

x-axis label

d. The price of tangerines decreases.

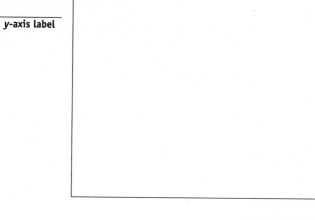

y-axis label

x-axis label

Problems

1. You are given the following information about demand in the competitive market for bicycles.

Price per bicycle	Quantity of bicycles demanded per week
$100	0
80	100
60	200
40	500
20	800
0	1,000

a. Draw the demand curve that reflects this demand schedule.

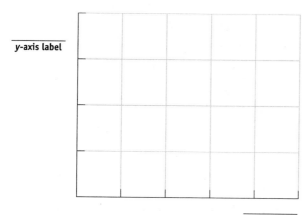

y-axis label

x-axis label

b. Suppose the price is initially $40. If price rises by $20, what happens to quantity demanded?

c. Suppose the price is initially $40. If price falls by $40, what happens to quantity demanded?

2. For each of the following situations in the table below, fill in the missing information. First, determine whether the situation causes a shift or a movement along the demand curve; then, if it causes a shift, determine whether the demand curve shifts to the right or to the left.

Situation	Specified market	Movement or shift	Rightward or leftward
People's income increases	Market for exotic vacations		
People's income decreases	Market for goods sold in secondhand shops		
Price of bicycles increases	Market for bicycles		
Price of tennis balls increases	Market for tennis racquets		
Price of movie tickets decreases	Market for popcorn at movie theatres		
Popularity of music-playing device increases	Market for music-playing device		
Popularity of branded clothing items decreases	Market for brand-name designer clothing		
Winter clothing is expected to go on sale next month	Market for winter clothing		
Increase in urban residents	Market for apartments in urban areas		

3. The following graph represents the supply curve for the production of widgets in Town Center.

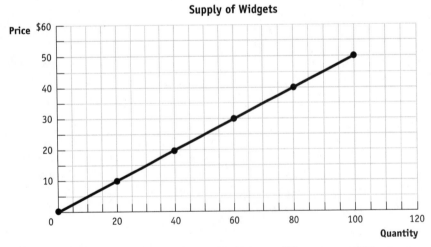

Supply of Widgets

a. At a price of $20, how many widgets are producers willing to supply?

b. At a price of $40, how many widgets are producers willing to supply?

c. Suppose there are ten widget producers in Town Center and the price of widgets is $50. If each producer produces the same number of widgets, how many widgets will each produce?

d. Suppose the price is initially $30 but then falls to $20. What is the change in quantity supplied?

e. Suppose the price is initially $30 but then rises to $50. What is the change in quantity supplied?

f. What price must suppliers receive in order to be willing to supply 80 widgets?

g. What price must suppliers receive in order to be willing to supply 40 widgets?

h. What does the slope of a supply curve imply about the relationship between price and quantity supplied?

4. For each of the following situations in the table below, fill in the missing information: first, determine whether the situation causes a shift or a movement along the supply curve; then, if it causes a shift, determine whether the supply curve shifts to the right or to the left.

Situation	Specified market	Movement or shift	Rightward or leftward
Labor costs for air travel and cruise ships increase	Market for exotic vacations		
Prices of office equipment and phone service rise by 40%	Market for call center services		
Price of bicycles increases	Market for bicycles		
Price of leather boots increases	Market for beef products		
Price of leather boots increases	Market for leather belts		
New technology for music-playing device revealed	Market for music-playing devices		
Price of brand-name designer clothing increases	Market for brand-name designer clothing		
Increase in number of coffee shop owners in the metro area	Market for coffee in the metro area		

5. The demand and supply schedules for Healthy Snacks, Inc., is provided in the table below.

Price	Quantity demanded	Quantity supplied
$0	1,000	0
10	800	125
20	600	275
30	400	400
40	200	550
50	0	675

a. Sketch the demand and supply curves for Healthy Snacks, Inc. Don't worry about drawing a precise graph. Focus on drawing the underlying relationships from the table. Your graph should be accurate with regard to x-intercepts and y-intercepts and indicate equilibrium.

b. What are the equilibrium price and quantity in this market? Show these on your graph.

c. Calculate the excess demand or excess supply at each price in the table below.

Price	Excess demand or supply?	Amount of excess demand or supply
$0		
10		
20		
30		
40		
50		

d. What is another term for excess demand?

e. What is another term for excess supply?

6. For each of the following situations, sketch a graph of the initial market demand (D_1), supply (S_1), equilibrium price (P_1) and equilibrium quantity (Q_1). Then sketch any changes in the market demand (D_2) and/or supply (S_2) curves and indicate the new equilibrium price (P_2) and quantity (Q_2).

a. Assume that bicycles and gasoline are substitutes and the price of gasoline increases significantly. What happens in the market for bicycles?

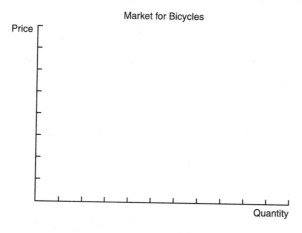

Market for Bicycles

b. The price of gasoline increases by 40 percent. What happens in the market for fuel-inefficient SUVs?

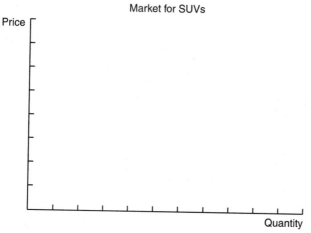

Market for SUVs

c. New technology for music-playing is developed. What happens in the market for the devices?

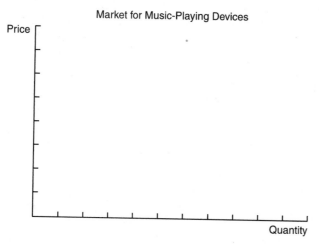

Market for Music-Playing Devices

d. The price of labor decreases. What happens in the market for fast-food restaurants?

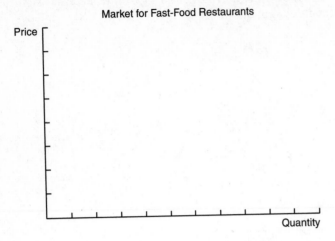

Market for Fast-Food Restaurants

Price

Quantity

e. Income increases and good X is a normal good. What happens in the market for good X?

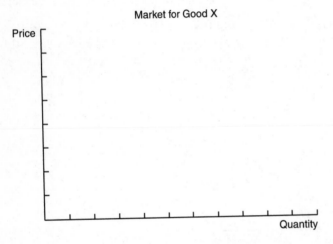

Market for Good X

Price

Quantity

f. Income increases and good X is an inferior good. What happens in the market for good X?

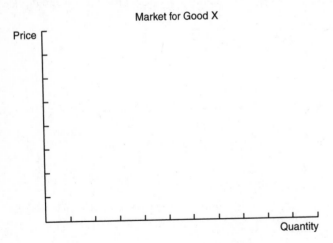

Market for Good X

Price

Quantity

7. Use the graph below to answer the following questions.

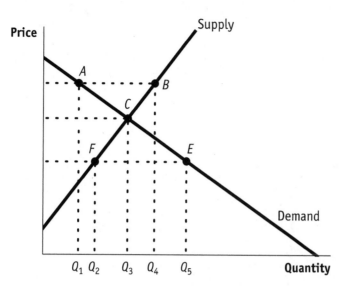

a. Identify the equilibrium price and the equilibrium quantity.

b. Suppose a price floor of P_3 is implemented by the government in this market. Describe what will happen to the price and quantity once this price floor is implemented.

c. Suppose a price floor of P_2 is implemented by the government in this market. Describe what will happen to the price and quantity once this price floor is implemented.

d. What must be true about a price floor in a market for a good or service in order for that price floor to be effective?

e. You are told that an effective price floor has been implemented in this market and that the resulting surplus is greater than Q_4 - Q_1. What do you know about the level of this price floor?

8. Use the graph below to answer the following questions.

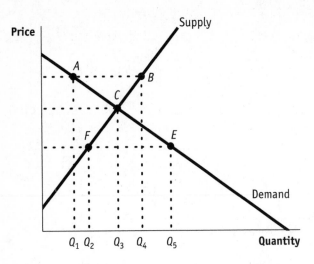

a. Identify the equilibrium price and the equilibrium quantity.

b. Suppose a price ceiling of P_2 is implemented by the government in this market. Describe what will happen to the price and quantity once this price ceiling is implemented.

c. Would both P_2 and P_3 be effective price ceilings? Explain.

d. Suppose a price ceiling of P_3 is imposed on this market. What quantity will be exchanged?

e. You are told that an effective price ceiling has been implemented in this market and that the resultant shortage is smaller than Q_5 - Q_2. What do you know about the level of this price ceiling?

9. Consider the market for housing in Metropolitan City, where all housing units are exactly the same. Currently the equilibrium price of housing is $2,000 a month and local residents consume 1,500 units of housing. The local residents argue that housing is too expensive and an effective price ceiling is implemented. When the price ceiling is implemented by the local government council, only 1,200 units of housing are supplied. Is this an efficient level of housing for Metropolitan City? Explain. To support your answer, provide two sketches: in the first sketch, indicate equilibrium quantity and price; in the second sketch, indicate the price ceiling and the quantity provided by the market. Is the price consumers are willing to pay for the last unit equal to the price suppliers must receive to supply the last unit? Explain.

10. The market for taxi rides in Metropolia this week is described in the following table. Assume that all taxi rides are the same in Metropolia.

Price of taxi rides	Quantity of taxi rides demanded per week	Quantity of taxi rides supplied per week
$1	200	40
2	180	60
3	160	80
4	140	100
5	120	120
6	100	140
7	80	160
8	60	180
9	40	200
10	20	220

a. What is the equilibrium price and quantity of taxi rides in Metropolia per week?

Suppose the government of Metropolia institutes a medallion system that limits the number of taxi rides available in Metropolia per week to 80 taxi rides.

b. At what price will consumers want to purchase 80 taxi rides per week? What is this price called?

c. At what price will suppliers be willing to supply 80 taxi rides per week? What is this price called?

d. What price will a taxi medallion rent for in this market? Explain your answer.

e. Draw a graph of the taxi ride market in Metropolia. On this graph, indicate the quota limit, the demand price, the supply price, and the medallion's rental price.

f. What is the total value of the taxi medallions per week in Metropolia?

Review Questions

Circle your answer to the following questions.

1. Competitive markets are characterized as having
   a. many buyers and a single seller.
   b. many buyers and a few sellers.
   c. many buyers and many sellers.
   d. a few buyers and many sellers.
   e. one buyer and many sellers.

2. Sue goes to the store to purchase a bottle of shampoo. When she gets to the store, she discovers that her brand of shampoo is on sale for $4 a bottle. According to the law of demand, we can expect that
   a. Sue will purchase one bottle of shampoo.
   b. Sue will not purchase the shampoo.
   c. Sue will likely purchase more than one bottle of shampoo.
   d. Sue will substitute for her usual brand of shampoo with an alternative brand.
   e. Sue will sell the shampoo she has at home.

3. Consider the market for mangos. Suppose researchers discover that eating mangos generates large health benefits. Which of the following statements is true? This discovery will
   a. not affect the market for mangos.
   b. cause the demand for mangos to shift to the right.
   c. cause the price of mangos to decrease due to a movement along the demand curve.
   d. cause a movement along the demand curve for mangos.
   e. cause the supply of mangos to decrease.

4. Consider the demand curve for automobiles. An increase in the price of automobiles due to a shift in the supply curve will
   a. cause a movement to the right along the demand curve for automobiles.
   b. result in a decrease in the demand for automobiles.
   c. have no effect on the quantity of automobiles demanded since the change was in supply.
   d. cause the quantity supplied of automobiles to increase.
   e. cause a movement to the left along the demand curve for automobiles.

5. Assume that ham and turkey are substitutes. If the price of ham decreases, then the demand for
   a. turkey will shift to the left.
   b. turkey will shift to the right.
   c. ham will shift to the left.
   d. ham will shift to the right.
   e. ham will not change.

6. Consider two goods: good X and good Y. Holding everything else constant, the price of good Y increases and the demand for good X decreases. Good X and good Y are definitely
   a. complements.
   b. substitutes.
   c. not related to one another.
   d. Cannot be determined
   e. normal goods.

7. Consider a supply curve. When the price of the good increases, this results in a movement along the supply curve resulting in a greater
   a. supply of the good.
   b. quantity supplied.
   c. supply.
   d. demand.
   e. equilibrium.

8. Research and development result in the discovery of a new technology for electricity generation. Holding everything else constant, this discovery will
   a. increase the supply of electricity.
   b. increase the quantity supplied of electricity.
   c. decrease the supply of electricity.
   d. decrease the quantity supplied of electricity.
   e. have no impact on the market for electricity.

9. The sawmill industry expects lumber prices to rise next year due to growing demand for the construction of new homes. Holding everything else constant, this expectation will shift
   a. the supply curve for lumber this year to the left.
   b. the supply curve for lumber this year to the right.
   c. the supply for lumber next year to the left.
   d. the supply for lumber next year to the right.
   e. the demand for lumber this year to the left.

10. In an equilibrium in a competitive market for a good, price has adjusted so that the quantity
    a. demanded is equal to the quantity supplied at that price.
    b. demanded is equal to the quantity supplied at all possible prices.
    c. supplied is greater than the quantity demanded at that price.
    d. demanded is greater than the quantity supplied at that price.
    e. demanded is equal to zero.

11. Consumers in Mayville consider houses and apartments to be substitutes. There is an increase in the price of houses in Mayville at the same time that three new apartment buildings are opened. In the market for apartments in Mayville, the equilibrium
    a. price will rise relative to its level before these two events.
    b. price will fall relative to its level before these two events.
    c. quantity will rise relative to its level before these two events.
    d. quantity will fall relative to its level before these two events.
    e. price will rise, but the equilibrium quantity will be unchanged.

12. An effective price floor will have what effect on the price of the product and the quantity sold?

	Effect on the price of the product	*Effect on the quantity sold*
a.	decreases	increases
b.	increases	increases
c.	decreases	decreases
d.	increases	no impact
e.	increases	decreases

13. A minimum wage that is higher than the market equilibrium wage will have what effect on the wage

	Wage	*Quantity of workers hired*
a.	increase	increase
b.	increase	decrease
c.	decrease	increase
d.	decrease	decrease
e.	increase	stay the same

Use the information in the table below to answer questions 14 and 15.

Price	Quantity demanded	Quantity supplied
$20	200	0
40	150	50
60	100	100
80	50	150
100	0	200

14. Suppose a price floor of $40 is implemented in this market. This results in
  a. an excess demand of 100 units.
  b. an excess supply of 100 units.
  c. no effect in this market, since the price floor is set below the equilibrium price.
  d. no effect in this market, since the price floor is set above the equilibrium price.
  e. an excess demand of 40 units.

15. Suppose a price ceiling of $40 is implemented in this market. This results in
  a. an excess demand of 100 units.
  b. an excess supply of 100 units.
  c. no effect in this market, since the price ceiling is set below the equilibrium price.
  d. a temporary shortage of the good while prices rise.
  e. a reduction in the demand for this good.

16. Black market or illegal activities increase with the imposition of price controls in markets. Black markets
  a. improve the situation of all participants in the price-controlled market.
  b. worsen the situation for those people who obey the rules imposed by the government.
  c. have little or no real impact in price-controlled markets.
  d. create greater respect in society for the need to obey all laws.
  e. do not exist because they are illegal.

17. An effective quantity control
  a. limits the price that suppliers can charge for the good or service in the regulated market.
  b. limits the price that demanders must pay for the good or service in the regulated market.
  c. limits the amount of the good or service available in the regulated market.
  d. increases the quantity of the good in the regulated market to a quantity above equilibrium.
  e. limits the price that suppliers can charge for the good or service in the regulated market without impacting the quantity exchanged.

18. A quota limit imposed on a market
   a. restricts the amount of the good available in that market.
   b. results in a payment being made by the government to the license holder.
   c. places a lower limit on the amount of the good provided in the regulated market.
   d. places an upper limit on the price of the good provided in the regulated market.
   e. restricts the amount of the good available in the market without having any impact on the price.

19. Which of the following statements is true of a quota?
   a. It places a wedge between the quantity demanded and the quantity supplied.
   b. It results in efficiency gains because quotas allow fewer goods to be sold, while price controls do not.
   c. It results in efficiency gains because quotas only restrict transactions that are not mutually beneficial.
   d. A price control results in efficiency gains because price controls allow fewer goods to be sold, while quotas do not.
   e. It restricts the sale of goods to those who value a good the least.

20. Quantity controls
   a. provide an incentive to engage in illegal activities.
   b. result in overproduction of the good in the market with the quota limit.
   c. result in a more efficient outcome than the market outcome.
   d. enable sellers to sell more of a good regardless of the market price.
   e. enable buyers to buy more of a good regardless of the market price.

Section ⑨ Behind the Demand Curve: Consumer Choice

Overview

This section looks more closely at the supply and demand model developed in Section 2 and presents several economic concepts used to evaluate market results. It introduces the concept of elasticity, beginning with the price elasticity of demand. It continues with several related concepts, including the income elasticity of demand and the price elasticity of supply. In addition, this section looks at how the price and quantity in a market affect consumer, producer, and overall welfare. Finally, it considers how consumers make choices to maximize their utility.

Featured Model/Graph: Consumer and Producer Surplus

This section uses the supply and demand model to calculate and interpret consumer surplus, producer surplus, and overall welfare and deadweight loss.

MODULES IN THIS SECTION

Module 46   Income Effects, Substitution Effects, and Elasticity

Module 47   Interpreting Price Elasticity of Demand

Module 48   Other Important Elasticities

Module 49   Consumer and Producer Surplus

Module 50   Efficiency and Deadweight Loss

Module 51   Utility Maximization

BEFORE YOU TACKLE THE TEST

Draw the Featured Model

Complete the Exercise

Problems

Review Questions

MODULE 46 | INCOME EFFECTS, SUBSTITUTION EFFECTS, AND ELASTICITY

BEFORE YOU READ THE MODULE

Summary

This module presents more detail about why demand curves slope downward and what the slope of the demand curve tells us. It introduces the income and substitution effects and the concept of elasticity (beginning with price elasticity of demand).

Module Objectives

Review these objectives before you read the module. Place a "√" on the line when you can do each of the following:

_____ **Objective #1.**   Explain the law of demand on the basis of income and substitution effects

_____ **Objective #2.**   Calculate the price elasticity of demand, a measure of consumer responsiveness to price changes

WHILE YOU READ THE MODULE

Key Terms

Define these key terms as you read the module:

Substitution effect:

Income effect:

Price elasticity of demand:

Midpoint method:

Practice the Model

Sally purchases two goods, bread and jam, at a local market. Data on the quantity of bread and jam Sally purchases at two different prices is given on the following page.

Jam			Bread		
Price	Quantity		Price	Quantity	
$10 per jar	100 jars		$8 per loaf	30 loaves	
$20 per jar	50 jars		$12 per loaf	10 loaves	

Use the midpoint method to 1) calculate the price elasticity of demand for bread and 2) determine how a 1% increase in price will change the quantity of bread demanded. This has been done for jam below.

Price elasticity of demand for jam	Price elasticity of demand for bread
1) $\dfrac{\dfrac{50-100}{50+100 / 2}}{\dfrac{20-10}{20+10 / 2}} = \dfrac{\dfrac{-50}{150 / 2}}{\dfrac{10}{30 / 2}} = \dfrac{\dfrac{-50}{75}}{\dfrac{10}{15}} = \dfrac{-2/3}{2/3} = -1$	
2) A 1% increase in price will decrease quantity by 1%.	

List questions or difficulties from your initial reading of the module:

AFTER YOU READ THE MODULE

Fill-in-the-Blanks

Fill in the blanks to complete the following statements. If you find yourself having difficulties, please refer back to the appropriate section in the text.

• When the price of a good decreases, it becomes cheaper relative to other goods, so consumers will purchase more of it and less of other goods. This is known as the **1)**_____ effect. Also when the price of a good decreases, a consumer's purchasing power increases. This is known as the **2)**_____ effect.

• The responsiveness of one variable to changes in another is measured using **3)**_____, which measures the percentage change in quantity demanded in response to a percentage change in **4)**_____. The midpoint formula for calculating this responsiveness is **5)**_____ (without the negative sign).

Multiple-Choice Questions

Circle the best choice to answer or complete the following questions or incomplete statements. For additional practice, use the space provided to explain why one or more of the incorrect options do not work.

6. If the price elasticity of demand is 3 and price increases by 10%, quantity demanded will
   a. increase by 30%.
   b. increase by 3%.
   c. decrease by 30%.
   d. decrease by 1/3%.
   e. decrease by 3%.

7. George buys 20 pounds of rabbit feed when the price is $11 and 30 pounds of rabbit feed when the price is $9. George's price elasticity of demand for rabbit feed between $9 and $11 is equal to
   a. 0.2.
   b. 0.25.
   c. 0.5.
   d. 2.
   e. 5.

Helpful Tips

- Be sure you know how to interpret elasticity as well as how to calculate it. It is helpful to think of the price elasticity of demand in terms of a 1% change in quantity demanded (since the percentage change in quantity demanded is in the denominator of the formula). For example, if price elasticity of demand is equal to 3, it means that for every 1% increase in price, there is a 3% decrease in quantity demanded since 3%/1% = 3.

- The midpoint method calculates the price elasticity of demand at the price and quantity that are midway between the starting and ending price and quantity. For example, if you use the midpoint formula to calculate price elasticity of demand between $4 and $6, you use a price of $5 (midway between $4 and $6) and the quantity that corresponds to that midpoint.

Module Notes

Elasticity is a very important and useful concept in economics and it is used in a variety of ways. So it is a good idea to understand the general idea of what is meant by "elasticity" before you begin working with the specific elasticities in this section. Elasticity measures the responsiveness of one thing to a change in another thing. For example, price elasticity of demand calculates the responsiveness of quantity demanded to a change in the price of the good. If you recognize that all elasticities measure how responsive one thing is to a change in another thing, you will better understand all the elasticities that you come across. However, if you think of each elasticity as completely different, it will take you more time and you will have to start over with every new elasticity. Every elasticity works the same way (same formula, same mathematical interpretation) – only the two relevant variables you consider are different.

   Any elasticity measures the percent change in one variable that results from the percent change in another variable. If the independent variable changes, the dependent variable will change in response. Elasticity is calculated as the percent change in the dependent variable divided by the percent change in the independent variable. With demand, price changes (it is the independent variable) and the quantity demanded responds (it is the dependent variable). Therefore, price elasticity of demand is calculated as the percent change in quantity demanded divided by the percent change in price.

Since most people are familiar with finding the percent change by dividing the change in a variable using the initial value of that variable, this module started with that simple approach to calculating percent changes. As the module explains, this approach will yield a different answer depending on where you begin. To overcome this problem, the module goes on to present the midpoint method. With the midpoint method, the percent change is found by dividing the change in the variable by the *average* of the starting and final values, rather than the initial value. In general, the midpoint method to calculating elasticity will always be

$$\frac{\% \text{ change in dependent variable}}{\% \text{ change in independent variable}} = \left(\frac{\dfrac{\text{Change in dependent variable}}{\text{Average value of dependent variable}}}{\dfrac{\text{Change in independent variable}}{\text{Average value of independent variable}}} \right)$$

For price elasticity of demand, this is
$$\left(\frac{\dfrac{\text{Change in quantity demanded}}{\text{Average quantity demanded}}}{\dfrac{\text{Change in price}}{\text{Average price}}} \right)$$

But remember, if you learn the approach in general, you can adapt it to any of the different elasticities you run into (in later modules or any time in the future!).

Economists calculate a variety of elasticities because these measures provide important insights into the relationship between different related variables. In fact, there are many more elasticities that are calculated than are in your text. You can calculate the elasticity of anything that changes in response to a change in something else. Remember that elasticities are unit-free (i.e. they are NOT percentages – they are the ratio of two percentages), making them an ideal measure of sensitivity of one variable to changes in another variable.

MODULE 47 INTERPRETING PRICE ELASTICITY OF DEMAND

BEFORE YOU READ THE MODULE

Summary

This module discusses interpreting and classifying price elasticity of demand. It also presents the major factors that affect price elasticity of demand.

Module Objectives

Review these objectives before you read the module. Place a "√" on the line when you can do each of the following:

_____**Objective #1.** Explain the difference between elastic and inelastic demand

_____**Objective #2.** Describe the relationship between elasticity and total revenue

_____**Objective #3.** Illustrate how the price elasticity changes along a demand curve

_____**Objective #4** Identify the factors that determine price elasticity of demand

WHILE YOU READ THE MODULE

Key Terms

Define these key terms as you read the module:

Perfectly inelastic demand:

Perfectly elastic demand:

Elastic demand:

Inelastic demand:

Unit-elastic demand:

Total revenue:

Practice the Model

When the price of spinach is $2 per bunch, people buy 20 bunches per month. When the price of spinach is $3 per bunch, people buy 15 bunches per month.

1) Calculate the price elasticity of demand using the midpoint formula.

2) Note that by using the midpoint formula you are actually calculating the price elasticity of demand for spinach at $2 (the price that is the midpoint between $2 and $3) where quantity is 15 bunches per month. Is price elasticity of demand elastic or inelastic? Can we say that of the demand for spinach at all prices? Explain.

3) Use the elasticity of demand to determine what will happen to total revenue if the price of spinach increases from $2 to $3 per bunch.

4) Check your answer. The total revenue that a seller would receive is price × quantity. So for a price of $2, a seller would receive a total revenue of $2 × 20 = $40. Calculate the total revenue a seller would receive from charging a price of $3. Is it greater than, less than, or the same as the amount the seller would get if he or she charged $2?

List questions or difficulties from your initial reading of the module:

AFTER YOU READ THE MODULE

Fill-in-the-Blanks

Fill in the blanks to complete the following statements. If you find yourself having difficulties, please refer back to the appropriate section in the text.

• When the percent change in the quantity demanded is equal to zero for *any* change in the price, the

price elasticity of demand is equal to **1)**_____ and the price elasticity of demand is known

as perfectly **2)**_____. A horizontal demand curve implies a price elasticity of demand equal to **3)**_____ and the price elasticity of demand is known as perfectly

4)_____.

- Demand is considered elastic when price elasticity of demand has a value that exceeds

  5)_____. When demand is elastic, an increase in price will lead to a(n)

  6)_____ in total revenue.

- Demand is considered inelastic when price elasticity of demand is less than **7)**_____.

  When demand is inelastic, an increase in price will lead to a(n) **8)**_____ in total revenue.

Multiple-Choice Questions

Circle the best choice to answer or complete the following questions or incomplete statements. For additional practice, use the space provided to explain why one or more of the incorrect options do not work.

9. If the price elasticity of demand of a good is 0.5, demand for the good is
   a. perfectly elastic.
   b. elastic.
   c. unit elastic.
   d. inelastic.
   e. perfectly inelastic.

10. If the price elasticity of demand of a good is 0, and the price of the good increases, total revenue will
   a. increase.
   b. decrease, but still be positive.
   c. be negative.
   d. equal zero.
   e. stay the same.

11. A seller wants to increase her total revenue. She knows that the price elasticity of demand for her good is elastic. Which of the following statements is true?
   a. She cannot increase revenue by changing her price.
   b. If she increases her price, total revenue will decrease.
   c. If she increases her price, total revenue will increase.
   d. If she increases her price, the quantity sold and total revenue will be zero.
   e. If she decreases her price, total revenue will decrease.

Helpful Tips

- When the price elasticity of demand is elastic, an increase in price will cause a decrease in total revenue. This is because consumers will respond to the price increase by decreasing the quantity that they purchase by a *greater* percentage than the price changed by. In other words, no matter what the percentage change in price is, consumers decrease their purchases by a greater amount.
  The opposite is true if the price elasticity of demand is inelastic. When price elasticity of demand is inelastic, an increase in price will cause an increase in total revenue. This is because consumers will

respond to the price increase by decreasing the quantity that they purchase by a *smaller* percentage than the price changed by.

- The effect of a price decrease on total revenue depends on elasticity in the same way. When price elasticity of demand is elastic, a price decrease will increase total revenue because consumers are very responsive to the price change and buy enough to more than offset the lower price. But when price elasticity of demand is inelastic, a price decrease will decrease total revenue because consumers are not very responsive to the price change and do not buy enough more to offset the lower price.

Module Notes

Now that you have learned the definition of price elasticity of demand and how to calculate it, you should focus on understanding what price elasticity of demand tells you. Even if you can calculate every elasticity value correctly, you do not truly understand elasticity unless you know what your answer means. While it is true that you will be asked to calculate the value of price elasticity of demand on an AP® exam, it will be much more important for you to understand what the value means and how to use it to answer questions (e.g. the effect on total revenue if a firm raises or lowers its price).

Make sure you understand total revenue and how to calculate it. Total revenue is equal to the price per unit times the quantity sold. Total revenue at any given price is equal to the area of a rectangle whose height is the price and whose width is the quantity sold at this price.

MODULE 48 OTHER IMPORTANT ELASTICITIES

BEFORE YOU READ THE MODULE

Summary

The previous modules addressed price elasticity of demand. This module explains how elasticity is used to understand the relationship between other important variables in economics. It presents cross-price elasticity, income elasticity, and price elasticity of supply.

Module Objectives

Review these objectives before you read the module. Place a "√" on the line when you can do each of the following:

_____**Objective #1.** Measure the responsiveness of demand for one good to changes in the price of another good using the cross-price elasticity of demand

_____**Objective #2.** Measure the responsiveness of demand to changes in income using the income elasticity of demand

_____**Objective #3.** Explain the significance of the price elasticity of supply, which measures the responsiveness of the quantity supplied to changes in price

_____**Objective #4** Identify and describe the factors that influence the size of these various elasticities

WHILE YOU READ THE MODULE

Key Terms

Define these key terms as you read the module:

Cross-price elasticity of demand:

Income elasticity of demand:

Income-elastic demand:

Income-inelastic demand:

Price elasticity of supply:

Perfectly inelastic supply:

Perfectly elastic supply:

Practice the Model

For each of the scenarios given:
   a)   Calculate the appropriate elasticity.
   b)   Interpret your answer.

Round your calculations to two decimal places. The first scenario has been done for you.

1) When the price of apples is $2 per pound, people buy 15 bananas. When the price of apples is $3 per pound, people buy 20 bananas.
   a) The cross-price elasticity between apples and bananas = $\frac{\frac{15-20}{(15+20)/2}}{\frac{2-3}{(2+3)/2}} = \frac{-0.29}{0.40} = -0.73$
   b) Apples and bananas are complements because the value is positive.

2) When the price of apples is $2 per pound, people buy 60 oranges. When the price of apples is $3 per pound, people buy 30 oranges.
   a)
   b)

3) When Sally's income is $50,000, she buys 10 boxes of chocolate per year. When Sally's income is $60,000, she buys 20 boxes of chocolate per year.
   a)
   b)

4) When Sally's income is $50,000, she buys 10 pounds of hamburger per month. When Sally's income is $60,000, she buys 5 pounds of hamburger per month.
   a)
   b)

5) When the price of wine is $10 per bottle, Meek Vineyards supplies 40 bottles per week. When the price of wine is $12 per bottle, Meek Vineyards supplies 45 bottles per week.
   a)
   b)

List questions or difficulties from your initial reading of the module.

Fill-in-the-Blanks

Fill in the blanks to complete the following statements. If you find yourself having difficulties, please refer back to the appropriate section in the text.

- When the price of one good changes, the quantity demanded of another good may increase or decrease. This "cross" effect on demand is measured by **1)**_____ elasticity. When this elasticity is positive, it tells us the two goods are **2)**_____. This elasticity for two goods that are consumed together, like flashlights and batteries, would be **3)**_____.

- The income elasticity of demand measures how a change in income will affect the **4)**_____ of a good. The income elasticity of demand is positive for a(n) **5)**_____ good and negative for a(n) **6)**_____ good.

- The two most important factors that affect the price elasticity of supply for a good are **7)**_____ and **8)**_____.

Multiple-Choice Questions

Circle the best choice to answer or complete the following questions or incomplete statements. For additional practice, use the space provided to explain why one or more of the incorrect options do not work.

9. When the price of cheese increases from $5 to $10, beef purchases increase from 20 pounds to 25 pounds. Which elasticity can be calculated using this information?
   a. income elasticity of demand for cheese
   b. income elasticity of demand for beef
   c. cross-price elasticity between cheese and beef
   d. price elasticity of supply for cheese
   e. price elasticity of demand for beef

10. If the income elasticity of demand for a good is -2, the good is a(n)
    a. normal good, so when income increases by $1, quantity demanded increases by 2 units.
    b. inferior good, so when income increases by $1, quantity demanded decreases by 2 units.
    c. normal good, so when income increases by 1%, quantity demanded decreases by 2%.
    d. inferior good, so when income increases by 1%, quantity demanded decreases by 2%.
    e. inferior good, so when income increases by any amount, quantity increases by 2%.

Helpful Tips

Use the following table to help keep track of the important elasticities, how to calculate them, and what the value means.

Table 48.1 An Elasticity Menagerie

Name	Elasticity values	Significance
Price elasticity of demand $= \dfrac{\% \text{ change in quantity demanded}}{\% \text{ change in price}}$ (dropping the minus sign)		
Perfectly inelastic demand	0	Price has no effect on quantity demanded (vertical demand curve).
Inelastic demand	Between 0 and 1	A rise in price increases total revenue.
Unit-elastic demand	Exactly 1	Changes in price have no effect on total revenue.
Elastic demand	Greater than 1, less than ∞	A rise in price reduces total revenue.
Perfectly elastic demand	∞	A rise in price causes quantity demanded to fall to 0. A fall in price leads to an infinite quantity demanded (horizontal demand curve).
Cross-price elasticity of demand $= \dfrac{\% \text{ change in quantity } \textit{of one good} \text{ demanded}}{\% \text{ change in price } \textit{of another good}}$		
Complements	Negative	Quantity demanded of one good falls when the price of another rises.
Substitutes	Positive	Quantity demanded of one good rises when the price of another rises.
Income elasticity of demand $= \dfrac{\% \text{ change in quantity demanded}}{\% \text{ change in income}}$		
Inferior good	Negative	Quantity demanded falls when income rises.
Normal good, income-inelastic	Positive, less than 1	Quantity demanded rises when income rises, but not as rapidly as income.
Normal good, income-elastic	Greater than 1	Quantity demanded rises when income rises, and more rapidly than income.
Price elasticity of supply $= \dfrac{\% \text{ change in quantity supplied}}{\% \text{ change in price}}$		
Perfectly inelastic supply	0	Price has no effect on quantity supplied (vertical supply curve).
Inelastic supply	Between 0 and 1	Upward-sloping supply curve
Unit-elastic supply	Exactly 1	Upward-sloping supply curve
Elastic supply	Greater than 1, less than ∞	Upward-sloping supply curve
Perfectly elastic supply	∞	Any fall in price causes quantity supplied to fall to 0. Any rise in price elicits an infinite quantity supplied (horizontal supply curve).

Module Notes

This module introduces some "other" elasticities. If you have learned the general approach to elasticity, all you need to do now is identify the two relevant variables involved in each of these new elasticities (and which is the independent, and which is the dependent variable).

Cross-price elasticity is very similar to the price elasticity of demand. However, instead of looking at the effect on the quantity demanded of a good from a price change of that good, it looks at the effect on the quantity demanded of a good from a price change of another good. The effect is across goods, hence the name *cross*-price elasticity. Quantity demanded is the dependent variable and price is the independent variable (just as with the price elasticity of demand), but the price and quantity are for two different goods. Why would we care about two different goods? They must be related goods for the quantity of one to respond to a change in the price of another. Remember that we studied related goods in Section 2 – complements and substitutes. We are interested in the cross-price elasticity because it tells us about the relationship between two goods.

Income elasticity of demand looks at effects on the quantity demanded from changes in income rather than price. The two relevant variables are quantity and income – with income as the independent variable. The effect on quantity when income changes determines whether the good is a normal good or an inferior good. Remember from Section 2 that a change in income can cause demand to increase or decrease, depending on what type of good we are studying.

Finally, the price elasticity of supply looks at the relationship between price and quantity *supplied*. Again, price is the independent variable. But here, we consider the responsiveness of the quantity supplied to changes in price. We learned in Section 2 that there is a positive relationship between price and the quantity supplied, so the price elasticity of supply will always be positive. The price elasticity of supply gives us more detail about the relationship between price and quantity supplied. According to the law of supply, the price elasticity of supply will be positive. With both the price elasticity of demand and the price elasticity of supply, the value determines the range of elasticity: elastic, inelastic, unit-elastic. Keep in mind that the negative sign is dropped from the value of the price elasticity of demand, and that there would never be a negative sign for a price elasticity of supply. But remember that whether the income elasticity of demand or the cross-price elasticity is negative or positive is very important. Keep your increases and decreases straight when working with these two elasticities. The sign (positive or negative) is an important part of interpreting them!

Economists calculate a variety of elasticities because these measures provide important insights into the relationship between two different variables. All elasticities are calculated as the ratio between the percentage changes in quantity (either the quantity demanded or the quantity supplied) to the percentage change in some other related variable. Elasticities are unit-free, making them an ideal measure of sensitivity of one variable to changes in another variable.

MODULE 49 CONSUMER AND PRODUCER SURPLUS

BEFORE YOU READ THE MODULE

Summary

This module introduces producer and consumer surplus, which we will use to measure the gains from trade and illustrate efficiency in markets in the next module. The benefits from being able to purchase a good are known as consumer surplus. The corresponding measure, producer surplus, measures the benefits sellers receive from being able to sell a good. Total surplus is the sum of consumer surplus and producer surplus.

Module Objectives

Review these objectives before you read the module. Place a "√" on the line when you can do each of the following:

_____**Objective #1.** Explain the meaning of consumer surplus and its relationship to the demand curve

_____**Objective #2.** Explain the meaning of producer surplus and its relationship to the supply curve

WHILE YOU READ THE MODULE

Key Terms

Define these key terms as you read the module:

Willingness to pay:

Individual consumer surplus:

Total consumer surplus:

Consumer surplus:

Cost:

Individual producer surplus:

Total producer surplus:

Producer surplus:

Practice the Model

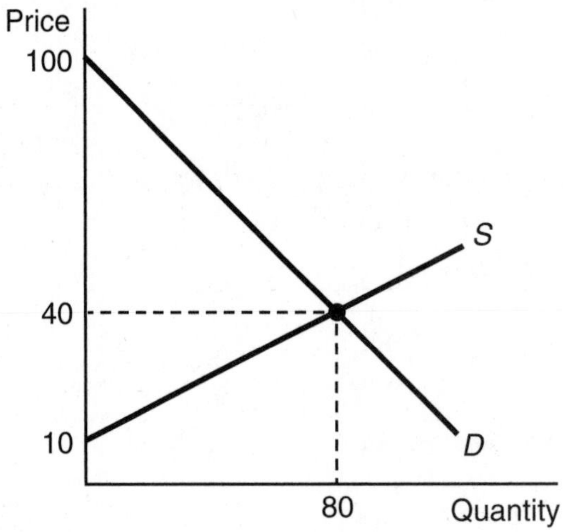

Use the figure above to calculate consumer and producer surplus at equilibrium. You can refer to Figures 49.3 and 49.8 in your textbook.

Consumer Surplus:

Producer Surplus:

List questions or difficulties from your initial reading of the module.

AFTER YOU READ THE MODULE

Fill-in-the-Blanks

Fill in the blanks to complete the following statements. If you find yourself having difficulties, please refer back to the appropriate section in the text.

- Consumer surplus measures the difference between the market price and the amount consumers are

  willing to pay for a good, as measured by the **1)**_____ curve. This means that consumer

  surplus is equal to the area below the **2)**_____ but above the **3)**_____.

- Producer surplus measures the difference between the market price and the lowest price at which

  producers are willing to sell a good, as measured by the **4)**_____ curve . This means

  producer surplus is equal to the area above the **5)**_____ but below the

  6)_____.

Multiple-Choice Questions

Circle the best choice to answer or complete the following questions or incomplete statements. For additional practice, use the space provided to explain why one or more of the incorrect options do not work.

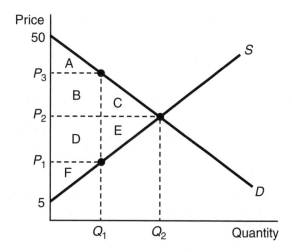

Use the preceding graph to answer questions 7 and 8.

7. What area of the graph represents the change in producer surplus if the price of the good increases from P_1 to P_2?

   a. F

   b. D + E

   c. A

   d. B + C

   e. C + E

8. What area of the graph represents the increase in consumer surplus if price decreases from P_3 to P_2?

   a. F

   b. D + E

   c. A

   d. B + C

   e. C + E

Helpful Tips

•   Consumer surplus and producer surplus are measured in dollars. Surplus measures *value* to consumers or producers.

•   When you are analyzing efficiency, think triangles! Producer surplus and consumer surplus are represented by triangles in our market graphs. You will need to understand what each of these areas represents and be able to identify the correct triangle on the graph. In some instances, you will need to calculate the area of the triangle. Recall from the Section 1 Appendix that the area of a triangle is ½ (base × height). The base is always the quantity that is being sold. For consumers, the height is the difference between the highest price that consumers are willing to pay (the price where the demand curve intersects the vertical axis) and the price that the consumers are actually paying. For sellers, the height is the difference between the lowest price that sellers are willing to accept (the price where the supply curve intersects the vertical axis) and the price that sellers are actually getting.

Module Notes

To master the key concept in this chapter, you must be able to locate the areas of consumer and producer surplus on supply and demand graphs. You will want to work with the concepts of consumer surplus, producer surplus, and total surplus until you feel confident that you can find these areas on your graphs. You also will want to be able to identify increases and decreases in consumer surplus and producer surplus when there is a change in price.

    A consumer's willingness to pay refers to the maximum price the consumer would pay to purchase an item. The demand curve is defined by the willingness of consumers to pay. An individual's consumer surplus is the difference between the individual's willingness to pay and the price he/she pays for the good: consumer surplus measures the net gain the consumer receives when he/she purchases the good. Total consumer surplus is the sum of the individual consumer surpluses achieved by all the buyers of the good. Total consumer surplus is equal to the area under the demand curve but above the market price. Holding everything else constant, a decrease in price increases consumer surplus while an increase in price decreases consumer surplus.

    The seller's price is the lowest price the seller is willing to sell the good for. Individual producer surplus is the difference between the price the good sells for and the lowest price the seller is willing to accept for the good. Individual producer surplus measures the net gain the seller receives from selling the good. Total producer surplus is the sum of the individual producer surplus achieved by all the sellers of the good. Total producer surplus is equal to the area above the supply curve but beneath the market price. Holding everything else constant, a decrease in price decreases producer surplus and an increase in price increases producer surplus.

MODULE 50 EFFICIENCY AND DEADWEIGHT LOSS

BEFORE YOU READ THE MODULE

Summary

This module introduces the concepts of total surplus and deadweight loss. Markets are an effective way to organize economic activity and generally make society as well off as possible given the available resources. In this module, consumer surplus and producer surplus are used to explain why this is so.

Module Objectives

Review these objectives before you read the module. Place a "√" on the line when you can do each of the following:

_____**Objective #1.** Define total surplus and discuss its relevance to market efficiency

_____**Objective #2.** Explain how taxes affect total surplus and can create deadweight loss

WHILE YOU READ THE MODULE

Key Terms

Define these key terms as you read the module:

Total surplus:

Progressive tax:

Regressive tax:

Proportional tax:

Excise tax:

Tax incidence:

Deadweight loss:

Administrative costs:

Lump-sum tax:

Practice the Model

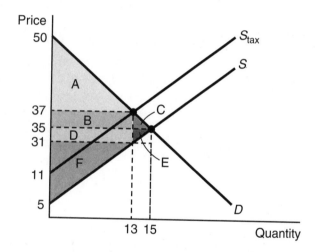

The preceding graph shows a market where a $6 excise tax has been imposed. Without the tax, the equilibrium price is $35 and 15 units are sold. With the tax, buyers pay $37, sellers receive $31, and 13 units are sold.

1) Area A + B + C represents the consumer surplus before the tax. The area is equal to ½ × 15 × (50 -35)= $112.50. Area D + E + F represents the producer surplus before the tax. Calculate the producer surplus before the tax.

2) What does total surplus (producer surplus plus consumer surplus) equal before the tax?

3) Consumer surplus is always the area below the demand curve and above the price that is paid by consumers. When a $6 tax is imposed, the consumer surplus is represented by area A. Calculate consumer surplus after the tax.

4) Consumer surplus before the tax was area A + B + C and consumer surplus after the tax was area A.
  i. The change in consumer surplus as a result of the tax is represented by what area?

  ii. Area B is no longer consumer surplus because it is now part of tax revenue. What happened to area C?

5) Producer surplus is always the area above the curve that represents producer costs and below the price that sellers receive. When a $6 tax is imposed, producer surplus is represented by area F. Calculate producer surplus after the tax.

6) Producer surplus before the tax was area D + E + F and producer surplus after the tax was area F.
  i. The change in producer surplus as a result of the tax is represented by what area?

  ii. Area D is no longer producer surplus because it is now part of tax revenue. What happened to area E?

7) Area B was consumer surplus that became part of tax revenue. This is the consumer's tax burden. Area D was producer surplus that became part of tax revenue. This is the producer's tax burden. Calculate area B and area D and compare them. Who pays a higher share of the tax? What determines how the burden of the tax is shared by consumers and producers?

List questions or difficulties from your initial reading of the module.

Fill-in-the-Blanks

Fill in the blanks to complete the following statements. If you find yourself having difficulties, please refer back to the appropriate section in the text.

•   The sum of consumer and producer surplus is known as the total **1)**_____ generated in a market. Consumer plus producer surplus is highest when the market is in equilibrium; therefore, any other outcome will **2)** (increase/decrease)_____ total surplus because the market equilibrium maximizes the gains from trade.

•   There are three caveats to the conclusion that market equilibrium maximizes the gains from trade. First, although a market may be efficient, it isn't necessarily *fair.* Economists refer to fairness as **3)**_____. Second, there are specific instances in which the economy experiences market **4)**_____ when markets do not maximize efficiency. Finally, market equilibrium maximizes **5)**_____ surplus, but does not necessarily result in the best outcome for every *individual* consumer and producer.

•   Taxes are an example of government intervention in a market that prevents the market from moving to equilibrium and results in a **6)**_____ loss that represents the total surplus lost to society because of the tax.

Multiple-Choice Questions

Circle the best choice to answer or complete the following questions or incomplete statements. For additional practice, use the space provided to explain why one or more of the incorrect options do not work.

7. Consumers will pay the entire burden of a tax when which of the following is true?
   a. Price elasticity of demand is elastic.
   b. Price elasticity of supply is perfectly elastic.
   c. Cross-price elasticity is perfectly inelastic.
   d. Price elasticity of demand is perfectly inelastic.
   e. Income elasticity of demand is perfectly inelastic.

8. Deadweight loss results from a tax because the tax creates which of the following?
   a. administrative costs
   b. a decrease in total surplus
   c. tax revenues
   d. equity
   e. increases in producer and consumer surplus

Helpful Tips

- Preventing a sale in a market that would have taken place at equilibrium may reduce both consumer and producer surplus, and will result in a loss of total surplus. Since a tax reduces the quantity sold, it causes deadweight loss.

- Operating at the market equilibrium when a market is perfectly competitive maximizes the sum of producer and consumer surplus. However, the market equilibrium does not necessarily provide equity or benefit the outcome for every individual buyer and seller.

- Markets can fail to be efficient as a result of a market failure. Market failures are discussed in a later section. Be careful not to draw the conclusion that all markets will automatically maximize welfare.

- The burden of a tax doesn't automatically fall on whoever is being taxed. Just because a tax is imposed on sellers doesn't mean that they pay the entire burden of the tax, or even the largest share of the tax. The burden of the tax will fall on whoever has the least elastic curve. Whoever has a more elastic curve can respond more, thereby reducing their burden of the tax.

Module Notes

This module analyzes the effect of an excise tax on total surplus. An excise tax is a tax charged on each unit of a good sold. Another type of tax is a lump-sum tax. Lump-sum taxes are the same for everyone, regardless of any actions people take. For example, a lump-sum tax does not change as the quantity bought or sold increases. Therefore, excise (or per unit) taxes change as quantity changes, but lump-sum taxes stay the same regardless of the quantity. When considering the effect of a tax, remember that it will be different depending on whether you are looking at a per unit or a lump-sum tax. A per unit tax will tend to increase price and decrease quantity, while a lump-sum tax will not affect price or quantity.

Total surplus is the sum of consumer and producer surplus. At the market equilibrium, total surplus is maximized: the market equilibrium allocates the consumption of the good among potential consumers and the sales of the good among potential sellers in order to achieve the maximum possible gains to society. In a perfectly competitive market, total surplus cannot be increased by reallocating consumption among consumers, reallocating sales among sellers, or by changing the quantity traded. In fact, each of these actions diminishes the level of total surplus in the market.

MODULE 51 UTILITY MAXIMIZATION

BEFORE YOU READ THE MODULE

Summary

This module looks at the theory of consumer choice. It explains how consumers make choices to maximize their utility.

Module Objectives

Review these objectives before you read the module. Place a "√" on the line when you can do each of the following:

_____**Objective #1**. Describe how consumers make choices about the purchase of goods and services

_____**Objective #2** Explain why consumers' general goal is to maximize utility

_____**Objective #3** Explain why the principle of diminishing marginal utility applies to the consumption of most goods and services

_____**Objective #4** Use marginal analysis to find the optimal consumption bundle

WHILE YOU READ THE MODULE

Key Terms

Define these key terms as you read the module:

Utility:

Util:

Marginal utility:

Marginal utility curve:

Principle of diminishing marginal utility:

Budget constraint:

Consumption possibilities:

Budget line:

Optimal consumption bundle:

Marginal utility per dollar:

Optimal consumption rule:

Practice the Model

Alex's total utility depends on his consumption of candy as given below.

Quantity of candy (in pieces)	Total Utility (Utils)	Marginal Utility (per piece of candy)
0	0	
1	10	10
2	19	9
3	27	__
4	34	__
5	40	__
6	45	__
7	49	__
8	52	__
9	54	__
10	55	__
11	55	__
12	54	__
13	52	__

1) Complete the table by calculating the marginal utility for each quantity of candy. The first few entries have been done for you.

2) What was the total utility gained from the 8th piece of candy? What was the marginal utility gained from the 9th piece of candy?

3) Suppose the price of candy is zero. Is Alex better off if he increases his consumption from 8 pieces to 9 pieces? What about increasing consumption from 10 to 11, and 11 to 12? Explain.

4) What is the amount of candy that maximizes Alex's utility?

List questions or difficulties from your initial reading of the module.

AFTER YOU READ THE MODULE

Fill-in-the-Blanks

Fill in the blanks to complete the following statements. If you find yourself having difficulties, please refer back to the appropriate section in the text.

- In models of consumer behavior, we measure personal satisfaction using the concept of

  1)_____ measured in hypothetical units called **2)**_____. Each time a person

  consumes an additional unit of a good, the increase in satisfaction is the **3)**_____ of that

  unit. According to the principle of diminishing marginal utility, each successive unit consumed adds

  4) (more/less) _____ to total satisfaction than does the previous unit.

- We assume that a person wants to get the highest personal satisfaction that is possible. However, a

  consumer must choose a consumption bundle that costs no more than his or her income.

  The **5)**_____ is the limit on the cost of different consumption bundles that a consumer

  can afford. We call the set of all of a consumer's affordable consumption bundles the consumer's

  6)_____. The consumption bundle that maximizes a consumer's total utility given the

  budget constraint is called the **7)**_____.

- The optimal consumption rule tells us that a consumer maximizes utility, given the budget constraint, when the **8)**_____ spent on each good or service in the consumption bundle is equal for all goods and services in the consumption bundle. This is written mathematically as

  9)_____.

Multiple-Choice Questions

Circle the best choice to answer or complete the following questions or incomplete statements. For additional practice, use the space provided to explain why one or more of the incorrect options do not work.

10. Owen spends his entire income on cheese and bacon and buys 20 pounds of cheese and 10 pounds of bacon. He receives 30 utils from purchasing the 20th pound of cheese and 30 utils from purchasing the 10th pound of bacon. If bacon costs $2 per pound and cheese costs $1 per pound, how might Owen increase his total utility?
   a. no change, since he is currently consuming the optimal bundle of bacon and cheese
   b. increase his consumption of bacon until he is buying the same quantity of bacon and cheese
   c. increase his consumption of both bacon and cheese
   d. increase his consumption of cheese until he is spending the same dollar amount on cheese as he is on bacon
   e. increase his consumption of cheese until he is getting the same marginal utility per dollar spent on cheese as he is on bacon

11. Cheyenne has $100 to spend on grapes and hummus. The price of grapes is $2 per pound and the price of hummus is $4 per package. Which of the following consumption bundles costs $100?
   a. 24 packages of hummus and 2 pounds of grapes
   b. 10 packages of hummus and 10 pounds of grapes
   c. 25 packages of hummus and 10 pounds of grapes
   d. 0 packages of hummus and 100 pounds of grapes
   e. 20 packages of hummus and 5 pounds of grapes

Helpful Tips

- Remember that there are two conditions to be met for a consumption bundle to be utility maximizing. First, all income must be spent and second, the marginal utility per dollar spent is the same for each good (or is as close as possible).

- Think of marginal utility per dollar spent as the "bang for your buck," where marginal utility is the "bang" you get from the last unit of consumption. For instance, suppose you were consuming hamburgers and fries, and your marginal utility per dollar spent on hamburgers is 5 units and your marginal utility per dollar spent on fries is 6 units. You are getting a better "bang per buck" on fries, so it would be rational to increase your consumption of fries and decrease your consumption of hamburgers.

Module Notes

Marginal analysis solves "how much" decisions by setting the marginal *benefit* of an activity equal to its marginal *cost*. In consumption decisions, marginal benefit is the additional satisfaction that we get from consuming one more unit of a good and marginal cost is the price that we pay to get that additional unit of the good.

Consumer utility refers to the satisfaction the consumer gets from the consumption of a bundle of goods and services. The level of utility received from consuming a good depends on each person's tastes. Utility is measured in utils. Total utility measures the total amount of satisfaction an individual gets from consuming different amounts of a good. As the quantity consumed increases, total utility increases at a decreasing rate. That is, additional units of the good provide diminishing marginal utility.

A consumer's budget constraint describes the consumption bundles that a consumer can afford and that exhaust the consumer's income. The budget constraint depends on the individual's income and the prices of the goods and services included in the consumption bundle. An individual can afford any points that lie in the area bounded by his or her budget line; these affordable consumption bundles represent the individual's consumption possibilities. The individual will not choose to consume at any of these points inside the budget line provided that his or her utility from consuming either good is positive and the utility of saving income is zero (this amounts to the assumption that the individual spends all of his or her income on the two available goods). Budget lines are downward sloping since the individual can afford to consume more of one good only if the individual consumes less of the other good.

The optimal consumption bundle is the one that maximizes the individual's total utility. The marginal utility per dollar spent on a good is equal to the marginal utility of the last unit consumed divided by the price of the good. The marginal utility per dollar for good X can be written as MU_X/P_X, where MU_X is the marginal utility from consuming that unit of the good and P_X is the price of good X. As additional units of the good are consumed, the marginal utility per dollar spent on the good decreases, because of the principle of diminishing marginal utility. The optimal consumption bundle for an individual is one in which the marginal utility per dollar spent on each good is equal. This idea can be expressed as $MU_X/P_X = MU_Y/P_Y$. When the price of a good changes, this changes the marginal utility per dollar spent on this good and therefore changes the optimal consumption bundle.

Draw the Featured Graph: Producer and Consumer Surplus

Use a supply and demand graph of a market in equilibrium (be sure you label both axes as well as the equilibrium price and quantity). Clearly illustrate the areas of consumer and producer surplus on your graph.

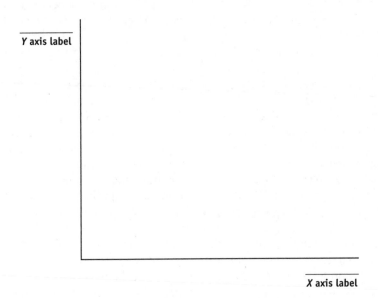

Y axis label

X axis label

Complete the Exercise

1) Summer Ice, a company that specializes in ice cream treats, wishes to raise its total revenue. It has two different groups of buyers: children and adults. Currently, its ice cream treats are priced at $2.00 per serving. The company is considering reducing the price of its treats to $1. From its market research, it knows that the two groups of buyers are likely to respond according to the data in the following table:

Price	Quantity demanded by children	Quantity demanded by adults
$2	100	100
1	300	120

a. What is the price elasticity of demand for each of these groups? Use the midpoint method.

b. What is Summer Ice's current total revenue if it sells its ice cream treats at a price of $2?

c. What is Summer Ice's total revenue if it sells its ice cream treats at a price of $1?

d. What is Summer Ice's total revenue if it prices its treats differently to the two groups and charges the higher price ($2) to adults and the lower price ($1) to children?

e. What is Summer Ice's total revenue if it prices its treats differently to the two groups and charges the lower price ($1) to adults and the higher price ($2) to children?

f. What pricing scheme in parts b. through e. results in the greatest total revenue for Summer Ice? Use price elasticity of demand to explain why this pricing scheme maximizes Summer Ice's total revenue.

Problems

1) This problem explores the midpoint method of calculating percentages and why this method is preferred when calculating price elasticity of demand or price elasticity of supply. Consider the demand curve in the following figure to answer this question.

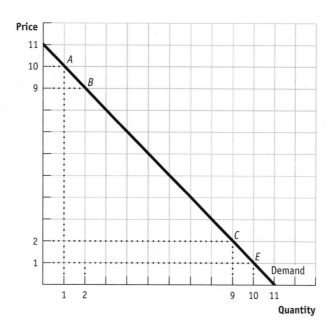

a. Suppose the initial price and quantity on the above demand curve is represented by point A and then the price and quantity change to point B. Calculate the percentage change in price and the percentage change in quantity using the following formula:

$$\text{Percent change} = \frac{\text{new value - old value}}{\text{old value}} \times 100$$

Note: we are purposefully *not* using the midpoint method for parts a. through e. of this problem so that we can compare these results to the results we would get if we used the midpoint method.

b. Using the percentage changes you calculated in part a., calculate the price elasticity of demand from point A to point B, using the following formula:

$$\text{Price elasticity of demand} = \left| \frac{\text{\% change in quantity demanded}}{\text{\% change in price}} \right|$$

c. Redo part **a.** starting at point B and moving to point A. Use the same formula as that given in part **a.**

d. Calculate the price elasticity of demand from point B to point A using the formula given in part **b.**

e. Are your values for the price elasticity of demand the same in parts **a.** and **d.**?

Now, let's recalculate the price elasticity of demand using the midpoint method.

f. Suppose you are initially at point A and that you move to point B. Calculate the percentage change in price and the percentage change in quantity using the midpoint formula.

$$\text{\% change} = \frac{\text{new value - old value}}{\dfrac{\text{old value + new value}}{2}} \times 100$$

g. Using the percentage changes you calculated in part **f.**, calculate the price elasticity of demand from point A to point B using the following formula:

$$\text{Price elasticity of demand} = \left| \frac{\% \text{ change in quantity demanded}}{\% \text{ change in price}} \right|$$

where both percentage changes have been calculated using the midpoint method.

h. Suppose you now start at point B and move to point A. Calculate the percentage change in price and the percentage change in quantity using the formula given in part f.

i. Calculate the price elasticity of demand from point B to point A using the formula given in part g.

j. Are the values you calculated for the price elasticity of demand using the midpoint method the same in parts g. and i.? Summarize the significance of the midpoint method when calculating the price elasticity of demand or the price elasticity of supply.

2. Use the following figure of a linear demand curve to answer this set of questions.

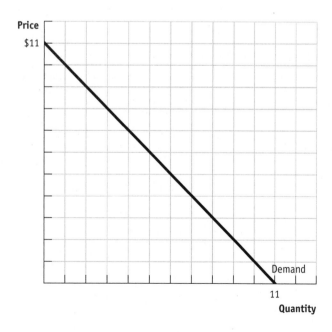

a. Based on the preceding figure, fill in the following table:

Price	Quantity demanded	Total revenue
$0		
1		
2		
3		
4		
5		
6		
7		
8		
9		
10		
11		

b. At what price is total revenue maximized? (Hint: this may be a price that is *not* included in your table.)

c. Suppose the price is initially $6, but it then decreases to $5. Calculate the elasticity of demand between these two points on the demand curve using the midpoint method.

d. Based on your calculations in part c., describe the relationship between the absolute value of the percentage change in the quantity demanded and the absolute value of the percentage change in price when moving from a price of $6 to a price of $5.

3. For each of the following pairs of goods, identify which good is likely to have the more elastic price elasticity of demand, and then provide an explanation for your choice.
   a. Apples and all fruit

   b. Gasoline and ice cream

c. Leisure travel and business travel

4. Suppose there are two goods, good C and good D. The cross-price elasticity of demand for these two goods is equal to - 0.2.
   a. What is the relationship between good C and good D? Explain your answer.

   b. Suppose the price of good C increases from $1 to $2. What do you estimate will be the percentage change in the quantity demanded of good D? (Use the simple formula for percentage changes rather than the midpoint method.)

   c. Suppose the cross-price elasticity of demand between two goods is negative and you would like to sell more units of one of these goods. What do you hope will happen to the price of the other good? Explain your answer.

5. When Mario's income increases by 10%, his consumption of noodles decreases from 100 units a year to 70 units a year, while his consumption of salmon increases from 20 units a year to 60 units a year.
   a. What is Mario's income elasticity of demand for noodles?

   b. What is Mario's income elasticity of demand for salmon?

   c. Is either of these goods income elastic for Mario?

   d. Is either of these goods income inelastic for Mario?

   e. From Mario's perspective, is either of these goods a luxury good? Explain your answer.

   f. From Mario's perspective, is either of these goods an inferior good? Explain your answer.

6. The following table describes a linear supply curve for bicycles in Microland.

Price	Quantity supplied of bicycles
$0	0
100	200
200	400
300	600
400	800
500	1,000

a. Graph this supply curve and then write an equation for it in slope-intercept form.

b. Suppose suppliers initially sell bicycles for $200 but then decrease their price to $100. Using the midpoint method, what is the value of the price elasticity of supply between these two points on the supply curve?

c. Suppose suppliers initially sell bicycles for $400 and then the price increases to $500. Using the midpoint method, what is the value of the price elasticity of supply between these two points on the supply curve?

7. The following table expresses the amount people are willing to pay to buy a new music-playing device. Use this information to answer this series of questions.

Name of person	Price willing to pay
Joe	$100
Mary	200
Lucinda	150
Pete	50
Mario	300

a. If the market price is $175, who will buy the good and what is the value of total consumer surplus?

b. Suppose the market price is $175, but a decision is made to allocate the two units of the good that are demanded at that price to Mario and Lucinda. What is the value of total consumer surplus in this case?

c. Why does the reallocation of the good in part b. reduce the value of consumer surplus? What are the implications of the reduction in consumer surplus that occurs when the good is not allocated to those buyers who place the highest value on the good?

8. The following table provides a list of sellers of organic apples and the lowest price each seller is willing to accept for a bushel of apples. Assume that each seller will only offer a single bushel of apples for sale. Use this information to answer this series of questions.

Seller	Lowest price seller is willing to accept for a bushel of apples
Ski Top Orchards	$6.00
J. Appleseed's Finest	7.25
Red's Organic	5.80
Pure Apples	8.25
Nature's Medicine	8.00

a. Suppose the market price of apples is $7.00 a bushel. At this price, which of the potential sellers will agree to sell a bushel of apples? What is the value of producer surplus when the market price of apples is $7.00 a bushel?

b. Suppose the market price of apples is $7.00 a bushel and that J. Appleseed's Finest is forced to sell a bushel of apples while Ski Top Orchards is forced to not sell a bushel of apples. When we reallocate sales according to this plan, what happens to the value of producer surplus in this market?

c. How does reallocation of sales away from the market-provided allocation alter the value of producer surplus? What implications does this result have if your goal is to maximize producer surplus?

9. George is considering the purchase of some new shirts for work. He is willing to pay $35 for the first shirt, $25 for the second shirt, and $15 for the third. Oxford Clothiers, his favorite shirt manufacturer, currently is selling shirts for $28 a shirt. What is the efficient number of shirts for George to buy? What is George's consumer surplus in this situation? Explain your answers.

10. Mark consumes ice cream and hamburgers. The following table provides information about the relationship between the quantity of ice cream and hamburgers and the total utility Mark gets from their consumption.

Utility from Ice Cream Consumption		Utility from Hamburger Consumption	
Quantity of ice cream (cones)	Total utility from ice cream (utils)	Quantity of hamburgers	Total utility from hamburgers (utils)
0	0	0	0
1	20	1	15
2	38	2	28
3	53	3	39
4	66	4	48
5	77	5	53
6	84		
7	89		
8	92		
9	94		
10	95		

Mark's income for expenditure on ice cream and hamburgers is $50 per month, the price of ice cream is $5 per cone, and the price of hamburgers is $10 per hamburger.

a. Complete the following table based on the above information.

Consumption bundle	Quantity of ice cream (cones)	Utility from ice cream (utils)	Quantity of hamburgers	Utility from hamburgers (utils)	Total utility (utils)
A	0		5		
B				48	86
C	6		2		
D		92			107
E	10		0		

b. Draw a horizontal line and label points along this line to correspond to the different combinations of ice cream and hamburgers Mark can afford given his income and the prices of the two goods. Moving from left to right along this horizontal line, the number of ice cream cones increases while the number of hamburgers decreases.

c. Graph the results from part **a.** using two different graphs. In the first graph, put the quantity of ice cream cones on the horizontal axis and the quantity of hamburgers on the vertical axis. Draw Mark's budget line and label consumption bundles *A* through *E* on this budget line. On a second graph drawn just below the first graph, draw Mark's total utility function: measure Mark's total utility on the vertical axis and the quantity of ice cream and the quantity of hamburgers on the horizontal axis—you practiced drawing this horizontal axis in part b. of this problem. Moving from left to right along the horizontal axis, the number of ice cream cones increases while the number of hamburgers decreases. Label consumption bundles *A* through *E* on Mark's total utility curve.

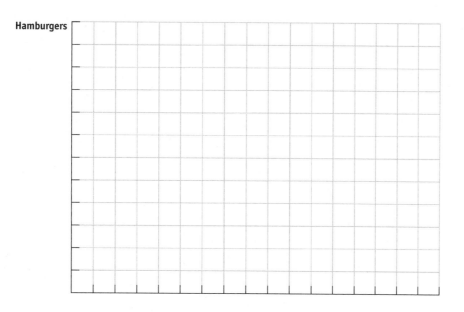

Hamburgers

Quantity of ice cream

Total utility

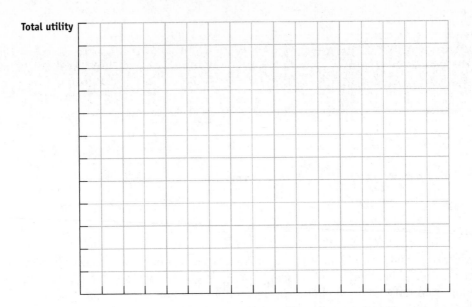

d. Given your work in part **a.** and the information you graphed in part **c.**, which consumption bundle is the optimal consumption bundle for Mark? Why is this bundle the optimal consumption bundle?

e. In the table on the following page, calculate Mark's marginal utility per ice cream cone (MU_{ic}), his marginal utility per dollar spent on ice cream (MU_{ic}/P_{ic}), his marginal utility per hamburger (MU_h), and his marginal utility per dollar spent on hamburgers (MU_h/P_h). Remember that the price of ice cream is \$5 per cone and the price of hamburgers is \$10.

Ice Cream				Hamburgers			
Quantity of ice cream (cones)	Utility from ice cream (utils)	MU_{ic} (utils)	MU_{ic}/P_{ic} (utils)	Quantity of hamburgers	Utility from hamburgers	MU_h (utils)	MU_h/P_h (utils)
0	0			0	0		
		20	4			15	1.5
1	20			1	15		
2	38			2	28		
3	53			3	39		
4	66			4	48		
5	77			5	53		
		7	1.4				
6	84						
7	89						
8	92						
9	94						
10	95						

f. Using the figure on the following page, draw a graph of Mark's marginal utility per dollar spent on ice cream and marginal utility per dollar spent on hamburgers. This graph's horizontal axis should be labeled in the same manner as the one you drew in part **b.** of this problem, while the vertical axis should measure Mark's marginal utility per dollar.

Marginal utility per dollar spent (utils)

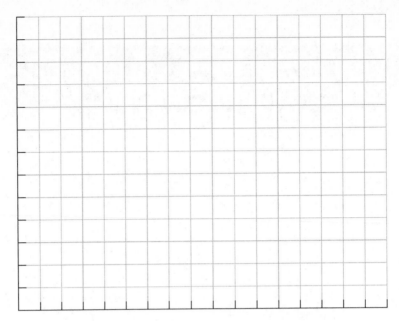

g. At the optimal consumption bundle *C*, what is the relationship between the marginal utility per dollar spent on ice cream and the marginal utility per dollar spent on hamburgers?

Review Questions

Circle your answer to the following questions.

1. The substitution effect measures
   a. the effect of a price change on the quantity of the good consumed.
   b. the change in the consumer's purchasing power when the price of the good changes.
   c. the degree to which good Y can be replaced by good X.
   d. the total utility an individual gets from consuming a particular consumption bundle.
   e. the additional utility an individual gets from consuming one more item.

2. When the price of a good increases and expenditures on that good represent a substantial amount of an individual's income, then the _____ effect makes that individual poorer since the price increase effectively _____ the individual's purchasing power.
   a. income   reduces
   b. substitution   reduces
   c. income   increases
   d. substitution   increases
   e. income   maintains

3. If the price is initially $10 and then increases to $15, the absolute value of the percentage change in price using the midpoint method is
   a. 4.
   b. 5.
   c. 25%.
   d. 40%.
   e. 50%.

4. A horizontal demand curve is
  a. perfectly inelastic.
  b. elastic
  c. unit elastic
  d. inelastic
  e. perfectly elastic.

5. Use the graph provided to answer this question. Suppose price is initially at P_1. Which of the following statements is true?

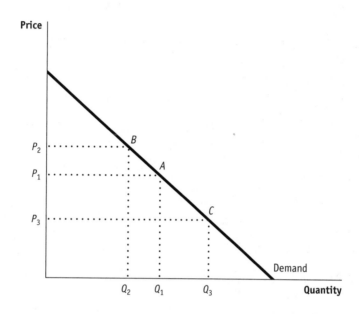

a. If price rises to P_2, then the quantity effect will dominate over the price effect and total revenue will increase.

b. If price falls to P_3, then the quantity effect will dominate over the price effect and total revenue will increase.

c. If price rises to P_2, then the price effect will dominate over the quantity effect and total revenue will increase.

d. If price falls to P_3, then the price effect will dominate over the quantity effect and total revenue will decrease.

e. If price falls to P_3, then the price effect will cancel out the quantity effect and total revenue will not change.

6. Which of the following statements is true?
  a. The shorter the time period of adjustment to a change in the price of the good, the more elastic the demand for that good.
  b. Goods that have many close substitutes typically have an inelastic demand.
  c. The demand for essential goods is more elastic than the demand for goods that are nonessential.
  d. Goods that make up a large proportion of expenditures will have more elastic demand than goods that make up a smaller proportion of expenditures.
  e. Goods that are habit forming have a higher elasticity of demand than goods that are not habit forming.

7. This year Joe's income increased by 15% while the quantity of bananas he demanded increased by 8% and the quantity of orange juice he demanded increased by 6%. Which of the following statements is true for Joe?
   a. Bananas are a normal good and orange juice is an inferior good.
   b. Bananas are an inferior good and orange juice is a normal good.
   c. Bananas and orange juice are both normal goods.
   d. Bananas and orange juice are both inferior goods.
   e. Bananas and orange juice are substitutes for Joe.

8. Use the data in the following table to answer this question. The table provides information about prices, quantity demanded, and income for Sue for two different years.

Year	Good	Price	Quantity demanded	Income
2014	Pizza	$6	10	
2014	Books	9	4	
2014				$200
2015	Pizza	6	7.5	
2015	Books	9	5	
2015				250

Calculate Sue's income elasticity of demand for pizza for this time period. Sue's income elasticity of demand for pizza equals _____ and pizza is a(n) _____ good.
   a. -1.3; normal
   b. -1.3; inferior
   c. -1.65; inferior
   d. -1.65; normal
   e. -1.65; complementary

9. Use the information in the following table to answer this question.

Good	Quantity demanded initially	Price initially	Quantity demanded after price change	New price
Pizza	10	$6	8	$6
Books	4	2	3	9

Calculate the cross-price elasticity of demand between the quantity demanded of pizza and the price of books. What is the relationship between pizza and books given this cross-price elasticity of demand value?
   a. Pizza and books are complements.
   b. Pizza and books are substitutes.
   c. Pizza is an inferior good and books are a normal good.
   d. Pizza is a normal good and books are an inferior good.
   e. Pizza is a necessity while books are a luxury.

10. Acme Manufacturing produces 1,000 widgets when the price of widgets is $20 per widget, and 1,200 widgets when the price of widgets is $22 per widget. Using the midpoint method, what is the value of the price elasticity of supply?
   a. - 0.5
   b. 0.5
   c. 0.6
   d. 1.9
   e. 2

Use the following table that expresses the amount people are willing to pay for a dinner tonight at Fast Eddy's Grill to answer questions 11 through 13.

Name of consumer	Price willing to pay
Matt	$20
Donovan	15
Savannah	8
Gertrude	12
Anna	7

11. If a dinner at Fast Eddy's tonight sells for $10, what is the value of Donovan's consumer surplus?
   a. $5
   b. $10
   c. $15
   d. $20
   e. $25

12. If a dinner at Fast Eddy's tonight sells for $9, what is the value of the total consumer surplus?
   a. $5
   b. $10
   c. $15
   d. $19
   e. $20

13. If a dinner at Fast Eddy's tonight sells for $11, who will not purchase a dinner at this restaurant?
   a. Matt & Donovan
   b. Savannah & Anna
   c. Donovan & Savannah
   d. Gertrude & Matt
   e. Savannah & Gertrude

14. For a given linear demand curve and linear supply curve, as the price increases, the value of consumer surplus _____ and the value of producer surplus _____.

	Consumer surplus	Producer surplus
a.	decreases	decreases
b.	is not affected by an increase in price	decreases
c.	increases	is not affected by an increase in price
d.	decreases	increases
e.	increases	decreases

Use the following table that expresses the number of dinners Fast Eddy's Grill is willing to prepare tonight at different prices to answer questions 15 through 17.

Total number of dinners prepared	Price per dinner
1	$3
2	6
3	10
4	12
5	15

15. If a dinner at Fast Eddy's tonight sells for $10, what is the value of Fast Eddy's producer surplus?
   a. $9
   b. $10
   c. $11
   d. $16
   e. $19

16. If the price of a dinner at Fast Eddy's tonight is $13, how many dinners will Fast Eddy sell?
   a. 1
   b. 2
   c. 3
   d. 4
   e. 5

17. Which of the following dinner prices will lead to Fast Eddy's highest value of producer surplus?
   a. $9
   b. $10
   c. $11
   d. $12
   e. $16

18. Use the following graph to answer this question.

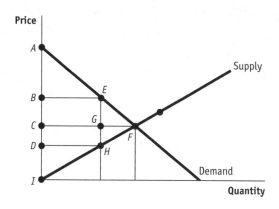

When this market is in equilibrium, total surplus is equal to area
a. *AFI.*
b. *BEHD.*
c. *BEFHD.*
d. *EFH.*
e. *AFH*

19. Use the following information about Joe's utility from consuming pizza to answer this question.

Number of slices of pizza	Total utility
1	100 utils
2	180 utils
3	240 utils
4	280 utils
5	300 utils
6	310 utils

Joe's marginal utility from consuming the fourth slice of pizza equals

a. 20 utils.
b. 40 utils.
c. 60 utils.
d. 280 utils.
e. 300 utils.

Use the following information about Maria's consumption of food and entertainment each month to answer questions 20 through 22. Assume Maria's monthly income for spending on food and entertainment is $400 and that each of the consumption bundles in the table are on her budget line.

Consumption bundle	Quantity of food in consumption bundle	Total utility from food consumption (utils)	Quantity of entertainment in consumption bundle	Total utility from entertainment consumption (utils)
A	200	280	0	0
B	150	240	25	80
C	100	180	50	110
D	50	100	75	130
E	0	0	100	140

20. Given the information in the table, what is the price of each unit of food and the price of each unit of entertainment?
   a. $2; $4
   b. $2; $1
   c. $4; $2
   d. $4; $1
   e. $2: $2

21. Maria maximizes her utility by consuming consumption bundle
   a. A.
   b. B.
   c. C.
   d. D.
   e. E.

22. Suppose Maria initially chooses consumption bundle A. She can increase her total utility by
   a. consuming more units of entertainment and fewer units of food.
   b. consuming more units of food and fewer units of entertainment.
   c. consuming no units of food and the same units of entertainment
   d. consuming no units of entertainment and the same units of food
   e. consuming more units of entertainment and more units of food

Section ⑩ Behind the Supply Curve: Profit, Production, and Costs

Overview

This section focuses on the factors that affect producer choice and the supply side of the supply and demand model. It begins with the concepts of profit and profit maximization as the goal of a firm and then investigates the firm's production function. This section also presents costs and cost curves and introduces the various market structure models economists use to understand how the supply side of the economy works.

Featured Graphs: The Production Function and Cost Curves

This section presents the firm's production cost curves (total, average, and marginal).

MODULES IN THIS SECTION

Module 52   **Defining Profit**

Module 53   **Profit Maximization**

Module 54   **The Production Function**

Module 55   **Firm Costs**

Module 56   **Long-Run Costs and Economies of Scale**

Module 57   **Introduction to Market Structure**

BEFORE YOU TACKLE THE TEST

Draw the Featured Model

Complete the Exercise

Problems

Review Questions

MODULE 52   DEFINING PROFIT

Summary

This module presents the different types of profit and how to calculate them.

Module Objectives

Review these objectives before you read the module. Place a "√" on the line when you can do each of the following:

_____ **Objective #1.**   Explain the difference between explicit and implicit costs and their importance in decision making

_____ **Objective #2.**   Describe the different types of profit, including accounting profit, economic profit, and normal profit

_____ **Objective #3.**   Calculate profit

WHILE YOU READ THE MODULE

Key Terms

Define these key terms as you read the module:

Explicit cost:

Implicit cost:

Accounting profit:

Economic profit:

Implicit cost of capital:

Normal profit:

Practice the Model

Jack is a musician who decided to give up performing professionally and open a music store. The table below summarizes the revenue and costs for Jack's music store in 2016 and 2017

	2016	2017
Total revenue	$200,000	$250,000
Explicit costs	180,000	210,000
Implicit costs	30,000	35,000

1) Give an example of an explicit cost and an implicit cost for Jack's music store.

2) Accounting profit is equal to total revenue minus explicit costs. Calculate accounting profit in both years.

3) Economic profit is equal to total revenue minus BOTH explicit costs and implicit costs. Calculate economic profit in both years.

4) In what year(s) did Jack make an accounting profit? In what year(s) did Jack make an economic profit?

5) Normal profit occurs when economic profit is equal to zero. This is a profit just high enough to keep a business engaged in its current economic activity.
a. Did Jack make a normal profit in either year?

b. Suppose that Jack knows that his business in the future will likely experience the same revenues and costs that he experienced in 2016. Will Jack stay in the music store business? Explain.

List questions or difficulties from your initial reading of the module.

Fill-in-the-Blanks

Fill in the blanks to complete the following statements. If you find yourself having difficulties, please refer back to the appropriate section in the text.

- A firm's profit is equal to **1)**_____ minus **2)**_____.

- The difference between accounting profit and economic profit is that accounting profit only considers

   3)_____ costs.

- The opportunity cost of capital is also called the **4)**_____ cost of capital.

- An economic profit of zero is also called a(n) **5)**_____ profit. When a firm is earning an

   economic profit equal to zero, the firm **6)**_____(will/will not) stay in that business.

Multiple-Choice Questions

Circle the best choice to answer or complete the following questions or incomplete statements. For additional practice, use the space provided to explain why one or more of the incorrect options do not work.

7. Which of the following statements about a firm's profits is true?
    a. Its profit is equal to total cost minus total revenue.
    b. Its accounting profit will be greater than its economic profit.
    c. Its economic profit must be greater than zero in the long run for it to continue producing.
    d. Its economic profit excludes its explicit costs.
    e. Its accounting profit excludes its explicit costs.

8. If a firm has total revenue equal to $5,000, total explicit cost equal to $3,000 and total implicit cost equal to $2,000, which of the following is true? The firm
    a. is earning accounting profit equal to zero.
    b. is earning economic profit equal to $2,000.
    c. will not continue in this activity.
    d. is earning a normal profit.
    e. is earning an accounting profit equal to $3,000.

Helpful Tips

- To calculate a firm's profit, subtract total cost from total revenue. If total cost is less than total revenue, the firm earns a (positive) profit. If total cost is greater than total revenue, the firm earns a negative profit.

- When people use the term profit, they often mean accounting profit. However, accounting profit ignores opportunity costs, and economists recognize that opportunity costs are very important. This is why economists mean economic profit when they use the term profit.

- It may sound strange that a firm would stay in business if it is making zero profit (in other words, a normal profit). A firm would definitely not stay in business if it were making an accounting profit equal to zero because that means it is only covering its explicit costs. However, if a firm is making an economic profit equal to zero, it is covering both its explicit and implicit costs and therefore could not do any better using its resources in any other activity. When a firm is earning an economic profit, it is earning an accounting profit that is greater than zero, because including implicit costs means that economic profit will be less than accounting profit.

- The idea of "earning" a *negative* profit can sound strange. When total cost is greater than total revenue, most people would say the firm is losing money. But "earning" a *loss* can also sound awkward. When a firm's total cost is greater than its total revenue, there are a variety of acceptable ways to refer to the situation. For example, it is correct to say that the firm is earning a negative profit or that it is earning a loss. But be careful to say one or the other – not both. For example, if a firm has total revenue of $1,000 and total cost of $1,500, the firm is earning a profit equal to –$500. It is also correct to say the firm is earning a negative profit equal to $500 or the firm is earning a loss of $500.

Module Notes

This module returns to the concept of opportunity cost. When economists measure costs, they include opportunity cost, or the benefit foregone when a choice is made. You may find it helpful to review the discussion of opportunity cost in Section 1. In this section, opportunity cost is discussed as implicit costs. When measuring costs, economists include both explicit and implicit costs. This means that opportunity costs are incorporated into the measures of costs that economists calculate. Economic decision making must include implicit costs.

It is important to understand the distinction between accounting and economic profits. Throughout this course, the focus is on economic profit, since it includes the opportunity cost of producing a good or service. Accounting profit, although often used by non-economists, does not include the implicit cost of producing a good or service. As you think about accounting versus economic profit, remember that business owners incur an opportunity cost associated with the use of their time and capital, and it is important to include this opportunity cost when evaluating a firm's profit.

MODULE 53 PROFIT MAXIMIZATION

BEFORE YOU READ THE MODULE

Summary

This module investigates how firms maximize their profits.

Module Objectives

Review these objectives before you read the module. Place a "√" on the line when you can do each of the following:

_____Objective #1. Perform marginal analysis

_____Objective #2. Determine the profit-maximizing level of output using the optimal output rule

WHILE YOU READ THE MODULE

Key Terms

Define these key terms as you read the module:

Principle of marginal analysis:

Marginal revenue:

Optimal output rule:

Marginal cost curve:

Marginal revenue curve:

Practice the Model

The following table shows costs, revenue, and profit for a bakery when the price of a cake is $22.

Quantity of cakes	Total Revenue	Marginal revenue	Total Cost	Marginal Cost	Profit
0	0		10		−10
		22		2	
1	22		12		10
		22		6	
2	44		18		26
		—		—	
3	66		28		38
		—		—	
4	88		42		46
		—		—	
5	110		60		50
		—		—	
6	132		82		50
		—		—	
7	154		108		
		—		—	
8	176		138		
		—		—	
9	198		172		
		—		—	
10	220		210		

1) Complete the table by calculating the entries for marginal revenue and marginal cost. The first two have been done for you.

2) The profit-maximizing rule is marginal cost is equal to marginal revenue. What quantity yields the highest total profit? What are marginal cost and marginal revenue at the profit-maximizing quantity?

3) Whenever marginal revenue is higher than marginal cost, the last unit costs less to produce than the revenue earned from selling it.
   a. Compare marginal cost to marginal revenue when the quantity is 4 cakes.

   b. Compare the marginal cost to the marginal revenue when the quantity is 8 cakes.

4) Profit is equal to total cost minus total revenue. Complete the profit column in the table. What quantity yields the highest total profit based on these values? Is this consistent with what you said in **2)**?

List questions or difficulties from your initial reading of the module.

AFTER YOU READ THE MODULE

Fill-in-the-Blanks

Fill in the blanks to complete the following statements. If you find yourself having difficulties, please refer back to the appropriate section in the text.

- The optimal output rule says that profit is maximized by producing at the quantity at which

  1)_____ is equal to **2)**_____. Given the firm's total cost of producing, whether

  or not the firm earns a profit at that quantity depends on the **3)**_____ of the product.

- If the firm sells every unit of its output for the same market price, then price is equal to marginal

  4)_____.

- In the long run, a firm will remain in business (decide to produce any output at all) only if it earns an

  economic profit equal to at least **5)**_____, also known as a **6)**_____ profit.

Multiple-Choice Questions

Circle the best choice to answer or complete the following questions or incomplete statements. For additional practice, use the space provided to explain why one or more of the incorrect options do not work.

7. If marginal cost is never exactly equal to marginal revenue, a firm should produce up to the last quantity where *MC* is
   a. greater than *MR*.
   b. less than *MR*.
   c. greater than zero.
   d. equal to zero.
   e. equal to average cost.

8. If marginal revenue is constant and price is greater than marginal cost, to maximize profit a firm should
   a. shut down.
   b. produce more.
   c. produce less.
   d. exit the industry.
   e. invest in more capital.

9. If the change in total revenue generated by an additional unit of output decreases as more output is produced and sold, the marginal revenue curve will
   a. be horizontal.
   b. have a positive slope.
   c. slope downward.
   d. be below the *MC* curve.
   e. be U-shaped.

Helpful Tips

• The optimal output rule says that to maximize profit, you should produce the quantity at which marginal revenue is equal to marginal cost ($MC = MR$). But what do you do if there is no output level at which marginal revenue exactly equals marginal cost? In that case, you produce the largest quantity for which marginal revenue exceeds marginal cost.

Module Notes

It is important to remember that the optimal level of production always occurs where marginal cost equals marginal benefit. As more of a good is produced, the marginal cost of producing it rises (due to diminishing returns) and the marginal benefit falls (due to diminishing marginal utility). If marginal cost is less than marginal benefit, it costs less to produce than the benefit it provides so more should be produced. As more is produced, the marginal cost rises and the marginal benefit falls until $MC = MR$ at the profit-maximizing quantity. If marginal cost is greater than marginal benefit, too much of the good is being produced because that unit costs more to produce than the benefit it creates. As the quantity produced decreases, marginal cost falls and marginal benefit increases until $MC = MR$ at the profit-maximizing quantity.

In the simple example in this module, the price of a good never changes, regardless of the quantity that is produced; so, the marginal revenue curve is a horizontal line at the market price. This is the special case of a perfectly competitive market structure (studied in Section 11). Since $P = MR$, the price stays the same regardless of the quantity that is produced. The optimal output rule can also be written as $P = MR = MC$.

MODULE 54 | THE PRODUCTION FUNCTION

BEFORE YOU READ THE MODULE

Summary

This module presents production functions and explains why they are often subject to diminishing returns to an input.

Module Objectives

Review these objectives before you read the module. Place a "√" on the line when you can do each of the following:

_____**Objective #1.** Discuss the importance of the firm's production function, the relationship between the quantity of inputs and the quantity of output

_____**Objective #2.** Explain why production is often subject to diminishing returns to inputs

WHILE YOU READ THE MODULE

Key Terms

Define these key terms as you read the module:

Production function:

Fixed input:

Variable input:

Long run:

Short run:

Total product curve:

Marginal product:

Diminishing returns to an input:

Practice the Model

The following table gives the relationship between the quantity of labor and the quantity of cakes produced at a bakery.

Quantity of labor (hours)	Quantity of cakes	Marginal product of labor
0	0	
		15
1	15	
		13
2	28	
		11
3	39	
		9
4	48	
		7
5	55	
		5
6	60	
		3
7	63	
		2
8	65	

1) Sketch a correctly labeled production function using the data given in the table. Use Figure 54.1 in your textbook as your guide.

2) Sketch a correctly labeled marginal product of labor curve using the data given in the table. Use Figure 54.2 in your textbook as your guide.

List questions or difficulties from your initial reading of the module.

AFTER YOU READ THE MODULE

Fill-in-the-Blanks

Fill in the blanks to complete the following statements. If you find yourself having difficulties, please refer back to the appropriate section in the text.

- The relationship between the quantity of output a firm produces and the quantity of inputs it uses is known as the firm's **1)**_____.

- The additional output produced as a result of hiring an additional unit of labor is known as the

  2)_____ of labor. There are diminishing returns to an input when an increase in the

  quantity of that input, holding the quantity of all other inputs fixed, **3)**_____ that input's

  marginal product. As a result, the firm's marginal product curve has a **4)**_____ slope.

- When the firm has sufficient time to adjust its use of any input, the firm is operating in the

  5)_____. When at least one input is fixed, the firm is operating in the

  6)_____.

Multiple-Choice Questions

Circle the best choice to answer or complete the following questions or incomplete statements. For additional practice, use the space provided to explain why one or more of the incorrect options do not work.

7. Which of the following is true in the long run? A firm may vary
   a. all of its inputs.
   b. none of its inputs.
   c. only one of its inputs.
   d. all but one of its inputs.
   e. labor but not capital.

8. When marginal product is increasing, what is happening to the firm's *MC*, ATC, and *APL*?

MC	*ATC*	*APL*
a. increasing	increasing	increasing
b. increasing	increasing	decreasing
c. increasing	decreasing	decreasing
d. decreasing	increasing	increasing
e. decreasing	decreasing	increasing

Helpful Tips

- The marginal product of labor is defined as the additional output produced when a firm hires one more unit of labor. The marginal product of any input is similar; it is the additional output produced when the firm hires an additional unit of the input. But what do we mean by a "unit" of labor? Is it an additional hour of labor, an additional week of labor, or some other units? It could be any of these. The important thing when answering a question is that you use the units that are relevant for the particular question.

- Don't think of the long run and short run as specific lengths of time. A firm is operating in the long run when it has enough time to vary all of its inputs; the amount of time that takes depends on what the firm is producing (and other factors specific to the firm).

Module Review

This module continues to use the concept of *marginal*. The marginal product of an input and the marginal cost of production are introduced. Both of these concepts consider changes. Marginal product of an input measures the change in output when an additional unit of an input is employed ($\blacktriangle Q / \blacktriangle L$), and the marginal cost measures the change in total cost due to a change in output ($\blacktriangle TC / \blacktriangle Q$). A change in output is considered when looking at both marginal product and marginal cost, but the change in output is in the numerator for marginal product and the denominator for marginal cost. Make sure you keep this difference straight when working with *MP* and *MC*!

   It is important that you understand the distinction between the short run and the long run. In the short run, at least one input is fixed, while in the long run all inputs are variable. An input is fixed if its level of usage does not change when the level of production changes. An input is variable when its level of usage varies as the level of production varies. There is no set length of time that determines the boundary between the short run and the long run: the short run is a time period so short that full adjustment to changes cannot take place, while the long run is a time period sufficiently long enough to allow full adjustment.

MODULE 55   FIRM COSTS

BEFORE YOU READ THE MODULE

Summary

This module looks at how a firm's production function can be used to develop its cost curves.

Module Objectives

Review these objectives before you read the module. Place a "√" on the line when you can do each of the following:

_____**Objective #1.**   Describe the various types of cost a firm faces, including fixed cost, variable cost, and total cost

_____**Objective #2.**   Explain how a firm's costs generate marginal cost curves and average cost curves

WHILE YOU READ THE MODULE

Key Terms

Define these key terms as you read the module:

Fixed cost:

Variable cost:

Total cost:

Total cost curve:

Average total cost:

Average cost:

U-shaped average total cost curve:

Average fixed cost:

Average variable cost:

Minimum-cost output:

Practice the Model

1) Max produces and sells muffins. In the space below, draw a correctly labeled graph showing Max's average total cost (*ATC*), marginal cost (*MC*), and average variable cost (*AVC*) curves. Label the horizontal axis "Quantity (in dozens)" and the vertical axis "Cost of unit."

2) Max's minimum cost output is 10 dozen, and marginal cost is $6 when quantity equals 10 dozen. Label this point "A" on your graph.

List questions or difficulties from your initial reading of the module.

AFTER YOU READ THE MODULE

Fill-in-the-Blanks

Fill in the blanks to complete the following statements. If you find yourself having difficulties, please refer back to the appropriate section in the text.

* There are many different ways to categorize a firm's costs. A cost that does not depend on the quantity

  of output produced is known as a **1)**_____ cost. A firm's total cost is equal to its

  2)_____ cost plus its **3)**_____ cost.

- The additional cost of producing an additional unit of output is known as **4)**_____ cost and the cost per unit is also known as **5)**_____ cost.

- The quantity of output that corresponds to the minimum average total cost is called the **6)**_____ output.

- **7)**_____ total and variable cost curves tend to be "U" shaped while **8)**_____ cost curves have a "swoosh" shape.

Multiple-Choice Questions

Circle the best choice to answer or complete the following questions or incomplete statements. For additional practice, use the space provided to explain why one or more of the incorrect options do not work.

Use the table below which describes the costs of production for a firm to answer questions 9 through 11.

Quantity	Fixed costs	Variable costs	Total costs	Marginal costs	Average total costs
0	40	0	40		
				2	
1	40	2	42		42
				6	
2	40	8	—		24
				8	
3	40	18	56		19
				14	
4	40	32	70		—
				—	
5	40	50	—		—
				22	
6	40	72	112		19
				26	
7	40	98	138		20
				30	
8	40	128	168		21
				—	
9	40	162	202		22
				38	
10	40	200	240		24

9. What is the total cost when quantity equals 2?

   a. 6
   b. 12
   c. 42
   d. 48
   e. 72

10. What is the average total cost when quantity equals 5?

   a. 18
   b. 22
   c. 36
   d. 50
   e. 90

11. Which of the following is the minimum cost output?

   a. 0
   b. 1
   c. 4
   d. 6
   e. 10

Helpful Tips

- Average cost is the cost of production *per unit*. To calculate average cost, divide the total cost by the number of units produced. For example, if it costs $100 to produce 10 units, the average cost is $100/10 = $10.

- When you draw average and marginal cost curves on the same graph, make sure the marginal cost curve intersects the average cost curve(s) at the minimum-cost output. That is, your marginal cost curve should intersect the average cost curve(s) at the lowest point. For example, suppose you form a basketball team with five players. To calculate the average height of your team, you would add up the heights of the five players and then divide by 5. Then, if you added another player, this additional player would represent a marginal addition to the height of your team. If this new player were taller than the team's average height, then the team's average height would increase. But, if the player were shorter than the team's average height, then the team's average height would decrease. This basic concept can be applied to a firm's costs: when the marginal cost exceeds the average total cost, the *ATC* must rise; and when the marginal cost is less than the average total cost, the *ATC* must fall.

- In addition to knowing the definition of each of the important costs (*TC, VC, FC, ATC, AVC, AFC, MC*), make sure you understand how the costs are related. Here is a summary of these relationships:

$$TC = FC + VC$$

$$ATC = TC/Q$$

$$AVC = VC/Q$$

$$AFC = FC/Q$$

$$ATC = AFC + AVC$$

$$MC = \blacktriangle TC/\blacktriangle Q$$

Module Notes

The study of cost curves, in and of itself, is not the most thrilling of undertakings. In the abstract, it can be difficult to understand why it is so important to know the definitions and relationships among the various types of costs. However, you will soon see how understanding cost curves is crucial to understanding the market structure models we develop in the following sections. Time spent learning about cost curves now is essential to understanding the analysis of market structures. So, as you study cost curves, keep in mind that the time spent will pay off later in terms of your ability to understand a major portion of the course and to analyze interesting real-world markets. Without cost curves, you won't be able to analyze firm behavior (a major goal of this course)!

You will need to learn the new terminology, the abbreviations for this terminology, and how to apply them. This might seem overwhelming at first, but a solid understanding of costs and cost curves will make the models in the next Sections much easier! Once you have learned the definitions and the abbreviations of all the new terms in the module, you should work on a thorough understanding of the graphs, particularly the graphs of ATC, AVC, and MC.

It is important that you understand the distinction between marginal cost and average cost. Marginal values always measure changes and average values are always per unit. Marginal cost measures the cost of producing an additional unit of output, while average cost measures the cost per unit produced.

MODULE 56 LONG-RUN COSTS AND ECONOMIES OF SCALE

BEFORE YOU READ THE MODULE

Summary

This module examines how a firm's costs behave in the short run and in the long run.

Module Objectives

Review these objectives before you read the module. Place a "√" on the line when you can do each of the following:

_____**Objective #1.** Explain why a firm's costs may differ between the short run and the long run

_____**Objective #2.** Describe how a firm can enjoy economies of scale

WHILE YOU READ THE MODULE

Key Terms

Define these key terms as you read the module:

Long-run average total cost curve:

Economies of scale:

Increasing returns to scale:

Diseconomies of scale:

Decreasing returns to scale:

Constant returns to scale:

Sunk cost:

Practice the Model

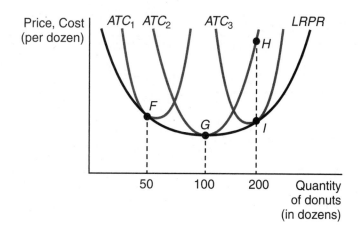

This graph shows the short-run and long-run *ATC* curves for a donut shop. Use the graph to answer the following questions.

1) Which of the points on the graph is associated with economies of scale?

2) Which of the points on the graph is associated with diseconomies of scale?

3) Which of the points on the graph is associated with constant returns to scale?

4) If the donut shop is operating on ATC_2 and is producing 200 dozen donuts, what is likely to happen in the long run? Explain.

List questions or difficulties from your initial reading of the module.

AFTER YOU READ THE MODULE

Fill-in-the-Blanks

Fill in the blanks to complete the following statements. If you find yourself having difficulties, please refer back to the appropriate section in the text.

• The lowest possible average total cost that can be achieved for each output level if the firm were to

   choose its fixed cost is used to determine a firm's **1)**_____ average cost curve. This curve initially has a negative slope, indicating that the firm is experiencing **2)**_____ returns to

scale (also known as economies of scale). In this situation, average cost **3)**_____ as output

increases. Eventually, this curve will have a positive slope, as the firm begins to experience

4)_____ returns to scale (also known as diseconomies of scale). In this situation, average

cost **5)**_____ as output increases.

- Specialization and initial set up costs lead to **6)**_____ returns to scale, while problems of

  communication and coordination lead to **7)**_____ returns to scale.

- **8)**_____ costs should be ignored in decision making.

Multiple-Choice Questions

*Circle the best choice to answer or complete the following questions or incomplete statements. For
additional practice, use the space provided to explain why one or more of the incorrect options do not
work.*

9. Dee produces baby toys and pays $500 per month in rent, $10 per hour in labor costs, and $3 per toy
for fabric and other materials. Which of the following is a fixed cost of production?
 a. rent only
 b. labor only
 c. fabric
 d. materials
 e. rent and labor

10. If a firm doubles the quantity of inputs that it uses and its output increases, but does not double, then
the firm is experiencing
 a. constant returns to scale.
 b. decreasing returns to scale.
 c. increasing returns to scale.
 d. diseconomies of scale.
 e. an average scale.

Helpful Tips

- It can be helpful to remember that economists say that "sunk costs don't matter." That is, producers
  don't consider sunk costs in decision making. This is because sunk costs have been paid and can't
  be recovered. They are gone regardless of what is done in the future.

- Do not think of long run and short run as being specific amounts of time. In the short run, at least one
  input is fixed. In the long run, all inputs can be varied.

Module Notes

Economies and diseconomies of scale refer to whether a firm's average cost increases or decreases as more output is produced in the long run. Firms experiencing economies of scale benefit from being relatively large, while firms with decreasing returns to scale find that getting larger is detrimental.

Returns to scale refer to what happened to output as more inputs are used. Increasing returns to scale occur when a firm doubles its inputs and its output more than doubles. With decreasing returns to scale, when a firm doubles its inputs, its output less than doubles.

Returns to scale and economies of scale are closely related. When a firm doubles its inputs and its output more than doubles (increasing returns to scale), its *ATC*, which is equal to *TC*/*Q*, will decrease since *TC* has doubled while *Q* has more than doubled.

With decreasing returns to scale, when a firm doubles its inputs, it doubles its costs but it produces less than double its output. The firm's *ATC*, which is equal to *TC*/*Q*, will increase since *TC* has doubled while *Q* has less than doubled.

Economies and diseconomies of scale explain why the long-run average cost curve is U-shaped. You should recall that diminishing returns explained why the short-run average cost curves were U-shaped. With diminishing returns, as more and more of a variable factor was added to a fixed factor, marginal product declined. Because a fixed factor is necessary for diminishing returns, it must be a short-run concept (since there are no fixed factors in the long run). Returns to scale, in contrast, is a long-run concept because all factors may be varied to produce any level of output. Be careful to distinguish between short-run and long-run cost concepts.

MODULE 57 INTRODUCTION TO MARKET STRUCTURES

BEFORE YOU READ THE MODULE

Summary

This module presents the four principal models of market structure economists use to study markets.

Module Objectives

Review these objectives before you read the module. Place a "√" on the line when you can do each of the following:

_____**Objective #1.**   Explain the meaning and dimensions of market structure

_____**Objective #2.**   Describe the four principal types of market structure —perfect competition, monopoly, oligopoly, and monopolistic competition

WHILE YOU READ THE MODULE

Key Terms

Define these key terms as you read the module:

Price-taking firm:

Price-taking consumer:

Perfectly competitive market:

Perfectly competitive industry:

Market share:

Standardized product:

Commodity:

Free entry and exit:

Monopoly/ Monopolist:

Barrier to entry:

Natural monopoly:

Patent:

Copyright:

Oligopoly/Oligopolist:

Imperfect competition:

Concentration ratios:

Herfindahl-Hirschman Index:

Monopolistic competition:

Practice the Model

List the market structure(s) in which firms MUST exhibit each of the following characteristics:

1) Many firms

2) Differentiated product

3) Economies of scale

4) High market share

5) Free entry and exit

List questions or difficulties from your initial reading of the module.

AFTER YOU READ THE MODULE

Fill-in-the-Blanks

Fill in the blanks to complete the following statements. If you find yourself having difficulties, please refer back to the appropriate section in the text.

- Market structure models are defined by the number of **1)**_____ in the market and the type

    of **2)**_____ sold. Economists consider four principle models of market structure: perfect

    competition, monopoly, oligopoly, and monopolistic competition.

- In perfect competition, there are many consumers and producers and both producers and consumers are

    3)_____ takers. Also, in a perfectly competitive market the product is

    4)_____. An industry controlled by a single producer is known as a **5)**_____.

    Single producers can persist in a market due to **6)**_____ to entry.

- A market structure in which firms compete but also possess market power is known as imperfect

    competition. Imperfect competition includes industries with only a few firms, known as

    7)_____ and industries with a large number of competing producers, differentiated

    products, and free entry, known as **8)**_____.

Multiple-Choice Questions

Circle the best choice to answer or complete the following questions or incomplete statements. For additional practice, use the space provided to explain why one or more of the incorrect options do not work.

9. In which market structure are firms price takers?
   a. perfect competition
   b. monopoly
   c. natural monopoly
   d. oligopoly
   e. monopolistic competition

10. Which market structure has free entry and exit and many firms that sell differentiated products?
   a. natural monopoly
   b. monopoly
   c. oligopoly
   d. perfect competition
   e. monopolistic competition

Helpful Tips

Use the following table to review the characteristics of the four market structure models.

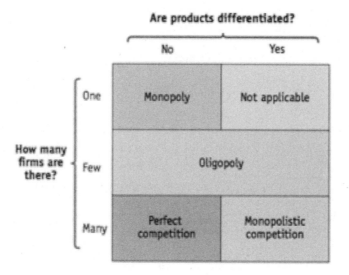

Module Notes

In reality, it is not always easy to definitively determine which market structure model fits a particular industry. In fact, economists often debate the appropriate model to use for some industries. It is best to think of markets in the real world as falling somewhere on a spectrum between monopoly and perfect competition. Where some specific markets fall on the spectrum can be between two of the market structures. For example, an industry can have a dominant firm that behaves in many ways like a monopoly, but there are several other small firms operating in the market. This industry falls between monopoly and oligopoly. Or an industry can have many firms, easy entry and exit, and a product that some see as essentially identical but others see as slightly differentiated. This industry falls between perfect competition and monopolistic competition. When using economic models, it is clear how firms in the different market structures behave. However, when looking at reality, differences are not always so clear-cut.

Draw The Featured Graph: Short-Run Cost Curves

Draw a firm's marginal and average cost curves (include average fixed, average variable, and average total cost curves), showing the typical shape of these curves. Be careful to correctly show where the marginal cost curve must cross the average variable and average total cost curves. Don't forget to label the axes on your graph!

Complete the Exercise

Discuss each of the following statements. Decide whether the statement is true or false and then justify your answer.

a. As output increases, if average total cost is decreasing, then marginal cost must be less than average total cost.

b. As output increases, if marginal cost is increasing, then marginal cost must be greater than average total cost.

c. As output increases, if marginal cost is greater than average fixed cost, then average fixed cost must be increasing.

d. As output increases, fixed cost decreases.

e. As output increases, variable cost increases.

Problems

1. Susie operates a business that prints designs on T-shirts. Susie's total revenue per year equals $500,000. The cost of labor per year is $125,000, the cost of raw materials and supplies is $200,000 per year, while the value of capital for the business is $200,000. Susie knows she could earn $50,000 per year working as a printer at a competitor's business. She also knows she could sell her business and the land it sits on for $600,000 and earn 10% a year on these funds. Each year her depreciation equals 5% of her capital expenditure.

a. What are Susie's explicit costs? Calculate the value for these explicit costs.

b. What are Susie's implicit costs? Calculate the value for these implicit costs.

c. What is Susie's accounting profit?

d. What is Susie's economic profit?

2. The following table describes the short-run production function for Harry's company. Harry uses labor and capital to produce can openers.

Quantity of labor (workers)	Quantity of capital (units)	Quantity of output (can openers)
0	10	0
1	10	50
2	10	80
3	10	100
4	10	115
5	10	125
6	10	133
7	10	138

a. How do you know that the table represents Harry's short-run production function? How is the short run different from the long run?

b. Economists make a distinction between variable inputs and fixed inputs. For the above short-run production function, which input is the fixed input and which one is the variable input? Explain your answer.

c. Draw Harry's total product curve for the production of can openers, holding the level of capital constant. In your graph measure the quantity of labor on the *x*-axis and the quantity of can openers on the *y*-axis.

d. Complete the following table using the information given above and assuming that capital is held constant at 10 units.

Quantity of labor (hours)	Quantity of output (can openers)	Marginal product of labor $MPL = \frac{\Delta Q}{\Delta L}$ (can openers per worker)
0	0	
		50
1	50	
2	80	
3	100	
4	115	
5	125	
6	133	
7	138	

e. Describe the results you found in part d. What is the relationship between the quantity of labor used and the marginal product of labor at Harry's can opener factory?

f. Graph Harry's marginal product of labor on a graph with the quantity of labor measured on the x axis and the marginal product of labor measured on the y-axis. Plot the marginal product values you found in part **d.** using the midpoint method. For example, the marginal product of labor from hiring the first unit of labor is equal to 50 can openers per worker: plot this information midway between 0 and 1 unit of labor.

g. What does it mean if the marginal product of labor curve is downward-sloping as you hire more units of the variable input?

3. The following table provides the short-run production function for Sherry's Hair Salon. Sherry uses only two inputs, labor and capital, to produce her output of stylish haircuts. The price of labor is $20 an hour and the price of capital is $50 per unit.

Quantity of capital (units)	Quantity of labor (hours of work)	Quantity of haircuts
10	0	0
10	10	15
10	20	28
10	30	38
10	40	44
10	50	48

a. Complete the following table of Sherry's costs given the above information. Round your calculations to one place past the decimal point.

Quantity of capital (units)	Quantity of labor (hours of work)	Quantity of haircuts	FC ($)	VC ($)	AFC ($)	AVC ($)	ATC ($)	TC ($)	MC ($ per unit of output)
10	0	0			—	—	—	500	
									13.3
10	10	15							
10	20	28							
10	30	38							
10	40	44							
10	50	48							

b. Does this production function exhibit diminishing marginal returns to labor? Explain your answer.

c. Graph the total cost function for Sherry's Hair Salon. Measure total cost on the vertical axis and the quantity of haircuts on the horizontal axis. Describe how increasing the quantity of haircuts affects the slope of the total cost curve.

d. Graph the marginal cost function for Sherry's Hair Salon using the midpoint method. Measure marginal cost on the vertical axis and the quantity of haircuts on the horizontal axis. Describe the slope of the *MC* curve and then explain why the *MC* is sloped this way.

e. In a new graph, draw Sherry's Hair Salon's *AFC* curve. Measure average fixed cost on the vertical axis and the quantity of haircuts on the horizontal axis. On your graph, indicate the area that corresponds to fixed cost if 15 haircuts are currently being produced.

f. In a new graph, sketch Sherry's Hair Salon's *ATC, AVC, AFC,* and *MC* curves. Measure cost per unit on the vertical axis and the quantity of haircuts on the horizontal axis. What must be true about the relationship between the *ATC* and *MC* curves?

4. For each of the following costs, decide whether it is a fixed cost or a variable cost for the firm in the short run. Provide a brief argument for your classification of the cost.

a. A one-year lease on the building in which the business is located

b. Annual property taxes that are assessed on the value of the land the business owns

c. The cost of a necessary metal used in the production of the firm's product

d. A ten-year-old metal stamping machine that has a useful life of twenty years in your business and is sufficient to produce any desired level of output for the firm

e. Sugar that the firm uses to make the cookies it sells

5. The following table provides some information about Stella's Delight, a business that Stella owns. Stella uses labor and capital as her only inputs in the production of her product.

a. Fill in the table below.

Quantity of labor (units)	Quantity of capital (units)	Quantity of output	VC ($)	FC ($)	AVC ($)	AFC ($)	ATC ($)	TC ($)	MC ($ per unit of output)
0	5	0			—	—	—		
1	5	10							
2	5	18			10				
3	5	24	15						
4	5	28							
5	5	30							
6	5	31							

b. What is the price of the variable input?

c. What is the price of the fixed input?

d. What is the marginal product of the fifth unit of labor?

e. What is the marginal cost of producing the twenty-fourth unit of output?

6. Suppose the firm represented in the following table is operating in the long run. This firm produces chairs using wood and labor. Some production information is provided in the table. Assume the price of wood and the price of labor do not change.

Quantity of wood	Quantity of labor	Quantity of chairs
4 units	5 units	20 chairs
8 units	10 units	45 chairs
12 units	15 units	90 chairs
24 units	30 units	150 chairs

a. If this firm is currently using 4 units of wood and 5 units of labor, does it experience increasing, decreasing, or constant returns to scale if it increases its wood use to 8 units and its labor use to 10 units? Explain your answer.

b. Is this firm's *LRATC* curve downward-sloping, upward-sloping, or constant in the range of production described in part **a.**?

c. If this firm is currently using 8 units of wood and 10 units of labor and it increases the use of both inputs by 50%, will the firm experience increasing, decreasing, or constant returns to scale?

d. Is this firm's *LRATC* curve downward-sloping, upward-sloping, or constant in the range of production described in part **c.**?

e. Suppose this firm is currently using 12 units of wood and 15 units of labor to produce chairs, and then the firm increases its input usage by 100% for both inputs. Will the firm experience increasing, decreasing, or constant returns to scale?

f. Is this firm's *LRATC* curve downward-sloping, upward-sloping, or constant in the range of production described in part **e.**?

7. The following table provides information about Sarah's Doughnut Shoppe, a small firm operating in a perfectly competitive industry. Use this information to answer the following set of questions.

Quantity of doughnuts	Total revenue	Total cost	Profit
100	$200	$250	
200	400	360	
300	600	530	
400	800	725	
500	1,000	950	

a. What is the market price for a doughnut?

b. Fill in the profit column of the table. At what level of output does Sarah's Doughnut Shoppe maximize its profits?

c. Calculate Sarah's Doughnut Shoppe's marginal cost and marginal revenue for each level of output. Use the following table to organize your results.

Quantity of doughnuts	Total revenue	Total cost	Marginal cost	Marginal revenue	Profit
100	$200	$250			
200	400	360			
300	600	530			
400	800	725			
500	1,000	950			

d. What is the relationship between marginal revenue and marginal cost at the profit-maximizing level of output for Sarah's Doughnut Shoppe? Explain the meaning of this relationship and how it relates to profitability.

8. You are given the following information about the five firms that produce soda in Bigtown. These five firms are the only producers of soda in Bigtown, and all soda consumed in Bigtown comes from these five producers.

Name of company	Quantity of soda sold (cans per month)
Fizzy Water	150
Cool Tonics	200
Carbonated Bliss	100
Mom's Pop	450
Taste of Eden	100

a. Given the above information, would you characterize the market for soda in Bigtown as perfectly competitive? Explain your answer.

b. Suppose market share is defined as the percentage of total sales represented by a firm's sales of soda over the given period. Calculate the market share of each of the companies producing soda in Bigtown.

c. Is the soda produced in this market likely to be standardized? Explain your answer.

9. Small Town initially has a single firm that serves good coffee and wonderful pastries. This firm is busy every morning with long lines of customers eager to get a hot cup of coffee and a breakfast pastry. The owner of the café is excited that he is earning $50,000 a year as his take-home pay, since in his former job he managed to earn only $30,000.

a. Is this scenario likely to be a long-run equilibrium situation? Explain your answer.

b. What do you anticipate will happen in the long run in Small Town?

c. The owner of the café is interviewed ten years after the initial story about his success. The reporter finds out that the café owner is no longer in business providing coffee and pastries. Can you think of a possible story to explain this owner's departure from the business? (Hint: the owner did not choose to retire—he simply exited the industry during this ten-year period.)

10. In October, Marissa paid an annual subscription fee of $600 to the local opera company for this season's five opera performances. This fee is nonrefundable and entitles Marissa to one ticket to each of the five performances. A friend of Marissa's invites Marissa to an all-expense paid weekend to Miami. Marissa discovers that the weekend her friend invites her to Miami is the same weekend as the first opera performance. Marissa estimates that the value of the trip to Miami is $1,000.

a. Marissa is trying to figure out the cost of going to Miami. Since she will miss the opera, she calculates that the cost of her going to Miami is $120 or the cost of one ticket to the opera. Do you agree with Marissa's reasoning? Explain your answer.

b. With respect to the opera, her friend says that the cost of going to Miami is $0 for Marissa, since whether she goes to the opera or not she will not get her $120 back. Do you agree with this reasoning? Explain your answer.

c. Marissa's roommate says that Marissa's cost of going to Miami is $1,120, since it should include the cost of the trip ($1,000) plus the cost of the missed opera performance ($120). Do you agree with this reasoning? Explain your answer.

Review Questions

Circle your answer to the following questions.

Refer to the following table about the production function for Terry's Widget Shoppe to answer questions 1 through 4. Assume labor is the only variable input Terry uses in the production of widgets.

Quantity of labor hired (workers)	Quantity of widgets per month
0	0
1	100
2	250
3	450
4	600
5	700

1. The marginal product of labor from hiring the third worker is
   a. 150 widgets per worker.
   b. 200 widgets per worker.
   c. 250 widgets per worker.
   d. 450 widgets per worker.
   e. 700 widgets per worker.

2. Diminishing returns to labor begins when Terry hires the
  a. first worker.
  b. second worker.
  c. third worker.
  d. fourth worker
  e. fifth worker.

3. Terry spends $200 a month to rent a building for his company, $600 a month for the capital he employs to produce widgets, and $10 per hour for every worker he employs. Terry's fixed cost per month equals
  a. $200.
  b. $600.
  c. $790.
  d. $800.
  e. $810.

4. Terry spends $200 a month to rent a building for his company, $600 a month for the capital he employs to produce widgets, and $10 per hour for every unit of labor he employs. Terry distinguishes between his fixed cost and his variable cost by
  a. deciding whether or not he is producing in the short run or the long run.
  b. whether or not the cost varies as his level of production changes.
  c. whether or not the cost exceeds $500.
  d. recognizing that capital is always a fixed cost while rent and labor are variable costs.
  e. doubling his inputs and observing what happens to his output.

Use the following information to answer the next four questions. The table provides production function information for Jimmy's Service Shop. Assume Jimmy hires only labor and capital to produce his services. The price of labor is $100 per worker per week and the price of capital is $10 per unit.

Quantity of labor (workers)	Quantity of capital (units)	Quantity of output produced per week (number of services per week)
0	10	0
1	10	200
2	10	400
3	10	600
4	10	700
5	10	750

5. Jimmy's fixed cost of production equals
  a. $0.
  b. $100.
  c. $110.
  d. $500.
  e. $750.

6. Jimmy's variable cost of production
   a. is constant and equal to $100.
   b. varies with the level of output that is produced.
   c. is always greater than his fixed cost.
   d. decreases as the level of production increases due to diminishing marginal returns.
   e. is always equal to average total cost times Q.

7. Jimmy's total cost of producing 700 units of output is
   a. equal to the sum of his average total cost and average variable costs.
   b. $700.
   c. greater than his total cost of producing 800 units of output.
   d. $500.
   e. $600.

8. Jimmy's marginal cost of producing the seven-hundredth unit of output is equal to
   a. $1 per unit of output.
   b. $10 per unit of output.
   c. $100 per unit of output.
   d. $400 per unit of output.
   e. $500 per unit of output.

9. The marginal cost curve is upward-sloping as output increases due to
   a. increasing returns to scale.
   b. decreasing returns to scale.
   c. diminishing marginal returns to the variable input.
   d. increasing marginal returns to the variable input.
   e. economies of scale.

10. In recent years there has been an increased demand for organic produce due to concerns about health issues related to food consumption. Holding everything else constant, in the short run this demand should lead to_____, while in the long run_____ .
    a. increases in the price of organic produce; entry of firms into the industry will reduce the price of organic produce
    b. increases in the price of organic produce; exit of firms from the industry will further increase the price of organic produce
    c. decreases in the price of organic produce; entry of firms into the industry will further reduce the price of organic produce
    d. decreases in the price of organic produce; exit of firms from the industry will increase the price of organic produce
    e. increases in the price of organic produce; exit of firms from the industry which will then decrease the price of organic produce.

11. Which of the following describes a perfectly competitive industry?
   a. Elementary school students are only allowed to attend the school in their attendance area.
   b. Water for household use is sold by the local water utility.
   c. An industry with a Herfindahl-Hirschman Index equal to 10,000.
   d. The price of oil is determined by global supply and demand. A total of five companies produce the world's supply of oil.
   e. The price of wine is determined by global supply and demand. A small share of the total world production of wine is produced in a local valley by ten companies.

12. Marginal revenue is the addition to total
   a. revenue from producing one more unit of the good.
   b. cost from selling one more unit of the good.
   c. revenue from selling one more unit of the good.
   d. profit from producing and selling one more unit of the good.
   e. revenue from hiring one more unit of labor.

13. Suppose Jerry calculates that if he produces one more box of pens his total cost will increase by $15, but that he can sell this box of pens for $14. Jerry will
   a. produce the pens and increase his revenues.
   b. not produce the pens, since the revenue from the additional pens is less than the cost of producing the additional pens.
   c. produce the pens, but wait to sell them until the market price of pens increases.
   d. shut down his pen production, since his addition to revenue from pen production is less than his addition to cost from pen production.
   e. shut down because he is making negative profit.

14. The optimal output rule for a perfectly competitive firm is to produce that quantity where
   a. $MR = MC$ in the long run, but in the short run to produce that quantity where $MC = ATC$.
   b. $MC = ATC$ in the short run.
   c. $MR = MC$ no matter what the time period, provided that marginal revenue is greater than average variable cost.
   d. $MR = MC$ no matter what the time period, provided that marginal revenue is greater than average total cost.
   e. $MC > MR$ in the short run.

15. Which of the following statements about a perfectly competitive firm is true?
   a. A firm profit maximizes by producing that output where $MR < MC$.
   b. A firm will produce in the short run provided that the price of the good exceeds its average variable cost.
   c. A firm in the long run can make positive economic profits.
   d. A firm that makes economic losses in the short run will shut down.
   e. A firm that makes normal profits in the short run will shut down.

16. When a perfectly competitive firm earns zero economic profit in the long run, this implies that accounting profits
   a. are also equal to zero.
   b. cannot be calculated.
   c. are negative.
   d. may be positive, negative, or equal to zero.
   e. are positive.

17. What is the Herfindahl-Hirschman Index for an industry with four firms that each has a 25% market share?
   a. 25
   b. 100
   c. 250
   d. 1,000
   e. 2,500

18. In the short run, the individual supply curve for a perfectly competitive firm is that firm's
   a. *MC* curve at or above the shut-down price.
   b. *ATC* curve above the *MC* curve.
   c. *ATC* curve below the *MC* curve.
   d. *MR* curve at or above the shut-down price.
   e. *MC* curve horizontal at the firm's price.

19. The long-run market equilibrium in a perfectly competitive industry with identical firms results in all firms
   a. earning positive economic profit.
   b. producing the quantity associated with their break-even price.
   c. producing the profit-maximizing quantity at which $MR = AVC$.
   d. producing the profit-maximizing quantity at which $MC = AVC$.
   e. earning negative economic profits.

20. A firm calculates that the cost of producing its tenth unit of output is $0.50, while the revenue from producing this tenth unit is $0.55. This firm
   a. should definitely produce the tenth unit.
   b. should definitely stop producing, since it knows it is profit maximizing and may risk reducing its profit if it produces any more units of the good.
   c. should definitely produce at least five more units if it hopes to profit maximize.
   d. cannot increase its production in the short run since its fixed inputs are constant.
   e. should definitely stop producing, since it is not making an accounting profit.

Section ⑪ Market Structures: Perfect Competition and Monopoly

Overview

Section 10 introduced several factors affecting a firm, including the number of firms in the industry, the type of product sold, and the existence of barriers to entry. It also introduced the four basic market structures found within these various environments—perfect competition, monopoly, oligopoly, and monopolistic competition. These four market structures fall along a spectrum from perfect competition at one end to monopoly at the other, with monopolistic competition and oligopoly lying somewhere in between. Section 11 begins an in-depth study of market structures by presenting the models at either end of the spectrum; perfect competition and monopoly.

Featured Models/Graphs: Perfect Competition and Monopoly

This section presents two important market structure models, perfect competition and monopoly, and shows how to interpret and draw graphs of perfectly competitive and monopoly firms and markets.

MODULES IN THIS SECTION

Module 58	**Introduction to Perfect Competition**
Module 59	**Graphing Perfect Competition**
Module 60	**Long-Run Outcomes in Perfect Competition**
Module 61	**Introduction to Monopoly**
Module 62	**Monopoly and Public Policy**
Module 63	**Price Discrimination**

BEFORE YOU TACKLE THE TEST

Draw the Featured Model

Complete the Exercise

Problems

Review Questions

MODULE 58 | INTRODUCTION TO PERFECT COMPETITION

BEFORE YOU READ THE MODULE

Summary

This module presents the model of perfect competition and uses it to analyze firms in the market.

Module Objectives

Review these objectives before you read the module. Place a "√" on the line when you can do each of the following:

_____ **Objective #1.** Determine the profit-maximizing quantity of output for a price-taking firm

_____ **Objective #2.** Assess whether or not a competitive producer is profitable

WHILE YOU READ THE MODULE

Key Term

Define this key term as you read the module:

Price-taking firm's optimal output rule:

Practice the Model

The following graph shows the marginal revenue, marginal cost, average total cost, and average variable cost curves for a perfectly competitive firm. According to this graph, minimum *ATC* is at a quantity of 4 and *MR = MC* is at a quantity of 8.

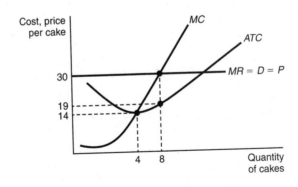

1) Calculate the firm's profit at Q = 4. Show your work.

2) Calculate the firm's profit at Q = 8. Show your work.

3) Will the firm choose to produce a quantity of 4 or 8? Explain.

List questions or difficulties from your initial reading of the module.

AFTER YOU READ THE MODULE

Fill-in-the-Blanks

Fill in the blanks to complete the following statements. If you find yourself having difficulties, please refer back to the appropriate section in the text.

- The price-taking firm's optimal output rule says that a price-taking firm's profit is maximized by

  producing the quantity of output at which the market price is equal to the **1)**_____ of the

  last unit produced.   In the case of a price-taking firm, **2)**_____ is equal to the market price.

- Accounting profit is calculated using only **3)**_____ costs of the firm. Economic profit also

  considers **4)**_____ costs. Whether or not a firm earns a profit or a loss depends on whether

  the market price is above or below the firm's **5)**_____ cost. When a firm's total revenue is

  6)_____ its total cost, the firm is earning a profit.

Multiple-Choice Questions

Circle the best choice to answer or complete the following questions or incomplete statements. For additional practice, use the space provided to explain why one or more of the incorrect options do not work.

7. A profit-maximizing perfectly competitive firm will produce at the level of output where
   a. *ATC* is lowest.
   b. *MC* = *ATC*.
   c. *MR* = *ATC*.
   d. *P* = *MC* = *MR*.
   e. *MC* is lowest.

8. If a profit-maximizing firm is producing 10 units at a total cost of $450 and the marginal cost of the 10th unit is $60, price must equal $____ and the firm is earning $____ profit.

Price	Profit
a. $45	$0
b. $50	-$50
c. $50	$50
d. $60	$45
e. $60	$150

Helpful Tips

- The demand curve for a perfectly competitive *firm* is always horizontal (perfectly elastic). But the demand curve for a perfectly competitive *market* is the same demand curve discussed in all of the sections so far – it is usually downward-sloping. It is important to remember that the horizontal demand curves in this module are the *firm's* demand curve, not the *market* demand curve. The market still usually has a downward-sloping demand curve and an upward-sloping supply curve which determines the market price. However, once the market price is established, the individual firm must take that market price as given, which means that the firm's demand curve is horizontal.

- To determine if a firm is profitable or not, consider the quantity that the firm will choose to produce (the profit-maximizing quantity, where $MC = MR$). At that quantity…

  … if $P > ATC$ → the firm is earning a profit

  … if $P < ATC$ → the firm is earning a loss

  … if $P = ATC$ → the firm is earning zero profit (a.k.a. "normal profit")

The optimal output rule says that to maximize profit, you should produce the quantity at which marginal revenue is equal to marginal cost. But what if there is no output level at which marginal revenue equals marginal cost? In that case, you produce the largest quantity for which marginal revenue exceeds marginal cost. An example of this is in your textbook in Table 58.1, where $MR > MC$ at an output of 5 bushels, but $MR < MC$ at an output of 6 bushels. In this case, you would choose to produce 5 bushels.

Module Notes

A perfectly competitive industry is an industry in which both the producers and consumers in the industry are price takers. A price-taking firm is one whose actions cannot affect the market price of the good sold; it can sell as many units of the good as it would like at the prevailing market price. A price-taking consumer is a consumer who cannot influence the market price of the good by his or her actions. The market price is therefore unaffected by the actions of either individual producers or individual consumers.

For an industry to be perfectly competitive, there must be many producers in that industry, and no single producer can have a large market share. The product sold in a perfectly competitive industry is a standardized product or commodity, and consumers must view each producer's product as a perfect substitute for any other producer's product. Perfectly competitive industries must also have no barriers to entry or exit. This is referred to as free entry and exit.

MODULE 59   GRAPHING PERFECT COMPETITION

BEFORE YOU READ THE MODULE

Summary

This module shows how to evaluate perfectly competitive firms in different situations and determine their profitability.

Module Objectives

Review these objectives before you read the module. Place a "√" on the line when you can do each of the following:

_____**Objective #1.** Evaluate a perfectly competitive firm's situation using a graph

_____**Objective #2.** Determine a perfectly competitive firm's profit or loss

_____**Objective #3.** Explain how a firm decides whether to produce or shut down in the short run

WHILE YOU READ THE MODULE

Key Terms

Define these key terms as you read the module:

Break-even price:

Shut-down price:

Short-run individual supply curve:

Practice the Model

Refer to the following graph of a firm to answer the questions.

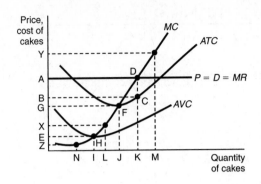

1) In which market structure does this firm operate? Explain how you know.

2) Identify the letter representing each of the following:
   i. What letter represents the profit-maximizing quantity?

   ii. What letter represents the cost-minimizing quantity?

   iii. What letter represents the market price?

   iv. What letter represents the price at which a firm would earn zero profit?

   v. What area represents the amount of profit that the firm would make when the price is $A?

   vi. What letter represents the shut-down price?

3) Suppose the price of this good increased to $Y. Would the firm be willing to produce M units in the short run? Would this firm earn a profit selling M units at a price of $Y?

4) Suppose the price of this good decreased to $X. Would the firm be willing to produce L units in the short run? Would this firm earn a profit selling L units at a price of $X?

5) Would the firm produce if the price decreased to $Z? Explain.

List questions or difficulties from your initial reading of the module.

AFTER YOU READ THE MODULE

Fill-in-the-Blanks

Fill in the blanks to complete the following statements. If you find yourself having difficulties, please refer back to the appropriate section in the text.

- Assume a firm is selling 100 units of output. If the market price is $10 and the firm's average total cost is $8, the firm's profit per unit equals **1)**_____ and its total profit equals

  2)_____.

- The minimum average total cost of a price-taking firm is called its **3)**_____.

- Since it cannot be changed in the short run, a firm's **4)**_____ cost is irrelevant to its decision about whether to produce or shut down in the short run. A firm should shut down in the short run if price is below **5)**_____. If the firm does not shut down in the short run, its individual supply curve is equal to its **6)**_____ curve.

Multiple-Choice Questions

Circle the best choice to answer or complete the following questions or incomplete statements. For additional practice, use the space provided to explain why one or more of the incorrect options do not work.

Refer to the graph on the following page for questions 7 and 8.

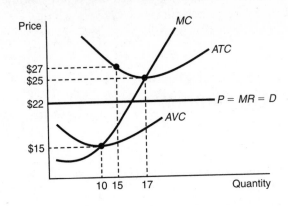

7. What is the profit-maximizing quantity when the price is $22?
   a. There is no profit-maximizing quantity because the firm would earn a loss.
   b. 0
   c. 10
   d. 15
   e. 17

8. What is the firm's profit at the profit-maximizing quantity?
   a. -$75
   b. -$51
   c. $0
   d. $51
   e. $75

Helpful Tips

- You will need to draw correctly labeled graphs of a perfectly competitive firm, showing correctly drawn and labeled cost curves (*MC, ATC, AVC*) and the demand and *MR* curve (at the market *P*). You should be able to show the profit-maximizing output level and area representing profit or loss on your graph. You need to be able to do this for each of the possible short-run situations the firm may face:
  - o   earning a profit
  - o   earning a normal profit
  - o   earning a loss (when the firm should shut down in the short run)
  - o   earning a loss (when the firm should continue to produce in the short run)

- However, don't try to memorize a graph for each possible situation. First learn to draw the basic graph and then understand the one difference between the four situations (as described below).

- Drawing a basic graph of a perfectly competitive firm

  1) Correctly label your axes. Your vertical axis measures costs and prices, while the horizontal axis measures the firm's level of output.

  2) Draw the demand/*MR* curve. A perfectly competitive firm is a price-taking producer, so the firm can sell as much as it would like at the market price. This means that the demand curve facing the

firm is a horizontal line. The fact that perfectly competitive firms are price takers means that the MR curve is the same as the demand curve and is equal to price. Get into the habit of labeling the horizontal demand curve with all three labels, $MR = D = P$, so you always have the relevant label on the graph.

3) Add the MC curve with its typical upward "swoosh" shape. Once you have MR and MC, you can find their intersection and draw a line down to the horizontal axis to show the profit-maximizing level of output and label it Q^*. Once you find the profit-maximizing output, every value you find for the firm will be found at Q^*.

4) Add the ATC curve. *Always make sure the ATC curve is U-shaped and that MC crosses at the minimum ATC.* (Review the previous modules if you don't remember why this must be true).

- Drawing the different situations

  If you are drawing a firm that is

…making a profit	→	**draw the ATC curve below demand** so that $P > ATC$ at Q^*
…making a loss/producing	→	**draw the ATC curve above demand and the AVC curve below demand** so that $AVC < P < ATC$ at Q^*
… making profit = 0	→	**draw the ATC curve with its minimum on demand** so that $P = ATC$ at Q^*
…making a loss/ not producing	→	**draw ATC and AVC curves both above demand**/price

Module Notes

The production conditions for a perfectly competitive firm can be summarized as follows:

When $P <$ minimum AVC (the shut-down price), the firm shuts down production in the short run since it can't cover its variable cost of production. The firm's profit when it produces 0 units of output in the short run is equal to the negative of its fixed cost.

When $P >$ minimum AVC (the shut-down price), the firm produces where $MC = MR$ in the short run; if $P <$ minimum ATC but is still above the minimum AVC, the firm is covering all of its variable cost and part of its fixed cost.

The long-run profitability conditions for a perfectly competitive firm can be summarized as follows:

When $P >$ minimum ATC, the firm earns a positive economic profit in the short run and firms enter the industry in the long run.

When $P =$ minimum ATC, the firm earns zero economic profit in the short run and firms do not enter or exit the industry in the long run.

When $P <$ minimum ATC, the firm earns a negative economic profit in the short run and firms exit the industry in the long run.

MODULE $\boxed{60}$ LONG-RUN OUTCOMES IN PERFECT COMPETITION

BEFORE YOU READ THE MODULE

Summary

This module presents the long-run situation in a perfectly competitive market and explains why perfect competition leads to some interesting and desirable market outcomes. In later modules, these outcomes are compared with the outcomes in monopoly and imperfectly competitive markets.

Module Objectives

Review these objectives before you read the module. Place a "√" on the line when you can do each of the following:

_____**Objective #1.** Explain why industry behavior differs between the short run and the long run

_____**Objective #2.** Discuss what determines the industry supply curve in both the short run and the long run

WHILE YOU READ THE MODULE

Key Terms

Define these key terms as you read the module:

Industry supply curve:

Short-run industry supply curve:

Short-run market equilibrium:

Long-run market equilibrium:

Long-run industry supply curve:

Constant-cost industry:

Increasing-cost industry:

Decreasing-cost industry:

Practice the Model

Assume the market price is $10. Draw a correctly labeled graph of a perfectly competitive firm in long-run equilibrium and label the profit-maximizing quantity Q^*.

List questions or difficulties from your initial reading of the module.

AFTER YOU READ THE MODULE

Fill-in-the-Blanks

Fill in the blanks to complete the following statements. If you find yourself having difficulties, please refer back to the appropriate section in the text.

- The **1)**_____ industry supply curve is the horizontal summation of the individual firms'

  supply curves. Short-run market equilibrium exists where the quantity **2)**_____ equals the

  quantity **3)**_____.

- The long run in perfect competition is different because of free **4)**_____ and

  5)_____. In the long run, perfectly competitive firms will earn an economic profit equal to

  6)_____.

Multiple-Choice Questions
Circle the best choice to answer or complete the following questions or incomplete statements. For additional practice, use the space provided to explain why one or more of the incorrect options do not work.

Use the following graph to answer questions 7 and 8.

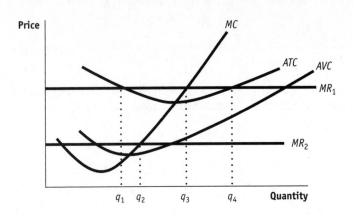

7. If the market price is the price associated with MR_1, then this firm is making a ____ profit and firms will ____ the industry, causing the market price to _____.
  a. positive   enter   increase
  b. positive   enter   decrease
  c. positive   exit   decrease
  d. negative   exit   decrease
  e. negative   exit   increase

8. If the market price is the price associated with MR_2, then this firm is making a ____ profit and firms will ____ the industry, causing the market price to _____.
  a. positive   enter   increase
  b. positive   enter   decrease
  c. positive   exit   decrease
  d. negative   exit   decrease
  e. negative   exit   increase

Helpful Tips

- When you consider profit, remember that the total cost used to calculate a firm's profit includes *opportunity costs* – the return a business owner could get by using his or her resources elsewhere. And so, when you see the term "profit," it is referring to *economic profit*. If the market price is above *ATC*, potential business owners can earn more in this industry than they could in the next best alternative.

Module Notes

In the short run in a perfectly competitive industry, there is no entry or exit of firms. Thus, positive or negative economic profit can persist. However, in the long run, there is free entry and exit in perfect competition. It is important to understand how this impacts the long-run situation for a perfectly competitive industry. Free entry and exit leads to the long-run equilibrium condition of zero economic profit (normal profit) for firms in perfect competition.

MODULE 61   INTRODUCTION TO MONOPOLY

BEFORE YOU READ THE MODULE

Summary

This module presents the monopoly model and uses it to look at the monopoly firm/market.

Module Objectives

Review these objectives before you read the module. Place a "√" on the line when you can do each of the following:

_____Objective #1.   Identify the profit-maximizing price and quantity for a monopolist

_____Objective #2.   Determine whether a monopoly is earning a profit or a loss

WHILE YOU READ THE MODULE

Key Terms

There are no new key terms in Module 61.

Practice the Model

Values for a monopolist's demand curve with the equation $Q_d = 10 - P$ are given in the following table.

P	Q	Total Revenue	Marginal Revenue
10	0	0	
9	1	9	—
8	2	16	—
7	3	21	—
6	4	24	—
5	5	25	—
4	6	24	—

1) Calculate the marginal revenue for each quantity in the table.

2) Plot the demand and marginal revenue curves on the following graph. Note in the space below the graph whether marginal revenue is above or below price for each quantity.

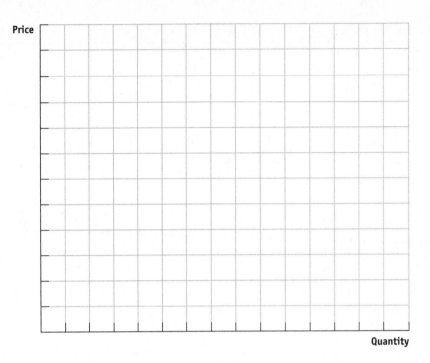

List questions or difficulties from your initial reading of the module.

AFTER YOU READ THE MODULE

Fill-in-the-Blanks

Fill in the blanks to complete the following statements. If you find yourself having difficulties, please refer back to the appropriate section in the text.

- A monopoly maximizes profit by producing the quantity of output where marginal cost equals

  1)_____. Because the demand curve for a monopoly slopes downward (it is the same as

  the market demand curve), the marginal revenue curve lies **2)**_____ the demand curve. In

  order to sell one more, a monopoly must **3)**_____ price on all units.

- A monopoly will earn a profit in the short run as long as price is **4)**_____ average total

  cost. However, a monopoly will earn a loss and shut down in the short run if price falls below

  5)_____ cost.

- In the long run, a monopoly can continue to earn a positive economic profit because of barriers to

  6)_____.

Multiple-Choice Questions

Circle the best choice to answer or complete the following questions or incomplete statements. For additional practice, use the space provided to explain why one or more of the incorrect options do not work.

Use the following figure to answer questions 7 and 8.

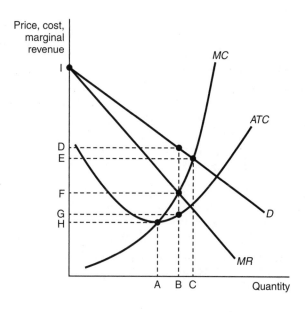

7. The profit-maximizing quantity and price for this monopolist are

Quantity	Price
a. A	H
b. B	G
c. B	F
d. B	D
e. C	E

8. At the profit-maximizing quantity, the monopolist will earn a per unit profit equal to
   a. DG.
   b. DF.
   c. FG.
   d. DH.
   e. EG.

Helpful Tips

• You will need to draw correctly labeled graphs of a monopoly, showing correctly drawn and labeled cost curves (*MC, ATC, AVC*) and the demand and *MR* curves. You should be able to show the profit-maximizing output level and price and the area representing profit or loss on your graph. You need to be able to do this for each of the possible short-run situations the firm may face:

o   earning a profit

o   earning a normal profit

o   earning a loss (when the firm should shut down in the short run)

o   earning a loss (when the firm should continue to produce in the short run)

- However, don't try to memorize a graph for each possible situation. First learn to draw the basic graph and then understand the one difference between the four situations (as described below).

- <u>Drawing a basic graph of a monopoly</u>
  1) Correctly label your axes. Your vertical axis is measuring costs and prices; the horizontal axis measures the firm's level of output.

  2) Draw the demand and *MR* curves. The demand curve is downward-sloping and *MR* begins at the same point on the vertical axis and lies below the demand curve.

  3) Add the *MC* curve with its typical upward "swoosh" shape. Once you have *MR* and *MC*, you can find their intersection and draw a line down to the horizontal axis to show the profit-maximizing level of output and label it Q^*. Once you find the profit-maximizing output, every value you find for the firm will be found at Q^*. The profit-maximizing price is found by going up to the demand curve at Q^* and over to the vertical axis.

  4) Add the *ATC* curve. *Always make sure the ATC curve is U-shaped and that MC crosses at the minimum ATC.* (Review the previous modules if you don't remember why this must be true).

- <u>Drawing the different situations</u>

  If you are drawing a firm that is

…making a profit	→	**draw the *ATC* curve below demand** so that $P > ATC$ at Q^*
…making a loss/producing	→	**draw the *ATC* curve above demand and the *AVC* curve below demand** so that $AVC < P < ATC$ at Q^*
… making profit = 0	→	**draw the *ATC* curve with its minimum on demand** so that $P = ATC$ at Q^*
…making a loss/ not producing	→	**draw *ATC* and *AVC* curves both above demand**/price

Module Notes

A monopoly is a market characterized by having a single producer of the good, when the good has no close substitutes. In contrast to perfect competition, a monopolist produces a smaller quantity and charges a higher price for its product. The monopolist is able to charge a price that is greater than the competitive price because it has market power: it is the only producer of the good and the good has no close substitutes. By charging a higher price and restricting output, the monopolist is able to increase its profit while maintaining positive profit in the long run.

Positive economic profit earned by the monopolist continues in the long run because effective barriers to entry prevent new firms from entering the industry. There are four principal barriers to entry: (1) the monopoly controls a scarce resource or input that prevents new firms from being able to compete in the industry; (2) the monopolist enjoys economies of scale and therefore can spread its fixed cost over a larger volume of output, resulting in the monopolist having lower average total costs than potential competitors; (3) the monopolist enjoys technological superiority over its potential competitors; and (4) the monopolist is protected from competition due to government-created barriers.

The monopolist's demand curve for its product is the market demand curve, since it is the only provider of the good in the market. Since the monopolist's demand curve is downward-sloping, this implies that the monopolist can only sell additional units of the good by lowering the price on all the units it sells: this results in the monopolist's marginal revenue (MR) curve being beneath the monopolist's demand curve. An increase in production by a monopolist has two opposing effects on revenue: a quantity effect and a price effect. A firm with market power will find that its MR curve always lies beneath its demand curve due to the price effect. Notice the relationship between the price elasticity of demand for the linear demand curve and its MR curve. Marginal revenue is positive in the elastic portion of the demand curve; marginal revenue equals 0 at the unit-elastic point (the midpoint) of the demand curve; and marginal revenue is negative in the inelastic portion of the demand curve.

MODULE 62 | MONOPOLY AND PUBLIC POLICY

BEFORE YOU READ THE MODULE

Summary

This module explains why monopoly leads to inefficiency and examines the policies governments adopt in an attempt to prevent this inefficiency.

Module Objectives

Review these objectives before you read the module. Place a "√" on the line when you can do each of the following:

_____**Objective #1.** Compare the effects of monopoly and perfect competition on society's welfare

_____**Objective #2.** Explain how policy makers address the problems posed by monopoly

WHILE YOU READ THE MODULE

Key Terms

Define these key terms as you read the module:

Public ownership:

Price regulation:

Practice the Model

Draw a correctly labeled graph of a natural monopoly. Assume that the monopoly is regulated to charge a price equal to average total cost. Label the profit-maximizing price P_M and the regulated price P_R. On your graph, lightly shade the area that represents the consumer surplus at the regulated price and darkly shade the area that represents the consumer surplus at the profit-maximizing price. Refer to Figure 62.2 in your textbook.

List questions or difficulties from your initial reading of the module.

AFTER YOU READ THE MODULE

Fill-in-the-Blanks

Fill in the blanks to complete the following statements. If you find yourself having difficulties, please refer back to the appropriate section in the text.

- Compared to a firm in perfect competition, a monopoly produces a **1)**_____ quantity and

  charges a **2)**_____ price. The monopoly redistributes surplus from **3)**_____ to

  4)_____. In addition, total surplus is **5)**_____. The change in total surplus

  created by the monopoly is known as **6)**_____ loss.

- When a single, large producer has lower average costs than one of many small producers, the market is

  a **7)**_____ monopoly. In this case, the government can address the inefficiency of

  monopoly through **8)**_____ ownership or price **9)**_____. Of course, in some

  cases "the cure may be worse than the disease," in which case the government should do

  10)_____.

Multiple-Choice Questions

Circle the best choice to answer or complete the following questions or incomplete statements. For additional practice, use the space provided to explain why one or more of the incorrect options do not work.

Refer to the following graph for questions 11 and 12.

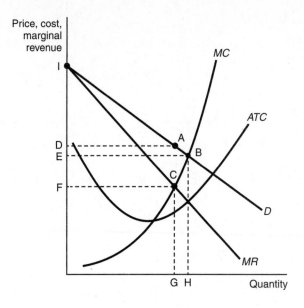

11. At the profit-maximizing price and quantity, consumer surplus is represented by what area?
    a. IDA
    b. IEB
    c. ABC
    d. IACF
    e. DACF

12. The deadweight loss associated with the profit-maximizing price and quantity is represented by the area _____.
    a. IAD
    b. IEB
    c. ABC
    d. IACF
    e. DACF

Helpful Tips

- Recall that the reason there is efficiency loss when there is a tax is because a tax decreases the quantity sold. The reason that there is efficiency loss with a monopolist is similar. The monopolist sells a lower quantity than a perfectly competitive firm would if a perfectly competitive firm had identical costs.

- For a perfectly competitive firm, the supply curve was the *MC* curve above the shutdown point. But this section has not said anything about a supply curve for a monopolist. That is because *monopolists don't have supply curves.* Remember that a supply curve shows the quantity that producers are willing to supply for any given market price. A monopolist, however, does not take the price as given; it chooses a profit-maximizing quantity, taking into account its own ability to influence the price.

Module Notes

In a perfectly competitive industry, each firm equates the marginal cost to the price of the good; in contrast, in a monopoly, the price of the good is always greater than the marginal cost at the profit-maximizing level of output. This tells us that the monopolist is not producing the efficient level of output, since the price consumers are willing to pay for the last unit produced is greater than the cost of producing the last unit. Too few resources are being devoted to the production of the monopolist product. A monopoly, compared with a perfectly competitive industry, restricts output, charges a higher price for the product, and earns a profit that is not eliminated through the entry of new firms in the long run.

Monopoly causes a net loss to society because the cost to the consumer is greater than the gain to the monopolist. The existence of a monopoly creates a deadweight loss due to the monopolist's restriction of output and its ability to charge a higher price for its product relative to the quantity and price decision made by a perfectly competitive firm. The deadweight loss created by the monopolist occurs because some mutually beneficial transactions do not occur: this is evident when we recall that for the last unit produced by the monopolist, the marginal cost of producing that unit is less than the price consumers are willing to pay for that unit. Because monopoly is inefficient, government policy often is used to offset some of its undesired effects.

Economies of scale result in lower costs of production as the size of the firm increases. In the case of a monopoly with economies of scale, the single firm finds that its cost of production falls throughout the relevant range of production. Any potential competitor would face higher costs per unit. Natural monopolies are an example of a monopoly that benefits from economies of scale.

If an industry is not a natural monopoly, then the best method for avoiding monopoly outcomes is to prevent monopoly from arising or to break up the monopoly if it already exists. Government policies used to prevent or eliminate monopolies are known as antitrust policy. If an industry is a natural monopoly, then breaking up the monopoly is not a clearly beneficial idea since large-scale producers have lower average total cost than smaller-scale producers. Two policy methods are used for regulating natural monopolies: public ownership and price regulation.

With public ownership, the government establishes a public agency to provide the good and to protect consumers' interests. With public ownership, it is possible to set the price at the efficient level so that $P = MC$ for the last unit being produced by the natural monopoly. Unfortunately, publicly-owned natural monopolies are not always successful at minimizing their costs or at providing high-quality products. Publicly-owned companies may also end up serving political interests.

Regulation typically takes the form of price regulation, where the private company is regulated with regard to what prices it can charge for the product. Local utilities are frequently regulated in this way. With price regulation, the monopolist produces a higher level of output and sells this output at a lower price. This is true provided that the regulated price is set at a level greater than the firm's marginal cost and is high enough that the firm at least breaks even on total output. Price regulation increases the area of consumer surplus because the regulation reduces the monopolist's profit and results in more output at lower prices.

MODULE 63 PRICE DISCRIMINATION

BEFORE YOU READ THE MODULE

Summary

This module explains how monopolists can increase their profit by engaging in price discrimination.

Module Objectives

Review these objectives before you read the module. Place a "√" on the line when you can do each of the following:

_____**Objective #1.** Explain the meaning of price discrimination

_____**Objective #2.** Discuss why price discrimination is common when producers have market power

WHILE YOU READ THE MODULE

Key Terms

Define these key terms as you read the module:

Single-price monopolist:

Price discrimination:

Perfect price discrimination:

Practice the Model

For each of the following scenarios, indicate whether it is an example of price discrimination and explain why or why not.

1) A coffee shop charges $5 for a latte in the morning and $3 for the same latte between 2 PM and 5 PM.

2) Mary uses a coupon for $3 off a medium pepperoni and sausage pizza. Roger does not use a coupon for a medium pepperoni and sausage pizza at the same restaurant.

3) An air-conditioning company offers a 20% discount for having air-conditioning service performed in December. It charges full price for having air-conditioning service performed in June.

4) A cell phone company has two pricing plans. One charges $40 per month plus $0.25 per text, while the other charges $80 per month with no charge for sending texts.

5) A gas station charges $4.05 per gallon for 87 octane gas, and $4.15 for 92 octane gas.

List questions or difficulties from your initial reading of the module.

AFTER YOU READ THE MODULE

Fill-in-the-Blanks

Fill in the blanks to complete the following statements. If you find yourself having difficulties, please refer back to the appropriate section in the text.

- Charging different customers different prices for the same good is known as **1)**_____.

  Firms engage in this practice in order to increase their **2)**_____. They will charge a higher

  price to the group of customers with a more **3)**_____ demand. When a monopolist is able

  to charge different prices so that consumer surplus is equal to zero, it is engaging in

  4)_____ price discrimination.

- A pricing scheme in which consumers pay a fixed fee up front in addition to the cost of items they

  purchase is called a **5)**_____.

- Government will prevent price discrimination when it results in serious issues related to

  6)_____.

Multiple-Choice Questions

Circle the best choice to answer or complete the following questions or incomplete statements. For additional practice, use the space provided to explain why one or more of the incorrect options do not work.

7. Perfect price discrimination
    a. maximizes consumer surplus.
    b. results in allocative efficiency.
    c. results in deadweight loss.
    d. results in zero producer surplus.
    e. is possible if a good can be resold.

8. When a monopoly price discriminates by charging different prices to two easily identifiable groups of consumers, which group will be charged a higher price? The group that has
    a. a more elastic demand.
    b. a less elastic demand.
    c. a lower demand.
    d. the ability to resell the product.
    e. a lower income.

Helpful Tips

- Price discrimination is defined as charging consumers different prices for the same good. However, often what seems to be price discrimination turns out not to be. To qualify as price discriminating, a company must charge different prices for the same good. When you consider whether price differentials are due to price discrimination, be careful that the different prices are for exactly the same good.

Module Notes

Price discrimination refers to a situation in which a firm with market power charges different prices to different customers. Instead of offering the good at a single price, the firm with market power offers the good at multiple prices depending on the characteristics of the consumer. The firm will find that its profit increases if it charges a higher price to the consumers of the good who have a more price inelastic demand, and a lower price to the consumers of the good who have a more price elastic demand. Common techniques for price discrimination include:

- Advance purchase restrictions—the earlier you purchase, the lower the price you pay.
- Volume discounts—the larger the quantity you buy, the lower the price per unit.
- Two-part tariffs—you pay an annual fee plus the cost of whatever items you purchase, thereby effectively creating a volume discount.

Perfect price discrimination occurs when the monopolist is able to capture the entire consumer surplus. The greater the number of prices the monopolist charges, the more money it extracts from consumers. In addition, the greater the number of prices the monopolist charges, the closer the lowest price will get to the marginal cost of producing the last unit of the good. A monopolist who practices perfect price discrimination does not cause any inefficiency, since the marginal cost of producing the last unit exactly equals the price of this last unit. But with perfect price discrimination, the consumer's surplus is equal to zero since this entire surplus is captured by the producer.

The Featured Models: Perfect Competition and Monopoly

Draw correctly labeled graphs of the following. Note that both should be earning a profit:

1)   a perfectly competitive firm

2) a monopoly

Complete the Exercise

Assuming identical costs, how do consumer surplus, producer surplus and deadweight loss for a monopoly industry compare to a perfectly competitive industry? Draw two sketches, with one sketch illustrating the perfectly competitive industry and its equilibrium market price and market quantity, and the other sketch illustrating the monopoly and its market price and market quantity. On both sketches, identify the area that corresponds to the consumer surplus, producer surplus, and deadweight loss.

Problems

1. What does it mean to be a price-taking firm? What does it mean to be a price-taking consumer? What is the relationship between market share and price taking?

2. The model of perfect competition is based on two necessary conditions and a third condition that is often present as well. Identify each of these conditions and then briefly discuss their importance in the model.

3. Use the following graphs of a perfectly competitive market to answer this set of questions.

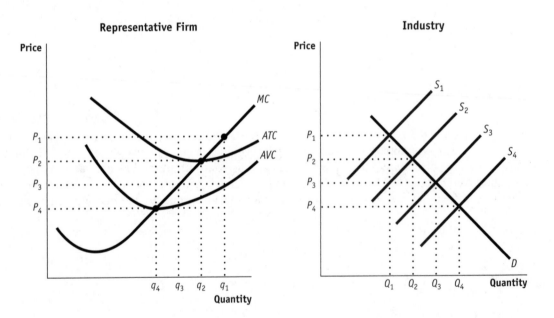

   a. Suppose in the short run the industry supply curve is given by S_1. Identify the short-run equilibrium market price and quantity and the quantity produced by the representative firm. State whether the firm is making positive, negative, or zero economic profit. Holding everything else constant, what will happen in the long run in this industry? In your answer to this question, identify the long-run equilibrium price and quantity in the industry, the quantity produced by the firm in the long run, and the level of profit for the firm in the long run.

b. Suppose in the short run the industry supply curve is given by S_4. Identify the short-run equilibrium market price and quantity and the quantity produced by the representative firm. State whether the firm is making positive, negative, or zero economic profit. Do you know with certainty what this firm's profit equals in the short run? Holding everything else constant, what will happen in the long run in this industry? In your answer to this question, identify the long-run equilibrium price and quantity in the industry, the quantity produced by the firm in the long run, and the level of profit for the firm in the long run.

c. You are told that this representative firm is currently making negative economic profit in the short run, but that it is covering all of its variable costs of production and some of its fixed costs. Given the price choices in the preceding graph, what is the current price for this good? In the long run, will there be entry of new firms into the industry or will existing firms exit the industry? Explain your answer.

4. In the long run, the model of perfect competition predicts that all firms in an industry will earn zero economic profits. Why would firms be willing to continue to produce in the long run if their economic profit is equal to zero?

5. Suppose the following table describes the market demand schedule for a monopoly.

Price ($)	Quantity demanded (units)
1,000	0
800	400
600	800
400	1,200
200	1,600
0	2,000

a. Draw a graph of this market demand schedule for the monopoly.

Price ... Quantity

b. Compute the firm's total revenue and marginal revenue figures for the following table. For the marginal revenue figures, use the midpoint method.

Price (dollars)	Quantity demanded (units)	Total revenue (dollars)	Marginal revenue (dollars per unit)
1,000	0		
800	400		
600	800		
400	1,200		
200	1,600		
0	2,000		

c. Draw the monopolist's marginal revenue curve on the graph you drew in part **a.** of this problem.

d. If the firm's marginal cost is constant and equal to $200, what is this monopolist's profit-maximizing level of output and what price will this monopolist charge for this good? Label this quantity and this price on your graph.

e. On the graph you drew in part a., shade in the area that corresponds to the consumer surplus and label it clearly. Then shade in the area that corresponds to producer surplus and label it clearly. Finally, shade in the area that corresponds to deadweight loss and label it clearly.

f. Calculate the value of consumer surplus, producer surplus, and deadweight loss for this monopoly.

6. The following graph represents a monopolist's cost curves and the demand curve for the monopolist's product. Use this graph to answer this set of questions.

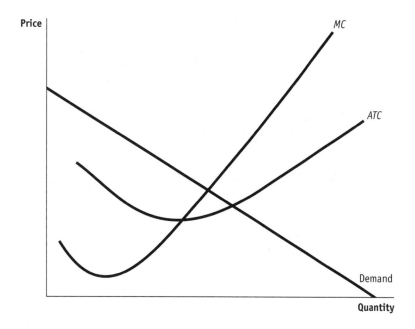

a. On the preceding graph, identify the monopolist's profit-maximizing level of output and label this amount Q_M (Hint: don't forget that you will need to first find the monopolist's MR curve to answer this question). On the graph, label the price the monopolist will charge for the good as P_M.

b. Does this monopolist make positive, negative, or zero economic profit in the short run? Identify the area that represents profit in the preceding graph if the firm earns positive or negative profit.

c. What do you expect will happen to the monopolist in the long run? In your answer, be sure to identify what happens to the firm's profit, level of production, and price.

7. Use the following diagrams to answer this set of questions. The left-hand graph depicts a monopoly with its market demand curve and its MC curve. The right-hand graph depicts a perfectly competitive industry with the same market demand curve and the MC curve for a representative firm. These two graphs are intended to allow you to compare a monopoly to a perfectly competitive industry.

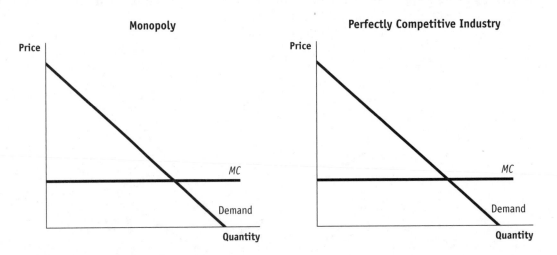

a. On each graph, identify the market level of output. On the first graph, label this output level Q_M, and on the second graph, label this output level Q_{PC}. (Hint: remember that you must first identify the MR curve before selecting the quantity that will be produced.)

b. On each graph, identify the market price for the good. On the first graph, label this price P_M, and on the second graph, label this price P_{PC}.

c. Compare the level of production and the price of the good in the two markets. Which market outcome is better for consumers? Explain your answer.

d. Is there a deadweight loss in either of the two graphs? If there is a deadweight loss, shade in the relevant area on the graph.

8. Discuss two different government policies for dealing with a natural monopoly. Describe each policy and then discuss any limitations or shortcomings that might arise from the implementation of the policy.

9. Use the following graph to answer this set of questions. Due to economies of scale, the firm in the graph is a natural monopoly.

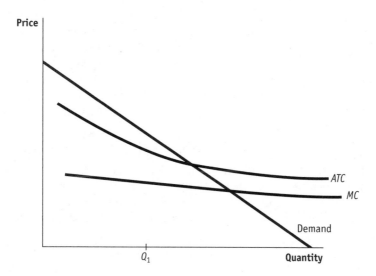

a. Why does this firm's economies of scale result in its being a natural monopoly?

b. Suppose that Q_1 units are provided in this market. On the graph provided, indicate the area that represents the total cost of production if this amount is produced by a single firm. Indicate the area that represents the total cost of production if this amount is produced by five identical firms. Is there an advantage to having a single firm produce this level of output versus having five firms produce this level of output?

c. Suppose this firm acts like a profit-maximizing monopolist. On the graph, find the quantity the monopolist will produce, and label this quantity Q_m. Also identify the price the monopolist will charge (P_m) and identify the area that represents the monopolist's profit, if there are any profits.

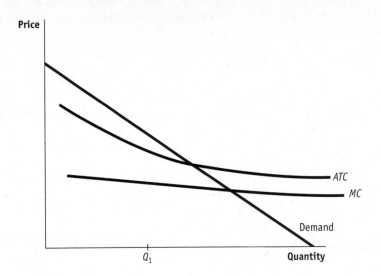

d. Suppose this firm is price regulated so that the price charged is exactly equal to the average total cost of production. On the graph in part c., identify the level of output the firm will produce when price regulated (Q_{pr}) as well as the price the firm will charge (P_{pr}). What is the economic profit equal to with this form of price regulation? Is the level of output (Q_{pr}) the efficient level of output? Explain your answer making sure to reference the relationship between price and marginal cost for the last unit produced.

e. Suppose this firm is price regulated so that the price charged is exactly equal to the marginal cost of production. On the graph in part c., identify the level of output that the firm will produce with this regulation (Q_{mc}) as well as the price the firm will charge (P_{mc}). Identify on the graph any area of profit that the firm earns with this form of price regulation. Is the level of output (Q_{mc}) the efficient level of output? Explain your answer making sure to reference the relationship between price and marginal cost for the last unit produced. Will the natural monopolist be willing to produce this level of output at this price? Can you think of a way to get the natural monopolist to produce this level of output?

10. Why does a price-discriminating monopolist charge a higher price to consumers with less elastic demand and a lower price to consumers with more elastic demand?

Review Questions

Circle your answer to the following questions.

1. Perfect competition requires that
  a. producers be able to enter or exit an industry in the short run.
  b. producers be able to distinguish their product from a rival producer's product.
  c. producers have no ability to exert influence over the market price of the product.
  d. consumers compete for the producers' product.
  e. there are many sellers and few buyers.

2. Suppose a perfectly competitive firm in the short run sells its product for a price that is less than the minimum point on its *ATC* curve. Which of the following statements is true?

   a. Firms in this industry will shut down in the short run because they are not covering all of their costs.

   b. Firms in this industry will exit in the long run until the market price increases to the minimum *ATC*.

   c. The firm will shut down in the short run if the price is greater than the shut-down price.

   d. Firms in this industry will exit in the long run until the market price increases to the minimum *AVC*.

   e. Firms will enter this industry because they expect a future increase in the price.

3. Suppose a perfectly competitive industry is initially in long-run equilibrium and demand increases due to a change in tastes and preferences. In the short run this will result in

   a. the product selling for a higher price, each firm producing more of the good, and positive economic profits for the firms in the industry.

   b. the product selling for a higher price, each firm in the industry producing the same level of the good as they did initially, since their capital is fixed, and each firm earning positive economic profit.

   c. the product selling for a higher price initially, but the industry will attract new firms, which will cause the price to fall back to its original level.

   d. the price staying constant, since the firms in this industry are price takers, and the output of each firm is increasing; therefore, each firm will earn positive economic profit.

   e. the product selling for a lower price and some firms exiting the industry.

4. Suppose a perfectly competitive industry is initially in long-run equilibrium. Demand for the product produced in this industry increases due to a change in tastes and preferences. In the long run this will result in

   a. the industry output decreasing, the price decreasing due to the entry of new firms into the industry, and some firms exiting the industry.

   b. the industry output of this good increasing, the price staying constant due to the entry of new firms into the industry, and each firm in the industry earning positive economic profit.

   c. the industry output of this good increasing, the price staying constant due to the entry of new firms into the industry, and each firm in the industry earning negative economic profit.

   d. the industry output of this good increasing, the price staying constant due to the entry of new firms into the industry, and each firm in the industry earning zero economic profit.

   e. the industry output of this good decreasing, the firm level of output increasing, the price increasing, and each firm in the industry earning zero economic profit.

5. A firm in the short run must decide whether or not it should produce any level of output. This means that the firm must

   a. equate marginal revenue to marginal cost to decide its level of output.

   b. consider whether its revenue is sufficient to cover its total costs of production.

   c. consider whether its revenue is sufficient to cover its average total costs of production.

   d. consider whether its revenue is sufficient to cover its average fixed costs of production.

   e. consider whether its revenue is sufficient to cover its variable costs of production.

6. A perfectly competitive firm's minimum-cost output corresponds to the level of output at which

   a. fixed cost is minimized.

   b. variable cost is minimized.

   c. average total cost is minimized.

   d. total cost is minimized.

   e. average variable cost is minimized.

7. Use the following graph of a perfectly competitive firm in the short run to answer the question.

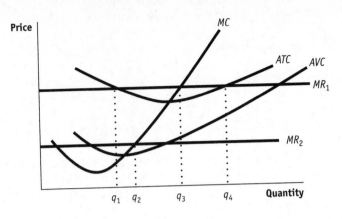

If the firm's marginal revenue is MR_2, then this firm profit maximizes by producing _____ units of output, and its economic profit will be _____.

   a. q_1; negative

   b. q_2; negative

   c. q_3; zero

   d. q_4; negative

   e. q_1; zero

8. For a firm to profit maximize, it must also be true that

   a. the firm is cost minimizing.

   b. the market price is greater than the shut-down price.

   c. the market price is equal to the break-even price.

   d. the firm is earning a positive accounting profit.

   e. the firm is producing a positive economic profit.

9. The short-run industry supply curve for a perfectly competitive market is

   a. perfectly elastic, since buyers can purchase as many units of the good as they desire at the prevailing market price.

   b. equal to the horizontal sum of the individual firms' entire MC curves.

   c. equal to the horizontal sum of the individual firms' MC curves at and above the AVC.

   d. perfectly inelastic, since buyers can purchase as many units of the good as they desire at the prevailing market price.

   e. equal to the horizontal sum of the individual firms' MC curves at or above the ATC.

10. The demand for the monopolist's product

   a. is horizontal.

   b. equals the market demand curve.

   c. is equal to the firm's MR curve.

   d. is less than the firm's MR curve.

   e. is vertical at the profit-maximizing quantity.

11. Which of the following statements is true for both a perfectly competitive firm and a monopoly?

   a. They have market power.

   b. They maximize profit by producing the quantity where $MC = P$.

   c. They must earn a normal profit in the long run.

   d. They have excess capacity.

   e. Their MC curve crosses the minimum point on the ATC.

Use the following graph of a monopolist to answer the next four questions.

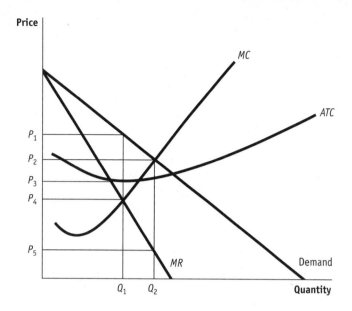

12. This monopolist will produce the profit-maximizing level of output ___ and sell each unit for___ .
    a. Q_1; P_1.
    b. Q_1; P_2.
    c. Q_2; P_2.
    d. Q_1; P_4.
    e. Q_2; P_2

13. If this monopolist were to act as if it were a perfectly competitive industry, then it would produce ___ units of the good and charge ___ for each unit.
    a. Q_1; P_2
    b. Q_1; P_1
    c. Q_2; P_2
    d. Q_2; P_5
    e. Q_2; P_1

14. The deadweight loss associated with this monopoly can be measured as the area
    a. $(1/2)(P_2 - P_4)(Q_2 - Q_1)$.
    b. $(1/2)(P_1 - P_4)(Q_1)$.
    c. $(1/2)(P_2 - P_4)(Q_1)$.
    d. $(1/2)(P_1 - P_4)(Q_2 - Q_1)$.
    e. $(1/2)(P_2 - P_4)(Q_2)$.

15. This monopolist earns
    a. positive economic profit equal to area $(P_1 - P_3)(Q_1)$.
    b. positive economic profit equal to area $(P_1 - P_4)(Q_1)$.
    c. negative economic profit equal to area $(P_1 - P_3)(Q_1)$.
    d. negative economic profit equal to area $(P_1 - P_4)(Q_1)$.
    e. zero economic profit.

16. Which of the following is true of both a perfectly competitive firm in long-run equilibrium and a perfectly price discriminating monopolist?
    a. They earn a normal profit in the long run.
    b. They produce the allocatively efficient level of output.
    c. They have market power.
    d. They face competition from firms entering the market.
    e. They maximize profit by setting $P = MC$.

17. At the midpoint of the monopolist's demand curve, the firm's marginal revenue is equal to
   a. *MC.*
   b. *AR.*
   c. *P.*
   d. one.
   e. zero.

Use the following information to answer questions 18 through 20.

An airline company is the only airline serving a market between several small cities. This monopolist finds that it can sell 500 tickets at a price of $300. The company also knows that it could sell an additional 200 tickets at $150. The marginal cost of providing a seat is $100.

18. If this airline company is only allowed to offer tickets at a single price, the company should sell____ tickets at a price of _____ and earn economic profit of _____ .
   a. 700; $300; $140,000
   b. 500; $150; $25,000
   c. 700; $150; $35,000
   d. 500; $300; $100,000
   e. 700; $100; $35,000

19. If this airline company is allowed to offer tickets at different prices, what is the maximum profit this airline company can earn?
   a. $100,000
   b. $110,000
   c. $35,000
   d. $180,000
   e. $140,000

20. When this company price discriminates, it
   a. increases its profit.
   b. increases consumer surplus.
   c. reduces deadweight loss.
   d. decreases demand.
   e. increases entry.

Section ⑫ Market Structures: Imperfect Competition

Overview

This section presents the two market structure models in the middle of the spectrum—oligopoly and monopolistic competition. These two models are at the same time more complicated and more realistic than those we studied in the previous sections.

Featured Models: Monopolistic Competition and Oligopoly

This section presents basic game theory – the approach used to analyze the behavior of oligopolists. It also presents the monopolistic competition model and how to interpret and draw graphs of monopolistically competitive firms and markets.

MODULES IN THIS SECTION

Module 64   **Introduction to Oligopoly**

Module 65   **Game Theory**

Module 66   **Oligopoly in Practice**

Module 67   **Introduction to Monopolistic Competition**

Module 68   **Product Differentiation and Advertising**

BEFORE YOU TACKLE THE TEST

Draw the Featured Model

Complete the Exercise

Problems

Review Questions

MODULE 64 — INTRODUCTION TO OLIGOPOLY

BEFORE YOU READ THE MODULE

Summary

This module presents the characteristics of oligopoly firms. In particular, it discusses how to determine whether a market has "a few" firms, as required for an oligopoly, and the role of interdependence in deciding whether a market is an oligopoly.

Module Objectives

Review these objectives before you read the module. Place a "√" on the line when you can do each of the following:

_____ **Objective #1.** Explain why oligopolists have an incentive to act in ways that reduce their combined profit

_____ **Objective #2.** Explain why oligopolies can benefit from collusion

WHILE YOU READ THE MODULE

Key Terms

Define these key terms as you read the module:

Interdependent:

Duopoly:

Duopolist:

Collusion:

Cartel:

Noncooperative behavior:

Practice the Model

Assume that two firms are the only producers of a good and the marginal cost of producing additional units of the good is zero for both firms. The demand schedule for the good is given below.

Price	Quantity	Total revenue
0	140	
1	120	
2	100	
3	90	
4	80	
5	70	
6	60	

1) Fill in the total revenue for each level of production shown in the table.

2) What quantity would be produced if the market were perfectly competitive and what combined total revenue would the firms earn from producing that output? Explain.

3) What level of output maximizes total revenue in the market?

4) How could the two firms maximize their joint profit in this market?

List questions or difficulties from your initial reading of the module.

AFTER YOU READ THE MODULE

Fill-in-the-Blanks

Fill in the blanks to complete the following statements. If you find yourself having difficulties, please refer back to the appropriate section in the text.

- The characteristic that sets oligopolies apart from other market structures is **1)**_____. An

    oligopoly market that consists of only two firms is known as a **2)**_____.

- When two firms cooperate to raise their joint profits, the firms are engaging in **3)**_____,

    the strongest form of which is called a **4)**_____. When firms act in their own self-interest,

    even though it has the effect of driving down everyone's profits, the firm is engaging in

    5)_____ behavior.

- A contract that requires cooperative behavior from firms in order to increase profits is unenforceable

    and **6)**_____ in the United States and many other countries.

Multiple-Choice Questions

Circle the best choice to answer or complete the following questions or incomplete statements. For additional practice, use the space provided to explain why one or more of the incorrect options do not work.

7. When firms ignore the effects of their actions on other firms, they are engaging in
   a. collusion.
   b. competitive behavior.
   c. duopolist behavior.
   d. noncooperative behavior.
   e. profit maximization.

8. Which of the following best explains the incentive to collude?
   a. Higher profits result from agreements to restrict output.
   b. Higher profits result from agreements to lower prices.
   c. Lower costs result from agreements to raise prices.
   d. Lower costs result from product differentiation.
   e. Lower costs result from direct price competition.

Helpful Tips

- It can be difficult to determine which real-world markets exhibit interdependence, which is an important key to distinguishing oligopoly from monopolistic competition. One way to tell is by looking at advertising in the industry. Oligopolies and monopolistic competitors both differentiate their products and therefore both use a considerable amount of advertising. Perfect competitors (who sell a standardized product) and monopolists (who are the only seller of a product) have no need to advertise to take sales away from other firms. A perfectly competitive market might advertise as a group (e.g. advertising to promote consumption of agricultural products like beef, pork, milk, chicken, raisins, etc.) and a monopoly might engage in "public relations" advertising, but monopolies don't have to try to take buyers away from their competitors.

- Oligopolies and monopolistic competitors account for a large portion of the advertising consumers see. If you look closely at the advertisements, you can get important clues about the level of interdependence in the market. If the advertisement mentions specific competitors (e.g. buy Pepsi, not Coke; buy Chevy trucks, not Ford trucks), the firms are likely experiencing interdependence. But if the advertisement simply promotes the firm's product as best (without mentioning other specific firms), there is no evidence of interdependence. In competitive markets, there are simply too many firms to attack each competitor. Too many firms means that there is not likely to be interdependence between individual firms.

Module Notes

Oligopolies are characterized as an industry in which there are a few producers. Each of these individual producers has some market power (like a monopoly) that enables it to set market prices, but each of these producers also competes against the other producers in the industry. This competition is different from perfect competition in that each producer is aware of the other firms in the industry and recognizes that each firm's behavior affects the other firms. The key aspect of oligopoly is the tension between cooperation and competition: each firm must decide whether and to what degree it wants to cooperate or compete with the other firms in its industry.

MODULE 65 GAME THEORY

BEFORE YOU READ THE MODULE

Summary

This module introduces game theory and shows how it is used to understand how oligopolists behave when faced with interdependent decision making.

Module Objectives

Review these objectives before you read the module. Place a "√" on the line when you can do each of the following:

_____**Objective #1.** Use game theory to enhance your understanding of oligopoly

_____**Objective #2.** Analyze a prisoners' dilemma using a payoff matrix

_____**Objective #3.** Determine dominant strategies and Nash equilibria in a variety of games

WHILE YOU READ THE MODULE

Key Terms

Define these key terms as you read the module:

Game theory:

Payoff:

Payoff matrix:

Prisoners' dilemma:

Dominant strategy:

Nash equilibrium:

Noncooperative equilibrium:

Practice the Model

Firm A and Firm B are the only two firms in a market. They are currently only open during the week, but each is deciding whether or not to also open on the weekend. The expected profits for both firms in each situation are included in the following payoff matrix. Use the information in the payoff matrix to answer the following questions.

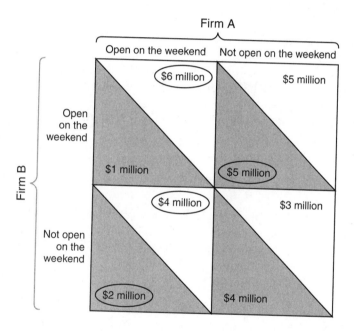

1) If Firm A and Firm B are both open on the weekend, how much profit does each earn?

2) Does Firm B have a dominant strategy? Explain.

3) Redraw the payoff matrix showing the new payoffs if demand increases on the weekends so that profits are $1 higher than shown in the payoff matrix for any firm that stays open.

List questions or difficulties from your initial reading of the module.

AFTER YOU READ THE MODULE

Fill-in-the-Blanks

Fill in the blanks to complete the following statements. If you find yourself having difficulties, please refer back to the appropriate section in the text.

- Because oligopolies are characterized by interdependence, economists use **1)**_____ to understand how oligopolists behave. Using this approach, economists represent the actions and payoffs for an oligopoly firm using a **2)**_____. One famous, and seemingly paradoxical, version of interdependence is illustrated by the **3)**_____ game.

- If a situation has a best action for a player regardless of the action taken by the other player, that action is considered a **4)**_____ strategy. When each player takes the action that is best, given the actions taken by other players, the situation is known as a **5)**_____ equilibrium.

Multiple-Choice Questions

Circle the best choice to answer or complete the following questions or incomplete statements. For additional practice, use the space provided to explain why one or more of the incorrect options do not work.

6. The payoff matrix in the prisoners' dilemma implies that
  a. each player has an incentive to benefit the other.
  b. neither player has an incentive to cheat.
  c. both players are better off if they cooperate.
  d. no dominant strategy exists in cases of mutual interdependence.
  e. noncompetitive equilibrium always benefits both players.

7. A player's best action regardless of the action taken by the other player in a game is known as the
  a. cooperative equilibrium.
  b. dominant strategy.
  c. Nash equilibrium.
  d. noncooperative equilibrium.
  e. payoff.

Helpful Tips

• Reading a payoff matrix can be challenging. Here's a suggestion for making this task easier. First, consider the payoff matrix from player 1's perspective as two separate columns: each column represents player 2 taking a particular strategy and sticking with it. Consider the payoff matrix from player 2's perspective as two separate rows: each row represents player 1 taking a particular strategy and sticking with it. When looking at different scenarios, use a piece of paper or your hand to cover up the strategy that is NOT being considered so you can only see the relevant sections of the payoff matrix. For example, cover the irrelevant column when considering player 1's choices or the irrelevant row when considering player 2's choices.

Module Notes

One common reaction to the prisoners' dilemma is to assert that it isn't really rational for either prisoner to confess. For example, a prisoner might not confess because of fear that the other would beat her up, or a prisoner would feel guilty about confessing. But this kind of answer is, well, cheating—it amounts to changing the payoffs in the payoff matrix. To understand the dilemma, you have to play fair and imagine prisoners who care *only* about the length of their sentences. Luckily, when it comes to oligopoly, it's a lot easier to believe that the firms care only about their profits.

MODULE 66 OLIGOPOLY IN PRACTICE

BEFORE YOU READ THE MODULE

Summary

This module explores a variety of oligopoly behaviors and how antitrust laws limit oligopolists' attempts to maximize their profits.

Module Objectives

Review these objectives before you read the module. Place a "√" on the line when you can do each of the following:

_____**Objective #1.** Discuss the legal constraints of antitrust policy

_____**Objective #2.** Explain how repeated interactions among oligopolists can result in collusion in the absence of any formal agreement

_____**Objective #3.** Explain the cause and effect of price wars, product differentiation, price leadership, and nonprice competition

_____**Objective #4.** Describe the importance of oligopoly in the real world

WHILE YOU READ THE MODULE

Key Terms

Define these key terms as you read the module:

Antitrust policy:

Strategic behavior:

Tit for tat:

Tacit collusion:

Price war:

Product differentiation:

Price leadership:

Nonprice competition:

Practice the Model

1) Why do firms with tacit price agreements engage in nonprice competition? Explain.

2) Which of the following are examples of nonprice competition?
    a. price wars
    b. price leadership
    c. product differentiation
    d. advertising

List questions or difficulties from your initial reading of the module.

AFTER YOU READ THE MODULE

Fill-in-the-Blanks

Fill in the blanks to complete the following statements. If you find yourself having difficulties, please refer back to the appropriate section in the text.

• Government efforts to make it difficult for oligopolistic industries to become monopolies or to behave

  like them are known as **1)**_____ policy. But even with this type of government policy and

  without explicit agreements, oligopolies can attempt to maximize their combined profits through

  2)_____ collusion, which is the normal state of oligopoly. However, oligopolists' ability to maximize their combined profits is made more difficult when the market has

3)_____, _____, _____, or _____. This difficulty

can be addressed by having one company tacitly set prices for the industry as a whole, known as price

4)_____. But if collusion breaks down, firms may find themselves in a

5)_____.

- Firms attempt to create the perception that their product is different by engaging in product

  6)_____.

Multiple-Choice Questions

Circle the best choice to answer or complete the following questions or incomplete statements. For additional practice, use the space provided to explain why one or more of the incorrect options do not work.

7. Which of the following make it more difficult for an industry to coordinate high prices?
   a. large numbers of firms
   b. standardized products
   c. shared interests
   d. large numbers of consumers
   e. tacit collusion

8. Firms in oligopolies attempt to convince buyers that their products are superior through
   a. price competition.
   b. price leadership.
   c. price wars.
   d. product differentiation.
   e. product standardization.

Helpful Tips

- The United States legally restricts the behavior of oligopolistic firms and prohibits the creation of monopolies. The Sherman Antitrust Act of 1890 marks the beginning of antitrust policy and the government's commitment to prevent oligopolistic industries from becoming or behaving like monopolies.

Module Notes

This is not the first (nor the last) time antitrust policy comes up in our study of the theory of the firm. Keep these specific examples of antitrust policy applied to oligopoly in mind (and recall the application of antitrust policy to monopoly) when the general topic of "public policy to promote competition" is covered in one of the last modules.

MODULE ⎡67⎤ INTRODUCTION TO MONOPOLISTIC COMPETITION

BEFORE YOU READ THE MODULE

Summary

This module presents the monopolistic competition market structure model and uses it to explain monopolistically competitive firm and market outcomes.

Module Objectives

Review these objectives before you read the module. Place a "√" on the line when you can do each of the following:

_____**Objective #1.** Determine prices and profit in monopolistic competition, both in the short run and in the long run

_____**Objective #2.** Explain how monopolistic competition can lead to inefficiency and excess capacity

WHILE YOU READ THE MODULE

Key Terms

Define these key terms as you read the module:

Zero-profit equilibrium:

Excess capacity:

Practice the Model

Draw a correctly labeled graph of a monopolistic competitor earning an economic profit in the short run. Be sure you show the firm's *D*, *MC*, *MR*, and *ATC* curves and the profit-maximizing quantity and price. Completely shade the area on the graph that shows profit.

List questions or difficulties from your initial reading of the module.

AFTER YOU READ THE MODULE

Fill-in-the-Blanks

Fill in the blanks to complete the following statements. If you find yourself having difficulties, please refer back to the appropriate section in the text.

- Monopolistic competition has a **1)**_____ demand curve in common with monopoly. And like perfect competition, monopolistic competition is characterized by free **2)**_____ and _____ . Monopolistically competitive firms maximize their profit by producing the level of output where **3)**_____ = _____.

- In the long run, monopolistic competitors will earn **4)**_____ economic profit. And since firms will not produce at the minimum average total cost in the long run, the industry will experience **5)**_____. However, consumers in the market benefit from product **6)**_____ and therefore it is hard to say whether or not monopolistic competition is inefficient.

Multiple-Choice Questions

Circle the best choice to answer or complete the following questions or incomplete statements. For additional practice, use the space provided to explain why one or more of the incorrect options do not work.

7. Excess capacity refers to the monopolistic competitor's inability to produce quantity sufficient to
   a. maximize price.
   b. maximize profits.
   c. maximize revenues.
   d. minimize marginal costs.
   e. minimize total costs.

8. The key to whether a monopolistic competitor is profitable in the short run depends on the relationship between
   a. its demand curve and its average total cost.
   b. its demand curve and its marginal cost.
   c. its marginal revenue and its marginal cost.
   d. its marginal revenue and its average total cost.
   e. its marginal revenue and its demand.

Helpful Tips

- Monopolistic competition is a blend of elements from the monopoly model and the perfect competition model. If you understand these similarities, you will see that you already understand monopolistic competition!

- The monopolistically competitive firm maximizes profit by producing the quantity where $MR = MC$. This is like both perfect competition and monopoly.

- A monopolistically competitive firm faces a downward-sloping demand curve and, therefore, the MR curve is beneath its demand curve. The price the monopolistically competitive firm charges for its good is found by taking the profit-maximizing quantity and looking at the firm's demand curve for the price associated with that quantity. These are the same as for a monopoly. In the short run, the monopolistically competitive firm can earn positive, negative, or zero economic profit.

- In the long run, the monopolistically competitive firm is subject to free entry and exit. This characteristic is the same for monopolistic competition and perfect competition. Free entry and exit means that a monopolistically competitive firm also earns zero economic profit in the long run.

Module Notes

Monopolistic competition shares characteristics with both monopoly and perfect competition. Product differentiation gives each monopolistic competitor a sort of "mini monopoly" for its somewhat unique product. This means that the demand curve for a monopolistic competitor is downward-sloping. However, since there are many similar products, the monopolistic competitor doesn't have very much market power; therefore, its demand curve is very flat (i.e. demand is very – but not perfectly – elastic). How flat? It depends on the specific situation. When drawing monopolistic competition graphs in the short run, they are very similar to monopoly graphs, but with a flatter demand curve. But since we don't really know how much flatter, we cannot distinguish short-run monopoly graphs from monopolistic competition graphs.

In the long run, monopolistically competitive firms experience free entry and exit just like perfectly competitive firms do. Free entry and exit lead to a normal profit for perfectly competitive firms in the long run and will lead to the same long-run result (a normal profit) in monopolistically competitive industries. So, just like a perfect competitor, a monopolistic competitor makes zero economic profit in the long run.

MODULE 68 PRODUCT DIFFERENTIATION AND ADVERTISING

BEFORE YOU READ THE MODULE

Summary

This module looks at how oligopolists and monopolistic competitors differentiate their products in order to maximize profit.

Module Objectives

Review these objectives before you read the module. Place a "√" on the line when you can do each of the following:

_____**Objective #1.** Explain why oligopolists and monopolistic competitors differentiate their products

_____**Objective #2.** Discuss the economic significance of advertising and brand names

WHILE YOU READ THE MODULE

Key Terms

Define this key term as you read the module:

Brand name:

Practice the Model

1) Draw a correctly labeled graph showing a monopolistic competitive firm's demand and marginal revenue curves.

2) On your graph, show the effect on these curves if the firm successfully differentiates its product through advertising.

List questions or difficulties from your initial reading of the module.

AFTER YOU READ THE MODULE

Fill-in-the-Blanks

Fill in the blanks to complete the following statements. If you find yourself having difficulties, please refer back to the appropriate section in the text.

- Product differentiation based on differences in people's tastes is known as differentiation by

  1)_____. Firms also differentiate by **2)**_____, by being the most

  convenient source of the good or service.

- Firms use **3)**_____ to provide information about their product or to convince consumers

  to buy it. And when a company does a good job of this, its product develops a **4)**_____

  name. This is considered efficient if the name conveys real **5)**_____, but inefficient if it

  creates market **6)**_____.

Multiple-Choice Questions

Circle the best choice to answer or complete the following questions or incomplete statements. For additional practice, use the space provided to explain why one or more of the incorrect options do not work.

7. Which of the following best explains why oligopolists differentiate their products?
    a. in order to increase competition
    b. in order to decrease market power
    c. in order to decrease costs
    d. in order to increase profits
    e. in order to decrease product quality

8. Which of the following is *not* used by competitors to differentiate their products in the minds of consumers?
    a. advertising
    b. location
    c. price wars
    d. quality
    e. style

Helpful Tips

- In the long run, the perfectly competitive firm produces at a level where price equals marginal cost, while the monopolistically competitive firm produces at a level where price is greater than marginal cost. The monopolistically competitive firm is interested in increasing demand for its good through advertising so that it can earn a profit in the short run. This helps us understand why monopolistically competitive firms advertise their product.

- Advertising is worthwhile in industries where firms have some market power. Advertising may help to establish the quality of a firm's product. Advertising may also convey important information. The establishment of a brand name may be a way of signaling quality to a consumer.

Module Notes

Remember to consider advertising as more than a way to increase sales, revenue, and profit in the short run. The use of advertising to create a brand name is a way that a firm can gain market power and create a barrier to entry. If a firm can establish its brand as the dominant brand in the market, the firm has made it difficult for a new, unknown brand to enter the market and compete. Thus, in the long run, product differentiation and advertising are used by firms to decrease competition, increase market power, and change the firm's location on the market structure spectrum (moving it toward the monopoly end).

Draw The Featured Models: Payoff Matrices and Monopolistic Competition

Assume there are two firms in the market for pickup trucks. They are deciding whether or not to develop and market a convertible pickup truck. If Firm 1 markets, it will earn a profit of $20 m. If Firm 2 markets, it will earn a profit of $25 m. If both firms market, Firm 1 will earn a profit of $10 m and Firm 2 will earn a profit of $15 m. Use this information to complete the payoff matrix. Not marketing will result in zero profit.

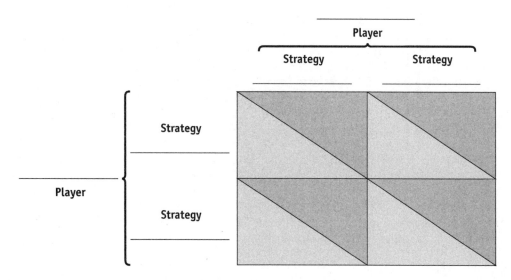

Graph a monopolistic competitor in long-run equilibrium. Label all axes and curves, and identify the equilibrium P and Q.

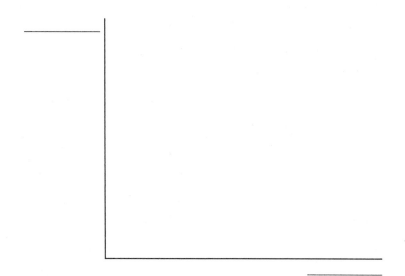

Complete the Exercise

Create your own example of a strategic oligopoly situation that has two players and two possible strategies. Fill in the players, strategies, and payoffs in the following payoff matrix. Does either player in your hypothetical game have a dominant strategy? Explain.

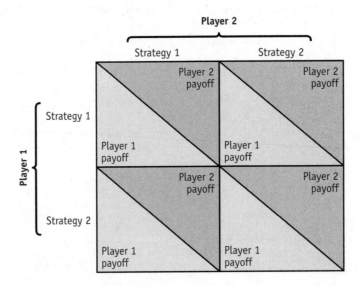

Draw a graph illustrating a monopolistic competitor in the short run that is (a) earning a profit and (b) experiencing a loss. Label all axes, curves, and profit-maximizing price and quantity.

a)

b)

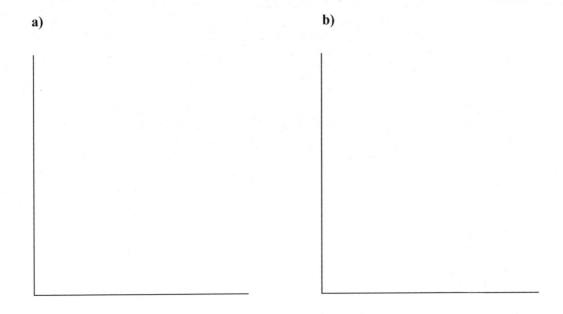

Problems

1. Suppose there are two firms in an industry that produces nuclear generators. Furthermore, suppose that each of these firms is able to produce a maximum of twenty generators a year due to their production facility. Would you predict that these two firms could successfully collude on price without a formal agreement? Why or why not?

2. The following payoff matrix provides information about the profits Apple Growers and Johnny Appleseed Company earn based on the advertising strategy the companies adopt. The first entry in the matrix cell gives the profit of Apple Growers, and the second entry provides the profit of Johnny Appleseed Company.

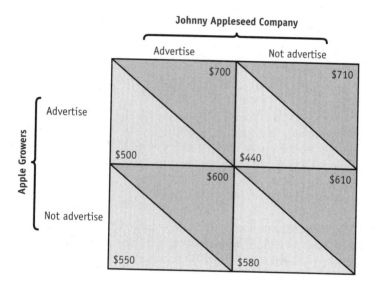

a. If these two firms could collude with one another and decide jointly on their advertising strategy with the goal of maximizing their joint profit, what combination of strategies would result in the greatest joint profit for these two companies?

b. Which strategy is Apple Growers' dominant strategy?

c. Which strategy is Johnny Appleseed Company's dominant strategy?

d. What is the Nash equilibrium for this game?

3. Two firms, Firm A and Firm B, compete against one another in a duopoly. These two firms have been in competition with each other for many years, and they anticipate that they will continue to compete against one another for many more years. Both firms are faced with two strategies they can pursue: they can either "Always Cheat" or they can pursue a strategy of "Tit for Tat" in which one firm punishes the other firm whenever the other firm cheats. Suppose that the payoff for playing the strategy of "Always Cheats" results in each firm earning a profit of $100 a year. If one firm plays the strategy of "Tit for Tat" while the other firm plays the strategy of "Always Cheat," the cheating firm will earn $150 the first year but only $90 for each subsequent year, while the "Tit for Tat" firm will earn $90 the first year but $100 for each subsequent year. If both firms play the "Tit for Tat" strategy, they will earn $130 a year.

a. Create a payoff matrix for Firm A and Firm B showing the profits these two firms earn given the strategies that are open to each of them.

b. Suppose that Firm A anticipates that Firm B is going to choose the strategy to "Always cheat." Given Firm B's choice, what is Firm A's best strategy if these two firms compete for a single year? Is this still the best choice if Firm A and Firm B are competing with each other for many more years?

c. Suppose that Firm B anticipates that Firm A is going to choose the strategy to "Always cheat." Given Firm A's choice, what is Firm B's best strategy if these two firms compete for a single year? Is this still the best choice if Firm A and Firm B are competing with each other for many more years?

d. If Firm A chooses the "Tit for Tat" strategy, what is the best strategy for Firm B to choose? If Firm B chooses the "Tit for Tat" strategy, what is the best strategy for Firm A to choose?

4. Discuss four different factors that make it difficult for a group of firms in an oligopolistic industry to achieve tacit collusion.

5. What is price leadership? How does it resolve the oligopoly's problem of deciding how to set the optimal price? If the firms follow a price leadership model, how do the firms then compete with one another if they all offer the good at the same price?

6. Suppose the existing firms in the fast-food restaurant business are currently earning positive economic profit in the short run.
   a. Draw a graph representing a monopolistically competitive firm in this situation. Identify the price of the good, the output the firm produces in the short run, and the area that represents this firm's profit.

   b. What do you anticipate will happen in the long run in this industry? How will the industry price and quantity change in the long run? How will each firm's profit change in the long run?

   c. Draw a graph representing a monopolistically competitive firm in long-run equilibrium. Identify the price of the good and the quantity the firm sells in the long run. What is the relationship between price and marginal cost for this firm in the long run? What is the relationship between price and average total cost for this firm in the long run?

7. Suppose the existing firms in the fast-food restaurant business are currently earning negative economic profit in the short run.
   a. Draw a graph representing a monopolistically competitive firm in this situation. Identify the price of the good, the output the firm produces in the short run, and the area that represents this firm's profit.

   b. What do you anticipate will happen in the long run in this industry? How will the industry price and quantity change in the long run? How will each firm's profit change in the long run?

   c. Draw a graph representing a monopolistically competitive firm in long-run equilibrium. Identify the price of the good and the quantity the firm sells in the long run. What is the relationship between price and marginal cost for this firm in the long run? What is the relationship between price and average total cost for this firm in the long run?

8. a. Compare the long-run equilibrium for a monopolistically competitive firm with the long-run equilibrium for a perfectly competitive firm. How are these two equilibriums similar? How are these two equilibriums different? Draw two sketches depicting the long-run equilibrium for these two market structures.

b. Compare the long-run equilibrium for a monopolistically competitive firm with the long-run equilibrium for a monopoly. How are these two equilibriums similar? How are these two equilibriums different? Draw two sketches depicting the long-run equilibrium for these two market structures.

9. Use the following graph of a monopolistically competitive firm to answer the next set of questions.

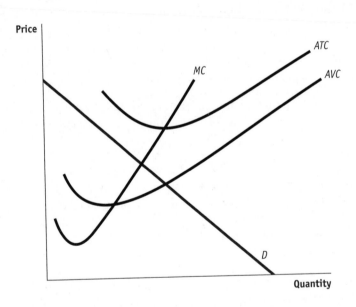

a. Label the profit-maximizing level of output and price for this firm in the short run.

b. Identify any profit the firm is making in the short run and decide whether these profits are positive or negative.

c. Draw the long-run equilibrium situation on this graph. Identify the long-run profit-maximizing quantity and the long-run price. What will this firm's profits equal in the long run?

d. Did entry or exiting of firms occur in the long run in this problem? Explain your answer.

10. What does it mean to say that a monopolistically competitive firm in the long run produces at a quantity where the firm has excess capacity? Is this a good or a bad outcome?

Review Questions

Circle your answer to the following questions.

1. An industry characterized by having a few firms, each with some market power, is an example of (a)n
  a. monopoly, since the firms have some market power.
  b. perfectly competitive industry, since there is more than one firm in the industry.
  c. monopolistically competitive industry, since the firms compete with one another while at the same time they have some market power.
  d. oligopoly, since the firms have market power and can therefore affect the market price, but there are only a few firms, so each firm recognizes the interdependence between firms.
  e. natural monopoly because economies of scale provide a large cost advantage.

2. Which of the following best describes interdependence in an oligopoly?
  a. The relatively large number of firms makes it possible to ignore the actions of other firms.
  b. The small number of firms makes it possible to ignore the effects of other firms' decisions.
  c. The small number of firms makes the profit of each firm dependent on the actions of other firms.
  d. Smaller firms in an oligopoly rely on the price leadership of larger firms to earn greater profits.
  e. Larger firms in an oligopoly rely on product differentiation to earn greater profits versus smaller firms.

3. Firms in a duopoly might collude as a way to
  a. stabilize prices.
  b. stabilize quantities.
  c. stabilize revenues.
  d. maximize each firm's profit.
  e. maximize joint profits.

Use the following information to answer the next three questions.

The following payoff matrix indicates the level of profits earned by Printers Press and Typesetters, the only two firms in the printing industry in an economy. The level of profit for each firm depends on whether they cooperate or compete with one another.

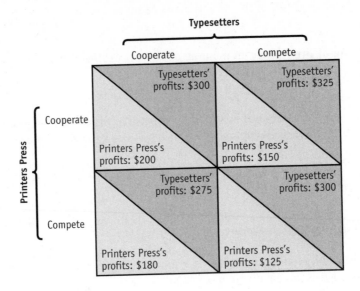

Typesetters

	Cooperate	Compete
Cooperate	Typesetters' profits: $300 / Printers Press's profits: $200	Typesetters' profits: $325 / Printers Press's profits: $150
Compete	Typesetters' profits: $275 / Printers Press's profits: $180	Typesetters' profits: $300 / Printers Press's profits: $125

Printers Press

4. What is Printers Press's dominant strategy?
  a. compete
  b. cooperate
  c. Printers Press does not have a dominant strategy.
  d. Both choices reflect a dominant strategy.
  e. collude with Typesetters

5. What is Typesetters' dominant strategy?
  a. compete
  b. cooperate
  c. Typesetters does not have a dominant strategy.
  d. Both choices reflect a dominant strategy.
  e. collude with Printers Press

6. When Printers Press and Typesetters pursue their dominant strategies, their joint profit
  a. is maximized.
  b. is not maximized.
  c. is shared equally.
  d. is greater than if they colluded.
  e. does not create an incentive to cheat.

Use the following information to answer the next four questions.

Two firms are the only producers in a market. Each firm is trying to decide whether or not to advertise. If Firm B advertises, Firm A earns $2,000 in profit if it does not advertise and $1,800 if it does. (The advertising increases its costs more than its revenues.) If Firm B does not advertise, Firm A earns $2,200 in profit if it does not advertise and $2,000 if it does. If Firm A advertises, Firm B earns $3,000 in profit if it does not advertise and $2,700 if it does. If Firm A does not advertise, Firm B earns $2,600 if it does not advertise and $2,400 if it does.

7. What is Firm B's dominant strategy?
   a. advertise
   b. do not advertise
   c. Firm B does not have a dominant strategy.
   d. Both options represent a dominant strategy.
   e. collude with Firm A

8. What is the Nash equilibrium?
   a. Firm A and Firm B will not advertise, and they will earn joint profits of $4,800.
   b. Firm A will advertise, Firm B will not advertise, and they will earn total profits of $5,000.
   c. Firm A will not advertise, Firm B will advertise, and they will earn total profits of $4,400.
   d. Firm A and Firm B will advertise, and they will earn total profits of $4,500.
   e. No Nash equilibrium exists for this game.

9. For these two firms, choosing the dominant strategy results in the best possible outcome for
   a. Firm A, but not Firm B.
   b. Firm B, but not Firm A.
   c. both Firm A and Firm B.
   d. neither Firm A nor Firm B.
   e. either Firm A or Firm B, but not both.

10. What would happen to the equilibrium payoffs for Firm A and Firm B if the government provided a $1,000 small business subsidy to advertise in the area?
    a. Both firms would choose to advertise and earn total profits of $6,500.
    b. Firm A would advertise and Firm B would not advertise, and they would earn total profits of $6,000.
    c. Firm A would not advertise and Firm B would advertise, and they would earn total profits of $5,400.
    d. Both firms would choose not to advertise and earn total profits of $4,800.
    e. No Nash equilibrium would exist in the presence of the government subsidy.

11. Which of the following statements is true for a monopolistically competitive firm?
    a. In the short run, the firm earns a positive economic profit whenever price is greater than average total cost.
    b. In the short run, the firm produces at the minimum average total cost level of production at which $MR = MC$.
    c. Monopolistically competitive firms engage in collusion so that they can set price at a level greater than marginal cost.
    d. Monopolistically competitive firms are able to earn positive economic profits in the long run because of decreased competition.
    e. Monopolistically competitive firms are economically efficient in the long run but not in the short run.

12. Monopolistically competitive firms resemble perfectly competitive firms because
    a. in the long run they earn zero economic profit.
    b. in the long run they produce at the minimum-cost point of their ATC curves.
    c. they compete with other firms that offer similar products.
    d. they are "price-takers."
    e. they profit maximize at the quantity of output where marginal cost equals demand.

13. Monopolistically competitive firms resemble monopolies because
   a. their *MR* curves lie above their demand curves.
   b. they charge a price that is greater than their marginal cost of production.
   c. entry and exit of firms in the long run ensure that profit equals zero in the long run.
   d. they produce a product with no substitutes.
   e. they produce at minimum average total cost.

14. When monopolistically competitive firms differentiate their products, the result is
   a. unprofitable, since differentiation costs money.
   b. unprofitable in the short run, since monopolistically competitive firms make zero economic profit in the short run.
   c. profitable in the short run, so long as consumers differ in their tastes.
   d. unprofitable in the short run, because differentiation results in a loss of market power.
   e. wasted effort, since consumers would be just as happy with identical products as they are with differentiated products.

15. Which of the following statements is true about monopolistically competitive industries that produce differentiated products?
   a. Firms in monopolistically competitive industries with differentiated products must operate at a loss in the short run.
   b. Monopolistically competitive industries with differentiated products are industries that find there is no value in diversity.
   c. Monopolistically competitive industries with differentiated products are able to sustain short-run positive economic profit into the long run.
   d. Monopolistically competitive industries with differentiated products must create barriers to entry to maximize revenues.
   e. Monopolistically competitive industries with differentiated products are characterized as having competition among sellers.

16. When Henry Ford produced his cars, he maximized his economies of scale, while General Motors decided to produce with excess capacity. This resulted in
   a. Ford being able to produce cheaper cars than General Motors initially, since Ford did not diversify the product it provided.
   b. Ford facing a trade-off between offering cars at a lower price with less differentiation or selling cars at a higher price with greater differentiation.
   c. consumers ultimately finding they did not prefer product differentiation as General Motors sold fewer cars than Ford.
   d. General Motors changing its strategy to offering fewer models of cars.
   e. Ford producing cars at a loss because the price of its cars could not cover its costs.

Use the following diagram of a monopolistically competitive firm to answer the next four questions.

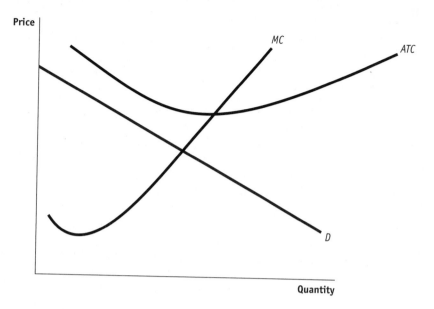

Price

MC

ATC

D

Quantity

17. To identify the profit-maximizing output for this firm in the short run, this graph needs
   a. the market price identified.
   b. the *MR* curve identified.
   c. the *AVC* curve identified.
   d. the *MR* and *AFC* curves identified.
   e. the *MR* and *AVC* curves identified.

18. Assuming this firm produces in the short run, this firm will earn
   a. negative economic profit, since its price is less than its average total cost.
   b. positive economic profit, since its price is greater than its marginal cost.
   c. zero economic profit, since entry of new firms will drive the profits of all firms down to that level where each firm earns zero economic profit.
   d. zero economic profit, since the exit of firms will cause profits of all existing firms to increase until all the firms left in the industry earn zero economic profit.
   e. a normal profit, since its price is equal to its marginal cost.

19. Assuming this firm produces in the short run, this firm will
   a. sell more units of the good if *MR* = *MC* at its selected level of production.
   b. sell fewer units of the good, if it currently is producing where marginal cost is less than price.
   c. sell the quantity at which *MC* equals *MR* and earn a negative profit.
   d. be reluctant to advertise, since this will only increase its costs.
   e. increase revenues by reducing product variety.

20. Relative to a perfectly competitive firm, a monopolistically competitive firm produces
   a. its product at a lower price.
   b. where its average total cost is increasing as output increases.
   c. at a point where the firm has excess capacity.
   d. at a point where its marginal cost is greater than quantity demanded.
   e. at a point where its marginal cost is equal to its average total cost.

Section 13 Factor Markets

Overview

This section examines factor markets, the markets in which the factors of production such as labor, land, and capital are traded. Factor markets, like goods markets, play a crucial role in the economy: they allocate productive resources to producers and help ensure that those resources are used efficiently.

Featured Model/Graph: The Labor Market

This section presents the markets for all factors of production (land, labor, and capital), but focuses on the market for labor.

MODULES IN THIS SECTION

Module 69   **Introduction and Factor Demand**

Module 70   **The Markets for Land and Capital**

Module 71   **The Market for Labor**

Module 72   **The Cost-Minimizing Input Combination**

Module 73   **Theories of Income Distribution**

BEFORE YOU TACKLE THE TEST

Draw the Featured Model

Complete the Exercise

Problems

Review Questions

MODULE 69   INTRODUCTION AND FACTOR DEMAND

BEFORE YOU READ THE MODULE

Summary

This module presents the factors of production and explains the distribution of income among those factors. It also explains what determines the demand for a factor of production.

Module Objectives

Review these objectives before you read the module. Place a "√" on the line when you can do each of the following:

_____ **Objective #1.** Describe features that make markets for factors of production — resources like labor, land, and capital — different from goods markets

_____ **Objective #2.** Explain how factor markets determine the factor distribution of income

_____ **Objective #3.** Discuss how the demand for a factor of production is determined

WHILE YOU READ THE MODULE

Key Terms

Define these key terms as you read the module:

Physical capital:

Human capital:

Derived demand:

Factor distribution of income:

Marginal revenue product (*MRP*):

Marginal revenue product curve (*MRPC*):

Practice the Model

Assume that the price of a car wash is $10 and the marginal product of labor at the car wash is given in the following table.

Quantity of labor L (workers)	Quantity of car washes Q	Marginal product of labor $MPL = \frac{\Delta Q}{\Delta L}$ (car washes per worker)
0	0	
1	6	___
2	11	___
3	15	___
4	18	___
5	20	___
6	21	___
7	21	___

1) Fill in the values for the *MPL* in the table.

2) Calculate the *MRPL* for each quantity of labor.

3) Draw a correctly labeled graph of the *MRP* curve in the space below.

List questions or difficulties from your initial reading of the module.

Fill-in-the-Blanks

Fill in the blanks to complete the following statements. If you find yourself having difficulties, please refer back to the appropriate section in the text.

- Resources used to produce goods and services are sold in **1)**_____ markets. The demand in these markets is different from demand in product markets because it is a **2)**_____ demand.

- Firms decide how much of a resource to use by comparing marginal costs and marginal benefits. The marginal cost of a worker in a perfectly competitive labor market equals the **3)**_____. The marginal benefit, which is the value of the extra output generated by a worker, is the **4)**_____ of labor. Perfectly competitive firms will hire labor up to the point where the **5)**_____ equals the **6)**_____ of labor.

- An individual producer's labor demand curve is the same as its **7)**_____ curve. The labor demand curve will shift if there is a change in **8)**_____, **9)**_____, or **10)**_____.

Multiple-Choice Questions

Circle the best choice to answer or complete the following questions or incomplete statements. For additional practice, use the space provided to explain why one or more of the incorrect options do not work.

11. The marginal revenue product of any factor of production equals its
    a. marginal product × marginal revenue.
    b. marginal product/number of factors of production.
    c. marginal product/marginal revenue.
    d. total product/wage.
    e. total product × wage.

12. Which of the following will shift the factor demand curve to the left?
    a. an improvement in technology.
    b. an increase in the wage rate.
    c. an increase in the marginal product of the factor.
    d. an increase in the supply of another factor used to produce the good.
    e. a decrease in the price of the good being produced.

Helpful Tips

- One of the key tips for working with factor markets is to recognize that the buyers in these markets are firms while the suppliers in these markets are individuals. Firms demand the services of land, labor, and capital, and households (or individuals) supply these services. This is in contrast to output markets where the buyers of the outputs are households and the suppliers of outputs are firms.

Module Notes

Factor markets and factor prices are critical in determining the allocation of resources among competing uses. There are two features that make factor markets special. First, the demand for a factor is a derived demand: this demand depends on or is derived from firms' decisions about how much output to produce. Second, for most of us, factor markets are the source of the largest share of our income. Factor prices play a key role in determining the income distribution in our economy, since it is these factor prices that determine how the total income in an economy is divided among labor, land, and capital.

MODULE 70 THE MARKETS FOR LAND AND CAPITAL

BEFORE YOU READ THE MODULE

Summary

This module looks more closely at the markets for land and capital. The labor market is discussed in Module 71.

Module Objectives

Review these objectives before you read the module. Place a "√" on the line when you can do each of the following:

_____ **Objective #1.** Determine supply and demand in the markets for land and capital

_____ **Objective #2.** Find equilibrium in the land and capital markets

_____ **Objective #3.** Explain how the demand for factors leads to the marginal productivity theory of income distribution

WHILE YOU READ THE MODULE

Key Terms

Define these key terms as you read the module:

Rental rate:

Equilibrium marginal revenue product:

Economic rent:

Marginal productivity theory of income distribution:

Practice the Model

1) What does it mean to say that the supply of a factor of production is perfectly inelastic?

2) Draw a correctly labeled graph showing the supply and demand for a factor of production with a perfectly inelastic supply curve and completely shade the area representing economic rent on your graph.

List questions or difficulties from your initial reading of the module.

AFTER YOU READ THE MODULE

Fill-in-the-Blanks

Fill in the blanks to complete the following statements. If you find yourself having difficulties, please refer back to the appropriate section in the text.

- The explicit cost of a unit of land or capital is called the **1)**_____ rate. Firms will employ more land or capital up to the point where the **2)**_____ of the land or capital equals this rate.

- Compared to capital, the supply of land is relatively **3)**_____. A decrease in the supply of land or capital will shift the factor supply curve to the **4)**_____, causing the factor price to **5)**_____.

- The **6)**_____ theory of income distribution says that each factor is paid the value of the output generated by the last unit of that factor employed in the factor market as a whole—its equilibrium marginal revenue product.

Multiple-Choice Questions

Circle the best choice to answer or complete the following questions or incomplete statements. For additional practice, use the space provided to explain why one or more of the incorrect options do not work.

7. A factor of production is earning economic rent when the payment for the factor is
   a. less than is economically efficient to employ the factor.
   b. in excess of the minimum necessary to employ the factor.
   c. creating a deadweight loss.
   d. less than the marginal revenue product for the factor.
   e. greater than the marginal revenue product for the factor.

8. The marginal productivity theory of income distribution explains
   a. the arbitrary nature of the division of income in the economy.
   b. how markets compensate factors of production in identical markets only.
   c. the distribution of income for different types of land, labor, and capital.
   d. the distribution of income for different types of labor only.
   e. how factors of production are compensated in imperfectly competitive markets only.

Helpful Tips

- The marginal productivity theory of income distribution says that each factor is paid the value of the output generated by the last unit of that factor employed in the factor market as a whole. This is equivalent to saying that each factor is paid the value of its marginal product. This theory implies that the division of income among the economy's factors is not arbitrary, but is instead determined by each factor's marginal productivity at the economy's equilibrium.

Module Notes

It's important to remember that the marginal productivity theory of income distribution says that *all* units of a factor get paid the factor's equilibrium marginal revenue product—the additional value produced by the *last* unit of the factor employed. The most common source of error is to forget that the relevant marginal revenue product is the equilibrium value. It is easy to confuse this with the marginal revenue products you calculate on the way to equilibrium. In looking at Table 69.2 in your textbook, you might be tempted to think that because the first worker has a marginal revenue product of $380, that worker is paid $380 in equilibrium. Not so: if the equilibrium marginal revenue product in the labor market is equal to $200, then *all* workers receive $200.

MODULE 71 THE MARKET FOR LABOR

BEFORE YOU READ THE MODULE

Summary

This module completes the development of the labor market by adding the supply of labor and determination of the equilibrium wage and quantity in the labor market.

Module Objectives

Review these objectives before you read the module. Place a "√" on the line when you can do each of the following:

_____**Objective #1.** Describe how a worker's decision about time preference gives rise to labor supply

_____**Objective #2.** Determine the equilibrium wage and level of employment in the labor market

WHILE YOU READ THE MODULE

Key Terms

Define these key terms as you read the module:

Time allocation:

Leisure:

Individual labor supply curve:

Marginal factor cost (*MFC*):

Monopsonist:

Monopsony:

Practice the Model

Draw a correctly labeled graph showing each of the following labor supply curves:

1) An individual labor supply curve when the substitution effect dominates

2) An individual labor supply curve when the income effect dominates

3) A firm labor supply curve in a perfectly competitive labor market

4) A labor supply curve in an imperfectly competitive market

List questions or difficulties from your initial reading of the module.

AFTER YOU READ THE MODULE

Fill-in-the-Blanks

Fill in the blanks to complete the following statements. If you find yourself having difficulties, please refer back to the appropriate section in the text.

- People work to earn income to purchase goods and services. Time spent working to earn income means less time spent not working, known as **1)**_____ time. A person is making an optimal labor supply choice when the marginal utility of an hour of **2)**_____ is equal to the marginal utility from the goods that can be purchased with the hourly **3)**_____.

- An individual's labor supply curve can have a positive or negative slope, depending on the relative size of the **4)**_____ and **5)**_____ effects. If the income effect dominates, a higher wage rate will **6)**_____ the quantity of labor supplied.

- The market labor supply curve will shift as a result of **7)**_____, _____, _____, or _____.

- A labor market in which there is only one firm hiring labor is called a **8)**_____. When the labor and product markets are not perfectly competitive, labor will be hired up to the point where the **9)**_____ of labor equals the **10)**_____.

Multiple-Choice Questions

Circle the best choice to answer or complete the following questions or incomplete statements. For additional practice, use the space provided to explain why one or more of the incorrect options do not work.

11. The income effect from an increase in wealth will
   a. shift the labor supply curve for these workers to the left.
   b. shift the labor supply curve for these workers to the right.
   c. increase the quantity of workers on the existing supply curve.
   d. decrease the quantity of workers on the existing supply curve.
   e. increase opportunities for these workers in alternative labor markets.

12. Why is the marginal factor cost curve above the supply curve for imperfectly competitive labor markets?
   a. The firms must hire workers at the market wage.
   b. The firms are able to pay wages below the marginal factor cost of labor.
   c. The marginal revenue product of labor decreases as the quantity of labor increases.
   d. The firm must offer a higher wage to each additional worker hired.
   e. The decision to hire workers is insignificant to the market for labor overall.

Helpful Tips

- Marginal product is the additional output produced as a result of hiring an additional unit of a factor. We started this module with the assumption that firms operate in a perfectly competitive industry. That means that the firm is a price-taker and therefore can sell any amount of output at the market price. Marginal revenue, the additional revenue received from selling one more unit of output, is equal to the price. So when firms determine their demand for a factor, they look at how much additional output the factor will produce (MP) and how much they will receive for that output (MR). The demand for a factor is equal to $MP \times P$ when the labor market is perfectly competitive.

- Both product markets and factor markets can be either perfectly competitive or imperfectly competitive (e.g. monopolies and monopsonies). When we drop the assumption of perfect competition in the product market--for example, if the firm is a monopoly--then the firm is not a price-taker. In this case, the firm will still determine its output by looking at how much additional output the factor will produce (MP) and how much it will receive for that output (MR). In this case, it is less than the price since the firm must lower the price in order to sell additional output. The demand for a factor is equal to $MP \times MR$, which is called MRP.

Module Notes

When the wage rate increases in the labor market, it causes both an income and a substitution effect for the individual. The wage increase causes the price (opportunity cost) of an hour of leisure to increase since the individual will now give up a greater amount of income if he or she elects to increase his or her consumption of leisure. Thus, the wage increase causes the individual to substitute away from leisure, the relatively more expensive good, toward income, the relatively cheaper good. However, the wage increase also creates an income effect: when the wage increases, the individual's income rises at every level of work effort and this increase in income causes the individual to demand more units of leisure, which is a normal good. Depending on the relative strength of the income and substitution effects, the individual may elect to work more or work less when the wage rate increases.

The factor market can also be either perfectly competitive or imperfectly competitive (e.g. a monopsony). If the firm can employ as much of a factor as it wants at a constant price, the factor market is perfectly competitive. For example, in a large city, a firm may be able to hire as many unskilled workers as it wants at an equilibrium wage rate. The firm does not have to offer higher wages to attract more workers – there are many workers and the firm is one of many small firms, so the supply curve of labor for the firm is horizontal at the market price. In this situation, the additional cost of hiring an additional worker (the marginal factor cost) is the market wage. If a firm operates in an imperfectly competitive factor market (for example, if the firm is a monopsonist), the firm will have to increase the wage it offers to hire more labor. Therefore, the MFC is above the market wage. Note that MFC is the general term for the additional cost of hiring additional units of a factor. The market wage (or rent) is the MFC in the case of a perfectly competitive factor market.

MODULE 72 COST MINIMIZING INPUT COMBINATIONS

BEFORE YOU READ THE MODULE

Summary

This module explains how firms decide the optimal combination of factors for producing the desired level of output.

Module Objectives

Review these objectives before you read the module. Place a "√" on the line when you can do each of the following:

_____**Objective #1.** Explain how firms determine the optimal input mix

_____**Objective #2.** Apply the cost-minimization rule for employing inputs

WHILE YOU READ THE MODULE

Key Terms

Define this key term as you read the module:

Cost-minimization rule:

Practice the Model

Assume that a firm is using the cost-minimizing combination of its only two inputs, capital and labor. If the price of a unit of capital is $200 and the price of a unit of labor is $50, what is the *MPL* of the last unit of labor if the marginal product of the last unit of capital is 2,000?

List questions or difficulties from your initial reading of the module.

AFTER YOU READ THE MODULE

Fill-in-the-Blanks

Fill in the blanks to complete the following statements. If you find yourself having difficulties, please refer back to the appropriate section in the text.

- When ATM machines reduce the need for bank tellers, capital and labor are **1)**_____ in production. When office workers are more productive as a result of better office computers, capital and labor are **2)**_____ in production. If alternative combinations of capital and labor can be used to produce the optimal level of output, a profit-maximizing firm will select the input combination with the **3)**_____ cost.

- The cost-minimization rule states that firms will adjust their hiring of inputs until the **4)**_____ per dollar is equal for all inputs.

- If the marginal product per dollar spent is higher for capital than it is for labor, then the firm should **5)**_____ its use of capital. When it does this, the marginal product of capital will **6)**_____, due to the law of diminishing returns, until the condition of the cost-minimization rule is met.

Multiple-Choice Questions

Circle the best choice to answer or complete the following questions or incomplete statements. For additional practice, use the space provided to explain why one or more of the incorrect options do not work.

7. In which situation should a profit-maximizing firm employ more labor?
   a. Marginal product per dollar of capital is greater than marginal product per dollar of labor.
   b. Marginal product per dollar of labor is greater than marginal product per dollar of capital.
   c. Marginal revenue product of capital is greater than marginal revenue product of labor.
   d. Marginal revenue product of labor is greater than marginal revenue product of capital.
   e. Marginal factor cost of labor is greater than marginal factor cost of capital.

8. Cost-minimizing firms employ factors of production up to the point at which
   a. the marginal product of all factors is equal.
   b. the marginal product per dollar of all factors is equal.
   c. the marginal product per dollar of labor is equal to one.
   d. the marginal product per dollar of capital equals the marginal revenue product of labor.
   e. the marginal revenue product of capital equals the marginal revenue product of labor.

Helpful Tips

• Profit-maximizing firms must satisfy two basic profit-maximizing rules. The first rule states that the firm will maximize profit when it produces the level of output at which marginal revenue equals marginal cost. The second rule says that a firm will maximize profit when it hires the level of factors at which the marginal factor cost of an additional unit of that factor is equal to the marginal revenue product of that factor. Although one of these rules focuses on the optimal output level while the other focuses on the optimal factor use, the two rules amount to the same principle: undertake production or hiring of a factor only up to the point where the marginal cost of that production or that factor usage is equal to the marginal benefit from that production or that factor usage. By this point this should be a familiar concept.

Module Notes

So far in this course, we have focused on profit maximization. For example, firms will maximize their profit by producing the level of output where $MC = MR$. An important related concept is the idea of cost minimization. For firms to maximize their profit, they need to produce their output using the least cost combination of inputs. Cost minimization and profit maximization go hand-in-hand. There are two scenarios in which a firm might apply the concept of cost minimization. A firm might determine its profit-maximizing output and then need to determine how to produce that level of output using the combination of inputs with the lowest cost. Alternatively, the firm might have a set budget for inputs and want to produce the highest possible level of output given that budget. In either case, the firm wants to achieve efficiency: no waste. A firm obviously can't maximize its profits if it is spending more than it has to for inputs or is getting less output than it could from the inputs it employs. The cost-minimization rule applies in either case and goes along with profit maximization.

MODULE 73 THEORIES OF INCOME DISTRIBUTION

BEFORE YOU READ THE MODULE

Summary

This module presents the marginal productivity theory of income distribution and discusses the extent to which it explains wage disparities between workers.

Module Objectives

Review these objectives before you read the module. Place a "√" on the line when you can do each of the following:

_____Objective #1. Explain the labor market applications of the marginal productivity theory of income distribution

_____Objective #2. Identify and describe sources of wage disparities and the role of discrimination

WHILE YOU READ THE MODULE

Key Terms

Define these key terms as you read the module:

Compensating differentials:

Unions:

Efficiency-wage model:

Practice the Model

1) Which of the following might cause an employer to pay an above equilibrium wage? *(Note that there may be more than one correct answer.)*
   a. an employee union
   b. providing incentives for performance and loyalty
   c. compensating differentials
   d. profit maximization
   e. cost minimization
   f. discrimination

List questions or difficulties from your initial reading of the module.

AFTER YOU READ THE MODULE

Fill-in-the-Blanks

Fill in the blanks to complete the following statements. If you find yourself having difficulties, please refer back to the appropriate section in the text.

- According to the marginal productivity theory of income distribution, the division of income among the economy's factors of production is determined by each factor's **1)**_____ at the economy's **2)**_____.

- There are three well-understood sources of wage differences across occupations and individuals that are consistent with the marginal productivity theory of income distribution. Across different types of jobs, wages are often higher or lower depending on how attractive or unattractive the job is. These wage differences are known as **3)**_____. Wages can also be different due to differences in individual ability or **4)**_____. A third reason for wage differences is an individual's education and training, known as **5)**_____.

- But some observers believe that wage differences may not be fully explained by differences in marginal productivity. They argue that wage differences may be due to **6)**_____ that arises when markets are not competitive, **7)**_____ wages used to motivate workers to work hard, or **8)**_____ against workers based on race, gender, or other characteristics.

Multiple-Choice Questions

Circle the best choice to answer or complete the following questions or incomplete statements. For additional practice, use the space provided to explain why one or more of the incorrect options do not work.

9. Which of the following is an example of a compensating differential?
   a. Computer programmers earn more than sales clerks.
   b. Men generally earn more than women.
   c. Union electricians earn more than non-union electricians.
   d. Experienced engineers earn more than engineers with no experience.
   e. Hazardous duty pay is added to earnings for military employees in war or actively hostile settings.

10. The marginal productivity theory of income distribution accounts for wage differences based on

    a. discrimination.

    b. education.

    c. efficiency wages.

    d. gender.

    e. market power.

Helpful Tips

- The marginal productivity theory of income distribution says that with a perfectly competitive market each factor is paid the value of the output generated by the last unit of that factor employed in the factor market as a whole. This is equivalent to saying that each factor is paid the value of its marginal product. This theory implies that the division of income among the economy's factors is not arbitrary, but is instead determined by each factor's marginal productivity at the economy's equilibrium.

- In the real world, there are wide disparities in income among people, and some people believe that some of this income disparity is not due solely to differences in marginal productivity or compensating differentials. They argue that wage differences may also reflect market power, efficiency wages, and discrimination.

Module Notes

When you study topics like income distribution, be sure to keep in mind two terms from early in this book: positive and normative. Remember that positive economics describes the way the economy actually works. For example, it looks at the extent to which the marginal productivity theory of income distribution explains the actual income distribution we see in the United States, or how efficiently factor markets work. Normative economics, on the other hand, makes prescriptive statements about how the economy should work. For example, it considers what the income distribution in the United States ought to be, or how equitable this distribution is. Positive economics tries to determine facts and to establish what income distribution exists. Normative economics draws on perceptions of equity and fairness to address what income distribution should exist. While no less important, addressing questions of equity is more complicated than determining actual income distributions. Therefore, economics more often focuses on questions of efficiency rather than equity.

The Featured Model: The Labor Market

Draw a graph of the labor market showing equilibrium wage and employment when (a) both the product and factor markets are perfectly competitive and (b) there is imperfect competition in the labor market. Be sure to clearly and correctly label all axes and curves with the correct labels specific to the labor market and the situation.

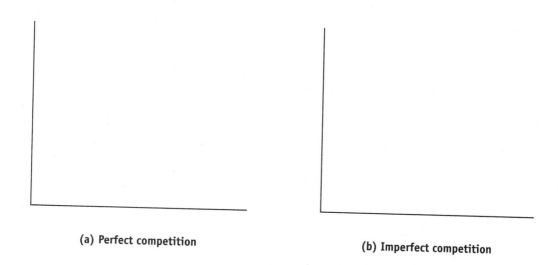

(a) Perfect competition   (b) Imperfect competition

Complete the Exercise

1. Suppose that a labor market is composed of two individuals, Sam and Anne. Sam's and Anne's individual supply of labor curves can be described by the following two equations:

   Sam's supply of labor: $W = 5 + (1/4)N$
   Anne's supply of labor: $W = 5 + (1/6)N$

   where W is the wage rate and N is the number of hours worked per week. Furthermore, you are told that the equilibrium wage rate in this labor market is $15 per hour.

   a. Find the market supply of labor curve by plotting the quantity supplied in the market at two different wage rates, assuming that Sam and Anne are the only two individuals supplying labor in this market.

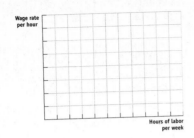 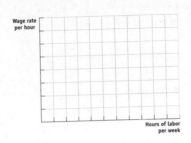 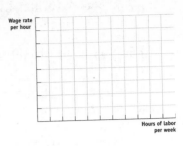

b. What is the total amount of labor supplied in this market at the equilibrium wage rate?

c. What is Sam's weekly income given the equilibrium wage rate?

d. What is Anne's weekly income given the equilibrium wage rate?

Problems

1. What is a derived demand? How is this term used to describe the demand for the services of land, labor, and capital?

2. Suppose that the government imposes a minimum wage law that is greater than the equilibrium wage rate in the economy. What will be the effect of this minimum wage law on employment? Use a graph to illustrate the effect of this minimum wage law on the labor market. Who is likely to be affected by this law?

3. Sarah operates a coffeehouse and her production function per week is given in the following table. The current equilibrium weekly wage in the perfectly competitive labor market is $400 per week, and Sarah sells each cup of coffee for $3 at her coffeehouse.

Quantity of labor (workers)	Quantity of coffee (number of cups)
0	0
1	300
2	450
3	550
4	600

a. Find the marginal product of labor for each worker and the marginal revenue product of each worker. Put your findings in the table below.

Quantity of labor (workers)	Marginal product of labor (cups of coffee per worker)	Marginal revenue product of labor (dollars per worker)
0	-	-
1		
2		
3		
4		

b. How many workers should Sarah hire?

c. Suppose the equilibrium wage rate fell to $300 per week. How would this change in the equilibrium wage rate affect Sarah's hiring decision? Describe in words how Sarah would determine how much labor she should hire.

4. Mike operates a sandwich shop and his production function is given in the following table. Suppose that the equilibrium weekly wage in the perfectly competitive labor market is $300 a week and that Mike sells his sandwiches for $5 each.

Quantity of labor (workers)	Quantity of sandwiches (number of sandwiches)
0	0
1	100
2	180
3	240
4	290

a. Using the preceding information, fill in the following table.

Quantity of labor (workers)	Marginal product of labor (sandwiches per worker)	Marginal revenue product of labor (dollars per worker)
0	-	-
1		
2		
3		
4		

b. Draw the marginal revenue product of labor curve for Mike's sandwich shop. Use this graph to determine how many workers Mike should hire at his sandwich shop.

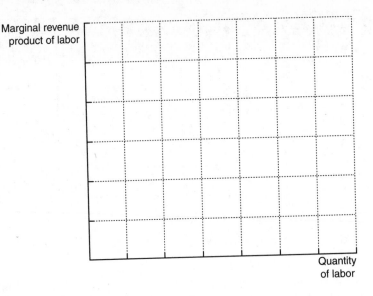

c. Suppose that the price of sandwiches falls to $4 each. Draw a new graph illustrating Mike's marginal revenue product of labor. How will this price change affect the amount of labor Mike chooses to hire?

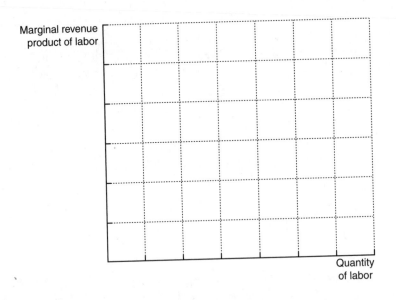

5. For each of the following situations, decide what the effect of the situation is on the firm's marginal revenue product of labor curve and on the amount of labor the firm will hire. Assume that the labor and product markets are both perfectly competitive for each of these situations.

a. The labor hired by the firm has an increase in its level of human capital.

b. The price of the firm's product decreases.

c. The technology used to produce the product changes and less labor is needed to produce each level of output than was necessary initially.

d. The firm decides to increase its use of capital and capital and labor are complements.

6. What are three reasons that workers might receive different wages?

7. A friend of yours argues that there is great wage disparity in the economy and therefore the marginal productivity theory of income distribution is not valid because it results in a highly unfair and inequitable income distribution. What do you think about this argument?

8. Joe hires labor in a perfectly competitive labor market. Joe and all the other employers in his economy would prefer to hire only men, even though women are equally productive workers. Why would profit maximization likely prevent gender discrimination in this market?

9. Suppose that Mark is willing to work 40 hours a week when his wage rate is $10 an hour, but when the wage rate increases to $15 an hour, he is only willing to work 36 hours a week.

   a. Draw Mark's labor supply curve given this information. In the following graph, measure wage rate per hour on the vertical axis and quantity of labor hours per week on the horizontal axis.

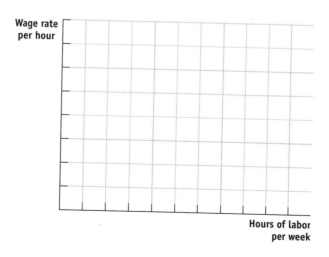

b. Given this information, what do you know about the income effect relative to the substitution effect of this change in wage rates for Mark?

c. What happens to the opportunity cost of an hour of leisure when Mark's wage rate increases from $10 an hour to $15 an hour?

d. Describe the income effect of this wage increase.

10. Suppose that Susan is willing to work 40 hours a week when her wage rate is $10 an hour, but when the wage rate increases to $15 an hour, she is willing to work 44 hours a week.

a. What is Susan's weekly income when the wage rate is $10 an hour? What is Susan's weekly income when the wage rate is $15 an hour?

b. Draw Susan's labor supply curve given this information. In the following graph, measure wage rate per hour on the vertical axis and quantity of labor hours per week on the horizontal axis.

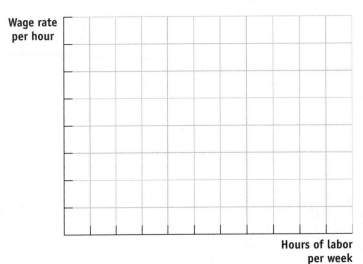

c. Given this information, what do you know about the income effect relative to the substitution effect of this change in wage rates for Susan?

d. Why would Susan choose to work longer hours when the wage rate is $15 an hour rather than $10 an hour?

Review Questions

Circle your answer to the following questions.

1. Human capital is
   a. the machines, tools, equipment, and buildings that humans own and that they use to produce goods and services.
   b. the improvement in labor productivity that reflects education and knowledge.
   c. relatively unimportant in determining labor's share of total income.
   d. a resource that is provided by nature since human capability is an innate endowment.
   e. innovation and risk-taking activities that bring resources together.

2. Capital refers to
   a. the dollars a household has invested in the stock market.
   b. the value of assets that are used by a firm to produce its output.
   c. physical capital only.
   d. resources provided by nature.
   e. the use of technology by entrepreneurs.

3. The improvement in labor that is due to greater education and knowledge is referred to as
   a. physical capital, since the labor has physically made the effort to get more education and knowledge.
   b. human capital, since more educated and knowledgeable labor is more productive.
   c. technological progress, since the knowledge is a result of computerized learning.
   d. entrepreneurship, since decisions are made to make labor more educated by management.
   e. labor improvement product, since this is the measure of the change in productivity from learning.

4. The demand for a factor of production is
   a. independent of the demand for the output the labor produces.
   b. a derived demand.
   c. dependent on the available supply of that factor.
   d. equal to the marginal product of labor.
   e. also known as the factor distribution of income.

5. The factor distribution of income
   a. describes the share of total income received by land, labor, and capital.
   b. indicates that total income in the economy is evenly divided between land, labor, and capital.
   c. indicates that most household income reflects the selling of capital.
   d. is unstable over time in the United States.
   e. does not include employee benefits like health insurance.

6. Labor's share of income in the United States over the past thirty-five years has
   a. remained relatively stable at about 70% of total income.
   b. increased rapidly until finally leveling off at 70% of total income.
   c. declined significantly until finally leveling off at 70% of total income.
   d. fluctuated from year to year and shows no discernible constancy.
   e. increased even as worker productivity declined.

7. Leisure is
   a. a normal good.
   b. an inferior good.
   c. a measure of the income effect on the wage rate.
   d. a measure of the substitution effect on labor quantity.
   e. a measurement of time spent goofing off.

8. A firm realizes that it has diminishing returns to labor. This means that
   a. its total output decreases as it hires additional units of labor.
   b. the marginal product of labor curve for this firm is upward-sloping.
   c. its total output increases as it hires additional units of labor, but it increases at a decreasing rate.
   d. it has hired too many workers.
   e. it must employ more capital.

9. Suppose the marginal cost of hiring an additional unit of labor is $10 while the marginal revenue product from hiring this additional unit of labor is $12. To profit maximize, this firm should
   a. hire more labor.
   b. hire less labor.
   c. raise the marginal cost of labor.
   d. lower the marginal cost of labor.
   e. enhance demand for the product produced.

10. The equilibrium wage rate in the labor market is $18. A perfectly competitive firm sells its product for $8. Suppose that the marginal product of the sixth unit of labor is 3 units of output, while the marginal product of the ninth unit of labor is 2 units of output. This firm should hire
    a. fewer than 6 units of labor.
    b. more than 9 units of labor.
    c. more than 6 units of labor but fewer than 9 units of labor.
    d. exactly 6 units of labor.
    e. exactly 9 units of labor.

11. Suppose the marginal factor cost of an additional unit of a factor is greater than the marginal revenue product of that additional unit of the factor. This means that hiring this additional unit of the factor will add more to the firm's
    a. costs.
    b. marginal product.
    c. marginal revenues.
    d. total product.
    e. total revenues.

12. The firm's demand curve for labor is equal to the
    a. firm's marginal product of labor curve.
    b. firm's marginal revenue product of labor curve.
    c. firm's marginal factor cost of labor curve.
    d. market-determined equilibrium wage rate.
    e. quantity of workers hired at each level of production.

13. If capital and labor are complementary resources, then for the profit-maximizing firm,
    a. an increase in the price of labor will increase the demand for capital.
    b. an increase in the price of labor will decrease the demand for capital.
    c. an increase in the productivity of capital will shift the marginal revenue product of labor to the left.
    d. a decrease in the productivity of capital will increase the marginal revenue product of capital.
    e. a decrease in the demand for labor will increase the marginal revenue product of capital.

14. A firm experiences a change in technology. This
  a. may cause the firm's demand for an input to increase or decrease depending on the nature of the technological change.
  b. causes the firm's demand for an input to increase.
  c. causes the firm's demand for an input to decrease.
  d. does not affect the firm's demand for other inputs, since the firm chooses how much of an input to demand based on its production function without regard to the technology that is available to the firm.
  e. increases the firm's demand for an input and all inputs like it.

15. In a perfectly competitive labor market, the equilibrium wage is the wage at which
  a. the quantity of labor demanded is equal to the quantity of labor supplied.
  b. all people who work in the labor market earn a living wage.
  c. the wage is equal to one half the marginal revenue product of labor.
  d. marginal resource cost equals the marginal product of labor.
  e. the cost-minimization rule is satisfied.

16. Because the supply of land is fixed,
  a. the supply curve is perfectly elastic.
  b. the quantity supplied is responsive to changes in the rental rate.
  c. changes in demand do not affect the rental rate.
  d. the rental rate is determined by the level of demand.
  e. land cannot earn in excess of the minimum necessary to employ it.

17. The marginal productivity theory of income distribution states that
  a. each factor is paid a payment equal to that factor's marginal productivity.
  b. each factor is paid a payment equal to the value of the output generated by the last unit of that factor employed in the factor market as a whole.
  c. factor income is distributed evenly and equally across all factors.
  d. all factors are paid less than the marginal revenue product.
  e. all factors are paid more than the marginal revenue product.

18. Which of the following explanations for wage disparities supports the marginal productivity theory of income distribution?
  a. unions
  b. efficiency wages
  c. gender differences
  d. discrimination
  e. differences in talent

19. The marginal productivity theory of income distribution provides
  a. a moral justification for the prevailing income distribution.
  b. a defense for discrimination in hiring practices.
  c. a critique of union involvement in the labor markets.
  d. a rebuke to the users of efficiency wages.
  e. an explanation for the division of income among the factors of production.

20. When an individual's labor supply curve bends backward, it indicates that the
  a. income effect is stronger than the substitution effect.
  b. income effect is weaker than the substitution effect.
  c. income effect is equal to the substitution effect.
  d. wage rate is creating a labor shortage.
  e. wage rate is creating a labor surplus.

Section ⑭ Market Failure and the Role of Government

Overview

This section explains how inefficiency can arise from positive and negative externalities, which cause a divergence between the costs and benefits of an individual's or firm's actions and the costs and benefits of those actions borne by society as a whole. In addition, it explains how the characteristics of goods often determine whether markets can deliver them efficiently. Finally, this section considers the role of government in addressing market failures.

Featured Model/Graph: Illustrating Externalities Using the Supply and Demand Model

This section uses the supply and demand model to show how positive and negative externalities create inefficiency in a market and how government policies can be used to correct inefficiency.

BEFORE YOU TACKLE THE TEST

Draw the Featured Model

Complete the Exercise

Problems

Review Questions

MODULE 74 INTRODUCTION TO EXTERNALITIES

BEFORE YOU READ THE MODULE

Summary

This module uses pollution as an example to introduce negative and positive externalities and presents private approaches to addressing the inefficiencies created as a result of externalities.

Module Objectives

Review these objectives before you read the module. Place a "√" on the line when you can do each of the following:

_____Objective #1. Explain what externalities are and why they can lead to inefficiency in a market economy

_____Objective #2. Discuss why externalities often require government intervention

_____Objective #3. Describe the difference between negative and positive externalities

_____Objective #4. Explain how, according to the Coase theorem, private individuals can sometimes remedy externalities

WHILE YOU READ THE MODULE

Key Terms

Define these key terms as you read the module:

Marginal social cost of pollution:

Marginal social benefit of pollution:

Socially optimal quantity of pollution:

External cost:

External benefit:

Externalities:

Negative externalities:

Positive externalities:

Coase theorem:

Transaction costs:

Internalize the externalities:

Practice the Model

1) Draw a correctly labeled graph showing the *MSC* and *MSB* of pollution. Assume that all pollution costs are external. On your graph, show each of the following:
  a. the market quantity of pollution if there is no government intervention
  b. the efficient quantity of pollution

List questions or difficulties from your initial reading of the module.

Fill-in-the-Blanks

Fill in the blanks to complete the following statements. If you find yourself having difficulties, please refer back to the appropriate section in the text.

- The quantity of pollution society would choose if all its costs and benefits were fully accounted for is called the **1)**_____ quantity of pollution. To find the socially optimal level of an activity, like pollution, we should compare the marginal social cost with the **2)**_____ .

- Uncompensated costs or benefits that an individual or firm imposes on others are called **3)**_____ costs or benefits. These kinds of costs and benefits are known jointly as **4)**_____. The idea that, in an ideal world, the private sector could indeed deal with all externalities is known as the **5)**_____ theorem. For this theorem to apply in the real world requires the assumption that **6)**_____ costs are low.

Multiple-Choice Questions

Circle the best choice to answer or complete the following questions or incomplete statements. For additional practice, use the space provided to explain why one or more of the incorrect options do not work.

7. Markets produce negative externalities, like pollution, when
   a. the marginal social cost of pollution is zero.
   b. the socially optimal quantity of pollution is greater than zero.
   c. the marginal social benefit of pollution is greater than the marginal social cost of pollution.
   d. the marginal social cost of pollution is greater than the marginal social benefit of pollution.
   e. the marginal social cost of pollution is equal to the marginal social benefit of pollution.

8. According to the Coase theorem, what is required to reach an efficient solution to negative externalities?
   a. government intervention in the market
   b. legal rights in favor of the polluter
   c. sufficiently low transaction costs
   d. an impartial third party to resolve legal issues
   e. knowledge of the socially optimal amount of the externality

Helpful Tips

- The key concept in this section is the idea that markets fail to produce the optimal amount of the good whenever there is a cost or a benefit that the market fails to include when deciding what the optimal quantity of the good will be in the market. A negative externality occurs when there is some kind of cost that is not internalized in the market, and a positive externality occurs when there is some kind of benefit that is not internalized in the market. When there is an externality in the market that is not internalized, the market does not produce the efficient level of output because it is not producing the level of output where the marginal social cost of production is equal to the marginal social benefit of consumption.

Module Notes

When discussing an economic "bad," like pollution, it is easy to conclude that we want none of it. While we would love to live in a world without pollution, it is important to realize that pollution has both costs and benefits. It may seem strange to think of the *benefits* of pollution. After all, it is something we would rather not have! But in order to live, we must produce and in order to produce, we create waste (pollution). The pollution created by production has to be dealt with somehow. We must either pay to create less pollution (e.g. installing scrubbers on smokestacks), pay to deal with the pollution created (e.g. build and operate landfills), or allow the pollution to be emitted into the environment. Therefore, the benefit of pollution is that we don't have to forego production, as long as we are willing to either pay to reduce pollution or pay to deal with it.

MODULE 75   EXTERNALITIES AND PUBLIC POLICY

BEFORE YOU READ THE MODULE

Summary

This module presents the policies governments use to deal with pollution and how economic analysis has been used to improve those policies.

Module Objectives

Review these objectives before you read the module. Place a "√" on the line when you can do each of the following:

_____**Objective #1.**   Address externality problems with specific public policies

_____**Objective #2.**   Explain why some government policies to deal with externalities, such as emissions taxes, tradable emissions permits, or Pigouvian subsidies, are efficient, although others, including environmental standards, are not

WHILE YOU READ THE MODULE

Key Terms

Define these key terms as you read the module:

Environmental standards:

Emissions tax:

Pigouvian taxes:

Tradable emissions permits:

Marginal private benefit:

Marginal social benefit:

Marginal external benefit:

Pigouvian subsidy:

Technology spillover:

Marginal private cost:

Marginal social cost:

Marginal external cost:

Network externality:

Practice the Model

1) Draw a correctly labeled graph showing a market with a positive externality. On your graph, label each of the following:
   a. Demand
   b. *MPB*
   c. *MSB*
   d. Supply
   e. *MPC*
   f. *MSC*
   g. The market quantity (Q_{MKT})
   h. The efficient quantity (Q_{OPT})

List questions or difficulties from your initial reading of the module.

AFTER YOU READ THE MODULE

Fill-in-the-Blanks

Fill in the blanks to complete the following statements. If you find yourself having difficulties, please refer back to the appropriate section in the text.

- Taxes designed to reduce external costs are known as 1)_____ taxes. In the case of pollution, tradable 2)_____, licenses to emit limited quantities of pollutants that can be bought and sold by polluters, are sometimes used to address external costs.

- To account for the true benefit to society of another unit of a good that creates a positive externality (like a flu shot), we use the marginal 3)_____ benefit of the good or activity to consumers *plus* the marginal 4)_____ benefit to society. Society can be induced to produce the socially optimal quantity of a good that produces a positive externality by using a Pigouvian 5)_____.

- An external benefit to consumers that occurs when many other consumers also own or use the same good is called a 6)_____ externality.

Multiple-Choice Questions

Circle the best choice to answer or complete the following questions or incomplete statements. For additional practice, use the space provided to explain why one or more of the incorrect options do not work.

7. Why might tradable emissions permits be an inefficient way to deal with negative externalities?
   a. Firms will not engage in transactions that allow other firms to reduce pollution.
   b. Firms have no incentive to take the marginal social cost of pollution into account.
   c. Tradable emissions permits increase deadweight loss in the market.
   d. The government assumes all firms have identical costs of pollution.
   e. The government may issue too many or too few permits to reduce pollution.

8. Which of the following policies would be the most effective way to correct for positive spillover benefits from vaccinating children?

    a. Establish a price ceiling for shots for children.

    b. Tax parents who choose not to vaccinate their children.

    c. Mandate that firms produce the socially optimal quantity of vaccine.

    d. Provide a subsidy to the producers of the vaccine.

    e. Tax firms producing less than the socially optimal quantity of vaccine.

Helpful Tips

- This module adds the distinction between private and social costs and benefits to the supply and demand model from Section 2. The demand curve has always represented marginal private benefits and the supply curve has always represented marginal private costs, but that terminology wasn't added until this Section. When there are no external costs and benefits, there is no difference between the marginal private and marginal social benefits and costs. In that case, the demand curve from Section 2 represents both MPB and MSB and the supply curve from Section 2 represents both MPC and MSC. But when there is an external benefit, the MSB curve is above the $D = MPB$ curve; when there is an external cost, the MSC curve is above the $S = MPB$ curve.

Module Notes

It might be confusing to think of marginal *social* cost—after all, up to this point we have always defined marginal cost as being incurred by an individual or a firm, not society as a whole. But it is easily understandable once we link it to the familiar concept of willingness to pay: the marginal social cost of a unit of pollution is equal to the *sum of the willingness to pay among all members of society* to avoid that unit of pollution. (It's the sum because, in general, more than one person is affected by the pollution.) But calculating the true cost to society of pollution—marginal or average—is a difficult matter, requiring a great deal of scientific knowledge. As a result, society often underestimates the true marginal social cost of pollution.

MODULE 76 PUBLIC GOODS

BEFORE YOU READ THE MODULE

Summary

This module explains how some goods are different from the private goods we have discussed in previous sections. It looks at how to classify public goods, common resources, and artificially scarce goods and how government intervention in the markets for these goods can make society better off.

Module Objectives

Review these objectives before you read the module. Place a "√" on the line when you can do each of the following:

_____**Objective #1.** Characterize public goods and explain why markets fail to supply efficient quantities of public goods

_____**Objective #2.** Define common resources and explain why they are overused

_____**Objective #3.** Define artificially scarce goods and explain why they are under consumed

_____**Objective #4.** Describe how government intervention in the production and consumption of these types of goods can make society better off

_____**Objective #5.** Discuss why finding the right level of government intervention is often difficult

WHILE YOU READ THE MODULE

Key Terms

Define these key terms as you read the module:

Excludable:

Rival in consumption:

Private good:

Nonexcludable:

Nonrival in consumption:

Free-rider problem:

Public good:

Common resource:

Overuse:

Artificially scarce good:

Practice the Model

1) Construct a matrix showing each of the possible combinations of rival/nonrival and excludable/nonexcludable characteristics of goods (see Figure 76.1 in your textbook). Leave room in your matrix to place each of the following goods in the appropriate box in your matrix.
  a. An apple
  b. Cable TV subscription
  c. Wheat
  d. Clean air
  e. National defense
  f. Wildlife
  g. Disease prevention
  h. Information goods

List questions or difficulties from your initial reading of the module.

AFTER YOU READ THE MODULE

Fill-in-the-Blanks

Fill in the blanks to complete the following statements. If you find yourself having difficulties, please refer back to the appropriate section in the text.

- Private goods have two important characteristics. They are **1)**_____, which means that suppliers of the good can prevent people who don't pay from consuming it. And they are **2)**_____ in consumption, which means the good cannot be consumed by more than one person at the same time. A good that has neither of these characteristics is called a **3)**_____ good. Clean water in a river has one, but not both, of these characteristics. It is an example of a **4)**_____. Pay-per-view movies on cable TV is an example of a good that has the other characteristic. They are known as **5)**_____ goods.

- If a rational consumer is not willing to pay for a good that benefits everyone because he or she decides to let everyone else pay for the good, that consumer is called a **6)**_____.

Multiple-Choice Questions

Circle the best choice to answer or complete the following questions or incomplete statements. For additional practice, use the space provided to explain why one or more of the incorrect options do not work.

7. Which of the following best explains why common resources are overused?
   a. They are nonrival in consumption.
   b. Individuals ignore the fact that their use of the resource reduces the amount available for others.
   c. The marginal social benefit of the resource is undefined.
   d. Taxes are unable to correct for the market level of consumption of the resource.
   e. Only the marginal social cost is considered by individuals in the market.

8. A good that is excludable but nonrival in consumption is known as
 a. an artificially scarce good.
 b. a common resource.
 c. an inferior good.
 d. a private good.
 e. a public good.

Helpful Tips

• This section looks at four types of goods—private goods, public goods, common resources, and artificially scarce goods—from the perspective of whether or not the good is rival in consumption and excludable. To understand this module, it is essential that you have a firm grasp on what it means to be rival in consumption versus nonrival in consumption and excludable versus nonexcludable. When a good is rival, this means that one person's consumption of the good effectively prevents another consumer from consuming that same unit of the good. When a good is nonrival, this means that one person's consumption of the good does not prevent another individual from consuming the same unit of the good.

• A good is excludable if a supplier can prevent someone from consuming the good if he or she does not pay for it. A good is nonexcludable if a supplier cannot prevent someone from consuming the good if he or she does not pay for it.

Module Notes

In the case of a good that is nonrival in consumption, it's easy to confuse the marginal cost of *producing* a unit of the good with the marginal cost of *allowing* a unit of the good *to be consumed*. For example, your local cable company incurs a marginal cost in making a movie available to its subscribers that is equal to the cost of the resources it uses to produce and broadcast that movie. However, *once that movie is being broadcast,* no marginal cost is incurred by letting an additional family *watch* it. In other words, no costly resources are "used up" when one more family consumes a movie that has already been produced and is being broadcast.

This complication does not arise, however, when a good is rival in consumption. In that case, the resources used to produce a unit of the good are "used up" by a person's consumption of it—they are no longer available to satisfy someone else's consumption. So when a good is rival in consumption, the marginal cost to society of allowing an individual to consume a unit is equal to the resource cost of producing that unit—that is, equal to the marginal cost of producing it.

MODULE 77 PUBLIC POLICY TO PROMOTE COMPETITION

BEFORE YOU READ THE MODULE

Summary

This module discusses government policies to promote competitive outcomes, including antitrust laws and direct government regulation.

Module Objectives

Review these objectives before you read the module. Place a "√" on the line when you can do each of the following:

_____ **Objective #1.** Identify the three major antitrust laws and describe how they are used to promote competition

_____ **Objective #2.** Explain how government regulation is used to prevent inefficiency in the case of natural monopoly

_____ **Objective #3.** Discuss the pros and cons of using marginal cost pricing and average cost pricing to regulate prices in natural monopolies

WHILE YOU READ THE MODULE

Key Terms

Define these key terms as you read the module:

Marginal cost pricing:

Average cost pricing:

Practice the Model

1) Draw a correctly labeled graph of a natural monopoly. On your graph, show each of the following:
a. The profit-maximizing price and quantity (P_1 and Q_1)
b. The quantity produced if the monopoly is regulated using average cost pricing (Q_A)
c. The quantity produced if the monopoly is regulated using marginal cost pricing (Q_M)
d. The loss incurred with marginal cost pricing

2) A monopoly creates deadweight loss in a market. What benefit of allowing a monopoly to exist in this case can offset the deadweight loss?

List questions or difficulties from your initial reading of the module.

AFTER YOU READ THE MODULE

Fill-in-the-Blanks

Fill in the blanks to complete the following statements. If you find yourself having difficulties, please refer back to the appropriate section in the text.

- Laws intended both to prevent the creation of more monopolies and to break up existing ones

  are called **1)**_____ laws. The cornerstone of these laws is the

  2)_____ Act, passed in 1890. In 1914, the Clayton Act outlawed four specific firm

  behaviors including **3)**_____, _____, _____, and

  _____. The third major law to address monopolization in the economy created

  the **4)**_____ to prohibit unfair methods of competition.

- The gains to producers from the cost advantages that come with a monopoly outweigh the loss to consumers from breaking up a monopoly in the specific case of a **5)**_____ monopoly. In this case, the average cost of production is lower with one firm, but firms will restrict output and raise price unless regulators apply **6)**_____ regulation.

Multiple-Choice Questions

Circle the best choice to answer or complete the following questions or incomplete statements. For additional practice, use the space provided to explain why one or more of the incorrect options do not work.

7. What important piece of antitrust legislation explicitly makes it illegal to charge different prices to different consumers for the same product?
  a. Sherman Antitrust Act of 1890
  b. Clayton Antitrust Act of 1914
  c. Federal Trade Commission Act of 1914
  d. The Price Discrimination Act of 1919
  e. The Price Regulation Legislation of 1929

8. Regulators of natural monopoly wanting to avoid providing a subsidy to the firm can set the price equal to
  a. demand.
  b. marginal cost.
  c. marginal revenue.
  d. average total cost.
  e. average variable cost.

Helpful Tips

- The average total cost curve for a natural monopoly isn't any different than *ATC* curves we have seen before. However, the relevant range of the *ATC* curve is the downward-sloping portion of the *ATC* curve. The *ATC* curve eventually slopes upward (like we are used to), but it doesn't happen until a quantity is so large that it isn't relevant. Since we know that when *ATC* decreases, *MC* is below it (and *MC* will cross *ATC* at the minimum point of the *ATC*), *MC* is below *ATC* at all relevant output levels.

Module Notes

In this module, we consider the case of a natural monopoly. A natural monopoly exists when the cost per unit to produce (the *ATC*) decreases as more output is produced. It is cheaper (per unit) to produce large quantities. For example, assembly lines that produce large quantities reduce the cost to produce each unit. In Section 11, monopolies were shown to be inefficient (i.e. to create deadweight loss). With a natural monopoly, the conclusion about efficiency is not so clear. A profit-maximizing monopoly would still prevent allocative efficiency ($P = MC$). But because of economies of scale, a monopoly is necessary to achieve productive efficiency (minimum *ATC*).

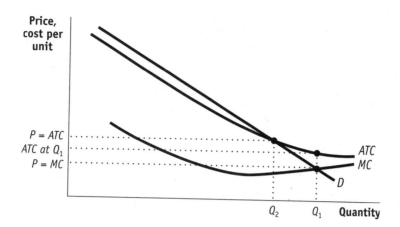

Another difference you will see when considering natural monopolies is the assumption that marginal cost is constant. This means that the additional cost of producing an additional unit of output is always the same, and the *MC* curve will be horizontal. It also means that, since each additional unit costs the same, the long-run average cost (cost per unit) is also constant. Economists assume that marginal cost is constant in cases in which it is likely to be true of the firm's production or when making the assumption simplifies the analysis to make it clearer.

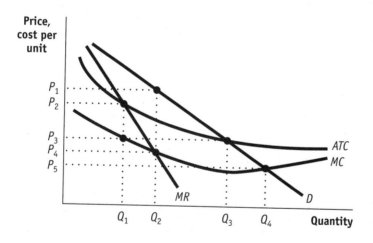

MODULE 78 INCOME INEQUALITY AND INCOME DISTRIBUTION

BEFORE YOU READ THE MODULE

Summary

This module discusses poverty, income inequality, and income distribution. It looks at how these have changed over time and government policies designed to affect them.

Module Objectives

Review these objectives before you read the module. Place a "√" on the line when you can do each of the following:

_____**Objective #1.** Define poverty and describe its causes and consequences

_____**Objective #2.** Explain how income inequality in America has changed over time

_____**Objective #3.** Discuss how Social Security and similar programs affect poverty and income inequality

WHILE YOU READ THE MODULE

Key Terms

Define these key terms as you read the module:

Poverty threshold:

Poverty rate:

Mean household income:

Median household income:

Lorenz curve:

Gini coefficient:

Means-tested:

In-kind benefit:

Negative income tax:

Practice the Model

Refer to the graph of the Lorenz curve shown below and answer the following questions.

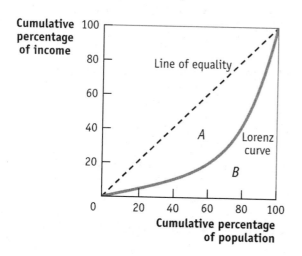

1) What does the Gini coefficient measure? Use the areas labeled on the graph to define the Gini coefficient.

2) If the Lorenz Curve were the same as the line of equality on the graph, what would the Gini coefficient equal and what would it tell you about the distribution of income in the economy?

3) If one person had all of the income in the economy, where would the Lorenz curve be shown on the graph and what would the Gini coefficient equal?

List questions or difficulties from your initial reading of the module.

AFTER YOU READ THE MODULE

Fill-in-the-Blanks

Fill in the blanks to complete the following statements. If you find yourself having difficulties, please refer back to the appropriate section in the text.

- The U.S. government establishes a minimum annual income that is considered adequate to purchase the necessities of life, called the **1)**_____.

- Mean household income, also called average household income, is the total income of all U.S. households divided by the **2)**_____. The **3)**_____ household income is the income of a household in the exact middle of the income distribution—the level of income at which half of all households have lower income and half have higher income.

- A single number that summarizes a country's level of income inequality is the **4)**_____ coefficient. As income inequality increases, the value of this coefficient will **5)**_____.

- Programs that provide help for low-income individuals in the form of goods and services are said to provide **6)**_____ benefits.

Multiple-Choice Questions

Circle the best choice to answer or complete the following questions or incomplete statements. For additional practice, use the space provided to explain why one or more of the incorrect options do not work.

7. Which of the following is not an important cause of poverty?
   a. lack of education
   b. lack of proficiency in English
   c. racial and gender discrimination
   d. income redistribution programs
   e. bad luck

8. Which of the following indicates the percentage of all income received by the poorest members of the population?
   a. poverty threshold
   b. poverty rate
   c. median household income
   d. Lorenz curve
   e. Gini coefficient

Helpful Tips

- The Lorenz curve illustrates income inequality on a graph. The farther the Lorenz curve is from the "line of equality," the more unequal the distribution of income. The Gini coefficient is a numerical measure of what the Lorenz curve shows. The Gini coefficient is between 0 (which means the income distribution is perfectly equal) and 1 (which means the income distribution is completely unequal – 1 person has it all!).

Module Notes

The discussion of income distribution necessarily involves the discussion of equity (i.e. fairness). Because individuals disagree about what is "fair," equity is not a well-defined concept (compared, for example, to the concept of efficiency). Keep in mind that much of the discussion of income distribution falls under the normative branch of economics. It is important to stay focused on what economics can offer these discussions and to be aware when personal opinions regarding equity enter into discussions.

Draw The Featured Model: Supply and Demand with Externalities

Draw a supply and demand graph showing the equilibrium price and quantity in the market if there is no government intervention. Then add the appropriate curve and show the optimal quantity of the good in the case of (a) a negative externality and (b) a positive externality. Be sure you label all axes and curves.

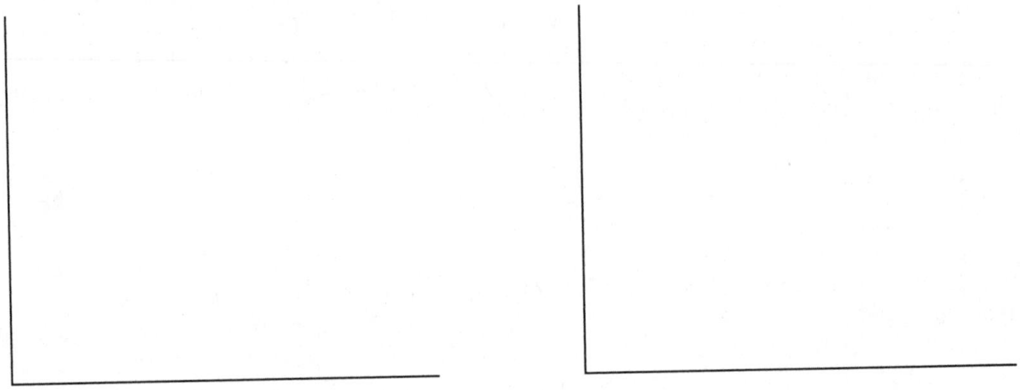

(a) Negative externality

(b) Positive externality

Complete the Exercise

1. Answer the questions below based on the following diagram of the market for bottled water that comes from aquifers deep underground. In the production of this product, the level of water in these aquifers is drawn down at a rate faster than the water can be replenished. This action results in a negative externality on the nearby communities that depend on these aquifers for their water, since the producers of the bottled water do not consider the effect of their production on the community's water source. In the following graph, Supply represents the marginal private cost of producing the good, *MSC* represents the marginal social cost (the external as well as private cost) of producing the good, and Demand represents the marginal social benefit from consuming the good. Assume that the externality per unit of the good produced is a constant amount per unit of bottled water.

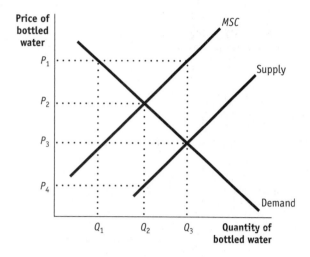

a. Without government intervention in this market, the market will provide how many bottles of bottled water?

b. Without government intervention, what is the price of a bottle of bottled water?

c. What is the socially optimal level of output for this market?

d. At the market-determined level of production in the above market, the deadweight loss due to the negative externality can be expressed as what area?

Problems

1. Classify each of the following situations as positive or negative externalities; then identify whether the externality occurs on the demand/consumption side of the model, or on the supply production side of the model.

    a. A manufacturing plant spews toxic gas into the environment as a by-product of its production of furniture.

    b. A group of teenagers gather on Saturday to play loud music and congregate in a downtown park, making it difficult for other people in the town to enjoy the park.

c. A property owner fills his front yard with trash and old tires.

d. A company develops a new technology for producing its product; the new technology can potentially help other companies produce more efficiently.

e. School-age children in a community do not get immunized prior to attending school.

f. A neighbor decorates the outside of her house with a tasteful holiday display.

g. A neighbor keeps his barking dog outside his house all day and all night.

h. Commercial fishermen catch too many fish and deplete the stock of fish.

2. Joan loves dogs and decides that she is going to buy one. She analyzes the benefit she will get from owning a dog and values that benefit at $500. Joan's next-door neighbor loathes dogs and is vehemently opposed to dogs being in the neighborhood. This neighbor, Mike, views the cost of an additional dog in the neighborhood as being $800. According to the Coase theorem, is it possible for Joan and Mike to amicably resolve this dilemma about the dog ownership? In your answer, identify how this conflict can be resolved provided that the rights to dog ownership are well defined. Also, in your answer, explain why it does not matter who owns the rights to dog ownership, provided that these rights are well defined.

3. A recent article reports that drunken driving has risen in communities that have imposed smoking bans in their bars and taverns. The gist of the problem is that smokers who also drink are now driving longer distances to get to bars that allow them to smoke while they are drinking. Does the decision to impose a smoking ban on the bars and taverns in the community create an externality? What do you think motivated policymakers to impose this smoking ban?

4. Suppose the consumption of a good generates substantial external benefits due to the presence of side effects. Suppose the government wishes to help the market generate the socially optimal consumption of this good. Will the market by itself generate the socially optimal amount of this good? Explain your answer. What type of policy or policies might the government engage in to meet this goal?

5. In the 1980s, there were two competing technologies for watching movies at home. The Beta system and the VHS system competed with one another for this particular market. Eventually, the VHS system became the dominant system, and those individuals who had purchased the Beta system found it difficult to find movies using this technology to show at home.

a. Is there an externality issue lying behind this story? If so, what kind of externality issue is it?

b. How would the term *positive feedback* apply to this situation?

c. Describe how this competition for the market for movies shown at home ultimately illustrates a network externality.

6. For each of the following situations, determine whether the good in the situation is (1) excludable or nonexcludable, and (2) nonrival in consumption or rival in consumption.

a. A community erects a lighthouse to guide ships navigating near its rocky shoreline.

b. A country builds a national defense system of missiles.

c. A community builds a toll road that has low levels of usage.

d. A community builds a toll road that has high levels of usage.

e. A radio station broadcasts the baseball game.

f. A community builds a non-toll road that has high levels of usage.

g. Police protection is hired for a community.

h. The environment of a community is improved.

7. Jimmy and Beth are the only residents of Smalltown. They both think the community would benefit from more parks, but neither Jimmy nor Beth is willing to contribute money to buy land to turn into parks. They both realize that once a park is provided, they can enjoy it even if they have not paid for it.

a. Describe Jimmy and Beth's behavior and why it represents a problem when trying to provide parks in their community.

b. Suppose Jimmy reveals that his marginal benefit from one park is equal to $50 per park, his marginal benefit from two parks is equal to $25 per park, and his marginal benefit from three parks is equal to $0 per park. Beth reveals that her marginal benefit from one park is equal to $60 per park, her marginal benefit from two parks is equal to $40 per park, and her marginal benefit from three parks is equal to $20 per park. What is the marginal social benefit of two parks equal to in their community? Explain how you found this answer.

c. Suppose the information in part **b.** is still true. Jimmy and Beth analyze the cost of providing parks in their community and find that the marginal social cost of providing parks is constant and equal to $55. What is the socially optimal amount of parks for this community? Explain how you got this answer.

d. If Jimmy and Beth are both willing to reveal their preferences with regard to parks (that is, they will tell the truth about the marginal private benefit they receive from the parks), will they both contribute to getting the socially optimal amount of parks for their community?

8. What two characteristics do private goods have that make it possible for markets to efficiently provide the good, and why are these characteristics so important?

9. Big Sports is a television company that has won the rights to broadcast next season's football games in the Big Group college football conference. To watch these televised games, viewers need to subscribe to the Super Cable package that costs an additional $15 per month.

a. Does Big Sports and its televised games represent a public good, a common resource, or an artificially scarce good? Explain your answer and why you have classified Big Sports in this manner.

b. What is the efficient price for consumers to pay for watching these football games? Explain your answer.

c. Does Big Sports produce the socially optimal, or efficient, level of televised football games for the Big Group college football conference? Explain your answer. If the level of production is not the socially optimal amount, is the amount produced in the market greater than or less than the socially optimal amount? Explain your answer.

10. For each of the following situations, decide whether the problem is a positive externality, negative externality, or natural monopoly.

a. The parent-teacher association at your child's elementary school is looking for parent volunteers to direct a fundraiser to raise money to replace the playground equipment.

b. Local community organizers are seeking people to serve on a committee to improve the beauty of the community through gardening and landscaping efforts.

c. The number of elephants in Africa is declining due to hunters killing them for their ivory tusks.

d. A local group is organizing a Saturday morning spring cleanup of the lakeshore in its community.

e. The quantity of salmon in the Great Lakes is declining due to too many salmon being caught by sport fishermen.

f. Once some children at an elementary school are vaccinated for childhood diseases, the risk of infection for those who are not vaccinated decreases.

g. The local cable television company charges an additional fee to the customer who wants to receive the channel that offers local sports coverage.

Review Questions

Circle your answer to the following questions

1. The optimal amount of pollution is
   a. the amount of pollution at which the marginal social benefit of the pollution exceeds the marginal social cost of the pollution.
   b. zero units of pollution, since pollution is harmful to people.
   c. the amount of pollution at which the marginal social benefit of the pollution is less than the marginal social cost of the pollution.
   d. the amount of pollution at which the marginal social benefit of the pollution equals the marginal social cost of the pollution.
   e. the amount of pollution at which the marginal private benefit is greater than the marginal social benefit of the pollution.

Use the figure on the following page to answer questions 2 through 4.

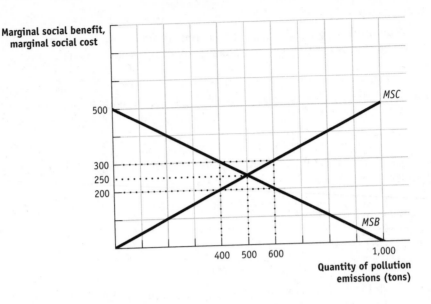

Marginal social benefit, marginal social cost

y-axis values: 500, 300, 250, 200

curves: MSC, MSB

x-axis values: 400, 500, 600, 1,000

Quantity of pollution emissions (tons)

2. The socially optimal amount of pollution emissions in the graph is
   a. 250 tons.
   b. 400 tons.
   c. 500 tons.
   d. 600 tons.
   e. 1,000 tons.

3. When 400 tons of pollution are emitted,
   a. the marginal social cost of pollution is less than the marginal social benefit of pollution.
   b. the marginal social cost of pollution is greater than the marginal social benefit of pollution.
   c. the marginal social cost of pollution is equal to the marginal social benefit of pollution.
   d. this economy would be worse off producing more pollution emissions.
   e. this economy should reduce pollution until the marginal social cost of pollution is equal to zero.

4. What is the appropriate emissions standard for this economy if there is only one producer and the goal is to produce the efficient level of pollution emissions?
   a. 400 tons
   b. 500 tons
   c. 600 tons
   d. 0 tons
   e. 1,000 tons

5. A government wants to enact a policy that will lead to a reduction in pollution emissions. One policy entails establishing an emissions standard; another policy entails implementation of an emissions tax. Which of the following statements is true?

   a. An emissions standard and an emissions tax are equally efficient methods for reducing pollution emissions.

   b. An emissions standard ensures that the marginal social benefit of pollution is equal for all sources of pollution.

   c. An emissions tax does not ensure that the marginal social benefit of pollution is equal for all sources of pollution.

   d. An emissions standard is the most effective and cost-minimizing approach to internalizing externalities.

   e. An emissions tax ensures that the marginal social benefit of pollution is equal for all sources of pollution.

6. Taxes that are designed to reduce external costs are known as

   a. excise taxes.

   b. income taxes.

   c. Pigouvian taxes.

   d. emissions taxes.

   e. proportional taxes.

7. Suppose a government decides to issue a limited number of tradable pollution permits. Which of the following statements is true?

   a. Firms that can easily and at low cost reduce their level of pollution will find it beneficial to purchase these tradable pollution permits.

   b. When the government issues these tradable pollution permits, it effectively creates a market for the right to pollute.

   c. Firms that sell their tradable pollution permits do not fully understand the costs they will incur when they try to reduce the level of pollution they create.

   d. The government will have little problem determining the optimal number of permits.

   e. Firms that find it more difficult to reduce pollution will find no benefit in tradable permits.

8. When the consumption of a good generates positive external benefits, the market tends to produce

   a. too much of the good because there are positive external benefits from the consumption of the good.

   b. too little of the good because the market does not take into account the positive external benefits from the consumption of the good.

   c. too much of the good because consumers look to maximize positive external benefits.

   d. the socially optimal quantity of the good because external benefits result from an efficient market.

   e. too little of the good because the additional benefit is less than the marginal social cost.

9. As the Lorenz curve moves closer to a 45 degree line from the origin, the income distribution in an economy becomes

   a. harder to determine.

   b. more equal.

   c. less fair.

   d. less equal.

   e. more fair.

10. A decrease in the Gini coefficient indicates that an economy's income distribution is becoming
   a. harder to determine.
   b. more equal.
   c. less fair.
   d. less equal.
   e. more fair.

11. For a market to efficiently deliver a good, the good must be
   a. rival in consumption and excludable.
   b. rival in consumption and nonexcludable.
   c. nonrival in consumption and excludable.
   d. nonrival in consumption and nonexcludable.
   e. a normal or superior good.

12. Madison has a number of city parks that are open to the public at no charge. Throughout the year these parks are often crowded, with long lines at the play structures. These public parks represent a good that is
   a. nonrival and nonexcludable.
   b. nonrival and excludable.
   c. rival and nonexcludable.
   d. rival and excludable.
   e. a normal or superior good.

13. Madison is in the middle of tornado country and, because of the imminent danger of tornadoes, has decided to invest in a tornado siren system. This tornado siren system is an example of a good that is
   a. nonrival in consumption and nonexcludable.
   b. nonrival in consumption and excludable.
   c. rival in consumption and nonexcludable.
   d. rival in consumption and excludable.
   e. a normal or superior good.

14. The Illinois Tollway that connects Rockford to Chicago is constantly congested with traffic jams. Motorists must pay a toll fee to use the Tollway. The Tollway is a good that is characterized as
   a. rival in consumption and nonexcludable.
   b. rival in consumption and excludable.
   c. nonrival in consumption and nonexcludable.
   d. nonrival in consumption and excludable.
   e. a normal or superior good.

15. Mason Street is a quiet residential street that is only three blocks long. There is no toll for driving on Mason Street, and the street gets very little traffic except from the people who live on the street. Mason Street is
   a. nonrival in consumption and nonexcludable.
   b. rival in consumption and excludable.
   c. nonrival in consumption and excludable.
   d. rival in consumption and nonexcludable.
   e. a normal or superior good.

16. Why do markets produce too little of nonexcludable goods?
  a. They suffer from inefficiently low consumption.
  b. Firms provide too few to keep prices high.
  c. More than one consumer can enjoy the good at the same time, thereby reducing demand.
  d. They tend to be luxury items with limited supplies.
  e. They suffer from the free-rider problem because individuals have no incentive to pay.

17. New Glarus has just built and opened a toll road connecting New Glarus to Old Glarus. This toll road is never congested no matter what time of day or what day of the week it is. Because the toll road is both nonrival in consumption and excludable, it is an example of an artificially scarce good. The marginal cost of letting an additional driver use the toll road is equal to
  a. the toll.
  b. zero.
  c. the toll divided by the number of drivers currently using the toll road.
  d. the toll divided by the population of the two communities.
  e. the total cost of the toll road divided by the amount of the toll.

18. Fishermen in Oceania report dwindling supplies of their favorite fish. These fishermen fish in open water with no limits placed on who can fish in the water and how many fish can be taken from the sea. This is an example of a(n)
  a. artificially scarce good because good fisheries management could eliminate the fish scarcity.
  b. public good because no one is paying to fish in the water and no one can be excluded from fishing in the water.
  c. common resource because the fishing grounds are nonexcludable but rival in consumption.
  d. private good because each fisherman catches his own fish, and then markets them at the local fish market.
  e. public good because the fish are a free and renewable source of income for the fishermen.

19. A good that is nonexcludable but rival in consumption is a(n)
  a. public good.
  b. positive externality.
  c. artificially scarce good.
  d. common resource.
  e. private good.

20. In the case of a common resource, the market tends to
  a. overconsume the good because the good is nonexcludable but rival in consumption.
  b. underconsume the good because the good is nonexcludable but rival in consumption.
  c. overconsume the good because the good is excludable but rival in consumption.
  d. underconsume the good because the good is excludable and nonrival in consumption.
  e. overconsume the good because the good is excludable and nonrival in consumption.

Preparing for the AP® Microeconomics Exam

I. OVERVIEW

As the grand finale of your economics classes, you will take the AP® Microeconomics exam in early May. There are a number of benefits that come from doing well on the exam. The benefits include, but are not limited to, becoming eligible to receive college credit for all of your hard work. Keep in mind that your AP® scores will become part of your academic record. Receiving AP® credit at a university is the same as completing the university's introductory microeconomics course. The credit means that you are a course closer to graduation, you don't have to pay tuition for the course, you are eligible to take courses for which introductory microeconomics is a prerequisite, and you gain credit hours that advance your academic standing and move you up the priority list for things like course registration. So, for these and a variety of other reasons, you want to make sure you do your best on the AP® exam. Doing your best requires that you have a plan to prepare and review for the exam. The material that follows is designed to help you as you prepare for and take the AP® Microeconomics exam.

Every year the number of students attempting the AP® Microeconomics exam grows. Annually, more than 50,000 microeconomics students take the AP® exam. The majority of test-takers are high school seniors, but this is not a requirement for taking the exam. A little more than 1/2 of those taking the exam scored a 3 or higher. According to the College Board, AP® test scores carry the following recommendations:

AP® SCORE	QUALIFICATION	TRANSLATION
5	Extremely well-qualified	Oh yeah!
4	Well-qualified	Most likely college credit
3	Qualified	Maybe college credit
2	Possibly qualified	Hmmm… probably not
1	No recommendation	Ugh!

Maximizing your performance on any AP® exam requires a well thought out preparation and review plan. Below is a suggested schedule for preparing for your AP® Microeconomics exam. Keep in mind that this suggested schedule will need to be modified to fit your individual circumstances. In particular, you will need to adjust the schedule based on any other AP® exams and activities that you will also have during this very busy time of year!

II. SAMPLE SCHEDULE

What follows is a general guide for creating a plan to prepare and review for the AP® Microeconomics exam. While each student's approach will differ, consider these suggestions for creating your own plan to maximize your performance on the exam!

1. At the start of your AP® Microeconomics course
During the first few weeks of your class, take some time to familiarize yourself with the course outline and AP® exam information. It will be helpful to have a general idea about the topics you will study and the format of the AP® exam. AP® Economics exams are not the same as AP® exams in other disciplines; be aware of the differences so that your approach to the class best prepares you to succeed. The AP® course outline and format of the exam are outlined in the following sections. Additional information about AP® exams is available on the College Board's AP® Central website.

2. During your AP® Microeconomics course
As you progress through each section of material, periodically refer to sample AP® exam questions to get an idea of course expectations. It is important to understand the level at which the material will be tested and to see how questions testing that material are typically written. You can find sample exam questions in the sections that follow and on the College Board's AP® Central website.

3. Six weeks before the exam
Approximately 6 weeks before the exam, you should begin planning for your exam preparation and review. Depending on what other exams and commitments you have, you may need to start your preparation right away or you may wait until the exam date is closer. Remember that AP® exams for all subjects are given over a two-week period. The economics exams have historically been given during the second week. So, if you are taking other AP® exams, you will need to complete your exam preparations before AP® exams begin, more than a week before the AP® Economics exam is scheduled.

4. Five weeks before the exam
About 5 weeks before your exam (end of March, beginning of April), you should use the diagnostic test provided in the following section to determine how much additional studying you will need and what specific areas you should emphasize as you allocate your additional study time. Follow the instructions provided to take the diagnostic test and use the score sheet and guidelines to help you determine your study and review schedule. At this point, there will still be several weeks of class left and therefore some

content will still need to be covered in class. Make sure that your plan includes this material and allows time for you to learn, practice, and review it.

5. The week before the exam

During the week preceding the AP® Economics exam (the last week in April), you should be finished studying for the exam and spend your available time reviewing. At this stage, you should be reminding yourself of things you have already learned and reviewing the topics that you had the most trouble mastering or remembering. The study sheets included in the following sections are a great way to review the most important models, formulas, and graphs you will need to understand for the exam. At this point, you can use one of the practice tests included below to help you get used to the exam process and format.

6. A night or two before the exam

Schedule time for one last review of the course material to make sure it is fresh in your mind. You may want to use the second practice test at this point. You can take the practice test as another mock exam; use it to review, or work through it with a study group. Your final review session should not be too long or intense (you have already done the hardest work!). Make sure you arrange to get a good night's sleep the night before the exam, have a good breakfast the morning of the exam, have everything you need to take to the exam with you, and get to your exam site early on the day of your exam!

III. THE AP® COURSE OUTLINE

The course outline for AP® Microeconomics is provided below. This outline shows the content areas covered in the course and the percentage of the course/exam devoted to that material. Be aware that the first section of the AP® Microeconomics course outline overlaps with the beginning sections of the AP® Macroeconomics course outline.

Content area (percentage of the exam – Multiple-Choice section)

I. Basic Economic Concepts   **(8–14%)**
- A. Scarcity, choice, and opportunity cost
- B. Production possibilities curve
- C. Comparative advantage, absolute advantage, specialization, and trade
- D. Economic systems
- E. Property rights and the role of incentives
- F. Marginal analysis

II. The Nature and Function of Product Markets   **(55–70%)**
- A. Supply and demand (15–20%)
  1. Market equilibrium
  2. Determinants of supply and demand
  3. Price and quantity controls
  4. Elasticity
  5. Consumer surplus, producer surplus, and allocative efficiency
  6. Tax incidence and deadweight loss
- B. Theory of consumer choice (5–10%)
- C. Production and costs (10–15%)
  1. Production function: short and long run
  2. Marginal product and diminishing returns
  3. Short-run costs
  4. Long-run costs and economies of scale
  5. Cost-minimizing input combination and productive efficiency

D.   Firm behavior and market structure (25–35%)
    1.   Profit
    2.   Perfect competition
    3.   Monopoly
    4.   Oligopoly
    5.   Monopolistic competition

III.   **Factor Markets**   **(10-18%)**
    A.   Derived factor demand
    B.   Marginal revenue product
    C.   Hiring decisions in the markets for labor and capital
    D.   Market distribution of income

IV.   **Market Failure and the Role of Government**   **(12 – 18%)**
    A.   Externalities
    B.   Public goods
    C.   Public policy to promote competition
    D.   Income distribution

IV. EXAM FORMAT

The AP® Economics exam is divided into two sections. The first section is comprised of 60 multiple-choice questions and the second is three free-response questions. The multiple-choice section counts for two-thirds of the overall exam grade weight, and the free-response counts for one-third. The number of questions you will be asked from each section of the course outline corresponds to the percentages provided in the course outline. For example, section III. Factor Markets.... 10 - 18% means that anywhere from six to eleven questions will be asked on the multiple-choice section over this topic.

Multiple Choice
You will have 70 minutes to complete the sixty questions on the multiple-choice section of the exam. Each multiple-choice question has five answer choices, only one of which is correct. The 70 minutes you are allotted to complete the multiple-choice section translates to 70 seconds per question. For each question answered correctly, you earn one point. No deductions are made for an incorrect response. This means that if you are unsure about the answer to a question, then your best strategy is to make an educated guess. You should always answer all of the multiple-choice questions – there is no penalty for guessing, but you are always wrong if you leave an answer blank! Remember that you are trying to rack up as many points as possible. So when in doubt, give it your best shot and guess; you just might get lucky. The worst thing that can happen is that no point will be earned.

    Unlike tests that you might take in a class, the AP® exams do not use all of the above, none of the above or true/false type questions. Instead, the multiple-choice questions you will encounter will come in several different formats.

Free-response
The second section of the AP® Microeconomics exam is made up of free-response questions. You must write all of your answers in the designated area of the test booklet provided. Answers should be written in blue or black ink only.

    The free-response is divided into three separate questions. The first question is the longest and most comprehensive of the three. You should allocate roughly half of your time, about 30 minutes, to answering it. The second and third free-response questions are shorter and typically test a particular area of the course outline. You should allocate roughly a quarter of the time available, or about 15 minutes, to each of the shorter questions. Allocate and monitor your time carefully so that you are able to provide at least a basic response to each question.

V. PLANNING YOUR TEST PREPARATION AND REVIEW

The following test is designed to help you assess the strengths and weaknesses in your knowledge of AP® Microeconomics. The test is comprised of 60 multiple-choice questions, each with 5 answer choices. This test is for diagnostic purposes and does not include free-response questions. Allow yourself 70 minutes to take this diagnostic test. The use of a calculator is not permitted on the AP® exam, so do not use one on this test either. If you are uncertain of the correct answer, make an educated guess.

The answers, along with explanations, are provided below for you to review once you have completed and graded your diagnostic test. In addition, the answer key correlates each question with a section on the AP® Course Outline. When you are finished, take time to review the answers to the questions you missed and assess which areas of the course outline you have mastered and which you need to review. Use your results to allocate your study time before the AP® exam. Good luck!

Diagnostic Test

1. Which of the following is an opportunity cost of going to college?
    a. tuition
    b. room and board
    c. books and supplies
    d. transportation
    e. forgone earnings

2. The following table shows the cost of purchasing different quantities of cookies at a bakery. Based on this information, what is the marginal cost of the third cookie?

Number of Cookies	Cost
0	0
1	$1.00
2	$1.75
3	$2.25
4	$2.50
5	$2.60

    a. $0
    b. $0.50
    c. $1.75
    d. $2.25
    e. $5.00

3. A market economy allocates resources primarily through which of the following?
   a. government agencies
   b. voluntary exchange of goods and services
   c. the decisions of large businesses
   d. social conventions
   e. historical preferences

Questions 4 and 5 refer to the following graph, which shows an economy's production possibilities curve for the production of goods "X" and "Y".

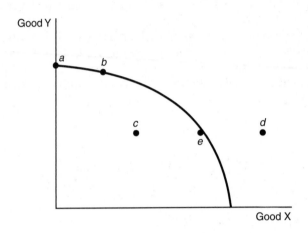

4. Which of the following points represents an inefficient use of resources?
   a. a
   b. b
   c. c
   d. d
   e. e

5. Given its current production possibilities, at which point(s) can this economy not produce?
   a. a
   b. b
   c. c
   d. d
   e. c or d

6. Which of the following can lead to an inward shift of the production possibilities curve?
   a. an increase in unemployment
   b. a decrease in the labor force
   c. an increase in prices
   d. a technological advance
   e. a recession

7. Which of the following will shift the demand curve for gasoline to the right?
   a. a decrease in the price of gasoline
   b. a decrease in the price of cars
   c. a decrease in the price of crude oil
   d. an increase in the average fuel efficiency of cars
   e. a decrease in the number of businesses that sell gasoline

8. An increase in the wages of textile workers will most likely lead to which of the following?
   a. an increase in the demand for textiles
   b. a decrease in the demand for textiles
   c. an increase in the supply of textiles
   d. a decrease in the supply of textiles
   e. an increase in both the supply and demand for textiles

9. If an increase in the price of good X leads to a decrease in the demand for good Y, which of the following must be true?
   a. X is a normal good.
   b. Y is an inferior good.
   c. Both X and Y are normal goods.
   d. X and Y are complements.
   e. X and Y are substitutes.

10. If both supply and demand for a good increase, which of the following is true?
    a. Price will increase.
    b. Price will decrease.
    c. Quantity will increase.
    d. Quantity will decrease.
    e. Quantity may increase, decrease, or remain the same.

11. Which of the following is true of an effective price ceiling?
    a. It is put in place to help producers.
    b. It must be set below equilibrium.
    c. It will increase the quantity of the good sold in the market.
    d. It will create a surplus in the market.
    e. It will not change the quantity of the good demanded or supplied.

12. If a 10% increase in price leads to no change in quantity demanded, the demand curve is
    a. indeterminate.
    b. downward-sloping.
    c. vertical.
    d. horizontal.
    e. asymptotic.

13. When price elasticity of demand is less than 1, what should a firm do if it wants to increase its total revenue?
    a. decrease the price
    b. raise the price
    c. produce less
    d. reduce costs
    e. sell more

14. When Yolanda's income increases from $40,000 to $60,000, she increases her purchases of good X from 90 to 110. Which of the following is true? Yolanda's income elasticity of demand for good X is
    a. .5 and X is a normal good.
    b. .5 and X is an inferior good.
    c. 2 and X is a normal good.
    d. 2 and X is an inferior good.
    e. -2 and X is an inferior good.

15. A decrease in the supply of a good will have what effect on consumer surplus, producer surplus, and total surplus in the market?

	Consumer surplus	Producer surplus	Total surplus
a.	increase	increase	increase
b.	increase	decrease	decrease
c.	decrease	decrease	decrease
d.	decrease	decrease	increase
e.	decrease	increase	decrease

Refer to the following graph of the gasoline market to answer questions 16 and 17.

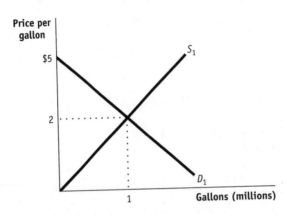

16. At equilibrium in this market, how much does total surplus equal?
  a. $1.0 million
  b. $1.5 million
  c. $2.5 million
  d. $4.0 million
  e. $5.0 million

17. If the government imposes a tax of $1 per gallon on sellers in the market, which of the following is true?
  a. Sellers will raise the price of gasoline by $1.
  b. Profit from gasoline sales will be reduced by $1 per gallon.
  c. Total surplus in the market will increase.
  d. The government will receive an increase in tax revenue of $1 million.
  e. The tax will lead to deadweight loss.

18. Which of the following will eventually decrease as an individual consumes additional units of a good?
  a. marginal utility
  b. average utility
  c. total utility
  d. marginal product
  e. marginal revenue product

The following table shows the marginal utility a consumer receives from consuming good X. Use the information in the table to answer question 19.

Q	MU
0	
1	10
2	8
3	5
4	4
5	3

19. The total utility the consumer receives from consuming 2 units of good X is equal to
   a. 2.
   b. 3.
   c. 8.
   d. 10.
   e. 18.

20. A consumer has $1,000 to spend on goods A and B. She is currently consuming 50 units of good A and 25 units of good B. The marginal utility she receives for good A is 50 and the marginal utility she receives from good B is 100. If the price of good A is $10 and the price of good B is $20, which of the following should she do in order to maximize her utility?
   a. continue to consume the current amounts of good A and good B
   b. consume less good B
   c. consume more good A and less good B
   d. consume less good A and more good B
   e. consume more good A and B

Units of labor	Output
0	0
1	8
2	18
3	26
4	32
5	36
6	38
7	36

21. The marginal product of the 4th unit of labor is equal to
    a. 84.
    b. 32.
    c. 8.
    d. 6.
    e. 4.

22. The average product of the second unit of labor is equal to
    a. 26.
    b. 18.
    c. 10.
    d. 9.
    e. 8.

23. A firm has a fixed amount of capital. As the firm increases production, the additional output that results from hiring additional units of labor declines. This is an example of which of the following?
    a. diseconomies of scale
    b. economies of scale
    c. diminishing returns
    d. declining marginal revenue product
    e. the law of supply

24. Which of the following is true in the short run?
    a. All inputs are fixed.
    b. There are no variable factors.
    c. At least one factor is fixed.
    d. The firm cannot vary its output level.
    e. Firms initially experience economies of scale.

25. A firm is producing the desired level of output using 40 units of capital and 120 units of labor. The marginal product of labor is 50 and the marginal product of capital is 48. The price of a unit of labor is $10 and the price of a unit of capital is $6. To minimize costs, the firm should
a. continue using the current combination of capital and labor.
b. use more capital and less labor.
c. use less capital and more labor.
d. use more capital and more labor.
e. shut down.

26. If a firm is earning a normal profit, what must be true of the firm's accounting profit? It is
a. zero.
b. negative.
c. positive.
d. increasing.
e. less than economic profit.

27. A firm will maximize profits by producing at the quantity where marginal cost
a. crosses the minimum of the average total cost curve.
b. is maximized.
c. is minimized.
d. equals marginal revenue.
e. begins increasing at a decreasing rate.

28. If average cost is decreasing, marginal cost must be
a. increasing.
b. decreasing.
c. above average cost.
d. below average cost.
e. equal to average cost.

29. Which of the following is true of the marginal revenue curve for a perfectly competitive firm?
a. It is equal to the average total cost curve.
b. It is equal to the demand curve.
c. It is equal to the marginal cost curve above average variable cost.
d. It is vertical at the profit-maximizing level of output.
e. The firm does not have a marginal revenue curve.

Use the information in the following table to answer questions 30 and 31.

Q	TC
0	$4
1	10
2	12
3	16
4	22
5	30
6	40
7	52
8	66
9	82

30. If price is $8, what is the firm's profit-maximizing level of output?
    a. 0
    b. 1
    c. 3
    d. 5
    e. 7

31. If the price is $8, what is the firm's maximum profit?
    a. $10
    b. $30
    c. $40
    d. $70
    e. 0

32. What will happen in a perfectly competitive market if firms are earning a profit?
    a. Supply and price will increase.
    b. Supply will increase and price will decrease.
    c. Demand and price will increase.
    d. Demand will increase and price will decrease.
    e. Demand will decrease and price will increase.

33. Which of the following is true of perfectly competitive firms in the long run?
    a. They differentiate their product through advertising.
    b. They engage in strategic decision making.
    c. They set price above where $MC = MR$.
    d. They earn an economic profit.
    e. They produce at minimum average total cost.

34. Allocative efficiency occurs when the market produces the level of output where price is equal to
    a. marginal revenue.
    b. demand.
    c. average total cost.
    d. marginal cost.
    e. minimum average variable cost.

Refer to the following graph to answer questions 35 – 36.

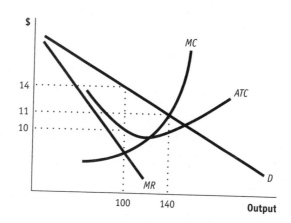

35. What are the profit-maximizing price and quantity for the monopoly shown on the graph?

	Price	*Quantity*
a.	10	100
b.	10	140
c.	11	140
d.	14	100
e.	14	140

36. The monopoly shown on the graph is earning a _____ equal to _____.
    a. profit; $100
    b. profit; $300
    c. profit; $400
    d. loss; $140
    e. loss; $560

37. Compared with firms in a perfectly competitive industry, a monopoly will
    a. produce a higher quantity.
    b. produce an efficient level of output.
    c. charge a lower price.
    d. produce at a lower average total cost.
    e. create deadweight loss.

Refer to the following graph to answer question 38.

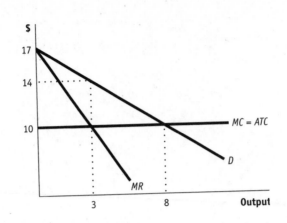

38. A monopoly in this industry would lead to a deadweight loss equal to how much?
   a. $0
   b. $4.5
   c. $10
   d. $12
   e. $28

39. Which of the following would result if a natural monopoly were required to charge a price equal to average cost? The monopoly would
   a. achieve allocative efficiency.
   b. achieve productive efficiency.
   c. operate at a loss.
   d. earn a normal profit.
   e. eliminate deadweight loss.

40. Which of the following is true of price discrimination?
   a. It occurs only in in oligopoly markets.
   b. It results in an increase in consumer surplus.
   c. It reduces the profit of firms that engage in it.
   d. It works best in markets in which goods can be resold.
   e. It can only be produced by firms with market power.

41. The oligopoly market structure is unique in that it assumes which of the following characteristics?
   a. interdependence of firms
   b. product differentiation
   c. barriers to entry
   d. more than one firm
   e. long-run normal profit

Refer to the following payoff matrix to answer questions 42 and 43.

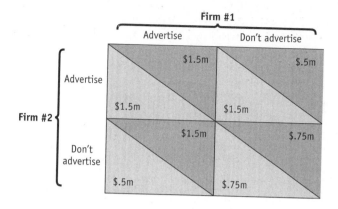

42. If Firm #1 decides to advertise, which of the following is true for Firm #2?
   a. Its dominant strategy is to advertise.
   b. Its dominant strategy is not to advertise.
   c. It does not have a dominant strategy.
   d. It may choose either to advertise or not to advertise.
   e. It will always choose not to advertise.

43. Collusion by the two firms will result in which of the following outcomes?
   a. Firm 1 advertises; Firm 2 does not.
   b. Firm 2 advertises; Firm 1 does not.
   c. Both Firm 1 and Firm 2 advertise.
   d. Neither Firm 1 nor Firm 2 advertises.
   e. It is impossible to determine what Firm 1 and Firm 2 will do.

44. Which of the following is a characteristic of monopolistically competitive firms?
   a. barriers to entry
   b. long-run economic profits
   c. standardized products
   d. a large number of buyers and sellers
   e. perfectly elastic demand curves

45. Which of the following is most likely to be true in the long run for a monopolistically competitive firm?
   a. $P = ATC = MR = MC$
   b. $P = MR = MC > ATC$
   c. $P > MR = MC = ATC$
   d. $P = ATC > MC = MR$
   e. $P > ATC > MC = MR$

46. The individual producer's demand for labor curve is the same as which curve when the product market is imperfectly competitive?
   a. marginal factor cost (*MFC*)
   b. marginal revenue (*MR*)
   c. marginal product (*MP*)
   d. marginal revenue product (*MRP*)
   e. marginal variable cost (*MVC*)

47. Which of the following will decrease the demand for bank tellers?
    a. an increase in the price of bank services
    b. a technological advance that makes bank tellers more productive
    c. an increase in the number of teller windows available for customers
    d. an increase in the number of trained bank tellers
    e. an increase in the popularity and availability of online banking

48. Which of the following is true of an individual's labor supply curve? It has a
    a. positive slope.
    b. negative slope.
    c. negative slope at low wage levels and a positive slope at higher wage levels.
    d. positive slope at low wage levels and a negative slope at higher wage levels.
    e. different slope depending on the demand for labor.

49. A monopsony employer hires labor up to the point where marginal factor cost equals
    a. the price of the product.
    b. marginal revenue.
    c. marginal product.
    d. marginal revenue product.
    e. the market wage.

50. Which of the following would lead to an increase in the supply of labor?
    a. an increase in career opportunities for women
    b. a decrease in population
    c. an increase in wealth
    d. a shift in the population from urban to rural areas
    e. an increase in worker productivity

51. Suppose a new regulation requires all auto mechanics to pass a test and pay a fee to obtain a license before they can work. How will this new policy affect the supply of auto mechanics, the equilibrium wage in the market for auto mechanics, and the price of auto repairs?

	Supply of Auto mechanics	Equilibrium Wage	Price of Auto repairs
a.	decrease	increase	increase
b.	decrease	decrease	increase
c.	increase	increase	increase
d.	increase	decrease	increase
e.	increase	decrease	decrease

52. If the marginal product of capital and labor are both equal to 100 while the wage is $10 and the rental rate is $12, which of the following is true? Assume the firm is currently producing the desired level of output. The firm
    a. is maximizing profits.
    b. is minimizing costs.
    c. should hire more capital and less labor.
    d. should hire more labor and less capital.
    e. should hire only labor.

53. Which of the following is the best example of a negative externality?
  a. Your neighbors allow you to have free access to their swimming pool.
  b. Your roommate provides a brand new TV for your living room.
  c. The government raises your income tax.
  d. You catch the flu from the student who sits next to you in math class.
  e. "Free riders" receive benefits from goods they did not help pay for.

54. Which of the follow is the best example of a good that is excludable?
  a. fire protection
  b. pollution
  c. a cable TV broadcast
  d. clean water in a river
  e. a public sewer system

Refer to the following graph for questions 55, 56, and 57. The graph shows the market for a good that generates external costs.

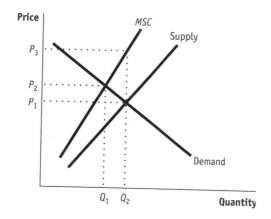

55. At the market equilibrium, the marginal external cost of producing this good is equal to
  a. P_3.
  b. P_2.
  c. P_1.
  d. $(P_3 - P_1)$.
  e. $(P_2 - P_1)$.

56. Without government action, the market will produce ____ which is ____ the efficient level of production.
  a. Q_1, greater than
  b. Q_1, less than
  c. Q_2, greater than
  d. Q_2, less than
  e. Q_2, equal to

57. The government can move production to the optimal level by instituting a Pigouvian ____ equal to ____.
    a. subsidy, marginal external cost
    b. subsidy, P_2
    c. tax, P_2
    d. tax, P_1
    e. tax, marginal external cost

58. Which of the following is the best example of a good that is rival in consumption?
    a. a cable television broadcast
    b. national defense
    c. clean water in a river
    d. a fireworks display
    e. an apple

59. Because of the free-rider effect, private markets produce
    a. the allocatively efficient quantity of output.
    b. too much of a public good, requiring the government to place a tax on the good.
    c. too little of a public good, requiring the government to provide the good.
    d. too much of a public good, requiring the government to place a quota on the production of the good.
    e. too little of a public good, requiring the government to place a tax on the good.

60. The marginal productivity theory of income distribution says that marginal productivity at the economy's equilibrium determines which of the following?
    a. how much each worker is worth
    b. the division of income among the factors of production
    c. whether or not there is discrimination in labor markets
    d. the price level in the economy
    e. the deadweight loss due to imperfect competition in factor markets

Place a "√" by the questions you answered correctly.

 # Correct in each section

I. Basic Economic Concepts

1_____ 2_____ 3_____ 4_____ 5_____ 6_____

IIA. Supply and Demand

7_____ 8_____ 9_____ 10_____ 11_____ 12_____
13_____ 14_____ 15_____ 16_____ 17_____ 18_____

IIB. Theory of Consumer Choice

18_____ 19_____ 20_____

IIC. Production and Costs

21_____ 22_____ 23_____ 24_____ 25_____

IID. Firm Behavior and Market Structure

26_____ 27_____ 28_____ 29_____ 30_____ 31_____
32_____ 33_____ 34_____ 35_____ 36_____ 37_____
38_____ 39_____ 40_____ 41_____ 42_____ 43_____
44_____ 45_____

III. Factor Markets

46_____ 47_____ 48_____ 49_____ 50_____ 51_____
52_____

VII. Market Failure and the Role of Government

53_____ 54_____ 55_____ 56_____ 57_____ 58_____
59_____ 60_____

Total # correct

Use your scores on the diagnostic test to determine how to prepare for the AP® Exam

Start by determining the percent of the questions that you answered correctly. Your total # correct divided by 60 is the percent of questions you answered correctly:

$$\boxed{} \div 60 = \boxed{}$$

Total # correct   **Total % correct**

To get an idea of how much you will need to study for your AP® exam, you can compare your performance to students who took the most recently released AP® Microeconomics exam. For example, of the students who scored a "3" on the AP® Microeconomics exam (the minimum score to receive college credit), 80% scored between 31 and 60 on the multiple-choice section. Sixty-seven percent of those scoring a "3" scored between 31 and 36 on the multiple-choice section. So if your score was below 50% on this diagnostic test, you need to allocate additional time to studying for the AP® exam, beyond the review time that all students need to spend in order to do well on the exam. If you scored above 50%, you should still plan to spend time studying the sections where you most need to improve your performance as well as taking time to review all of the sections in the week leading up to the exam.

Next, determine how to allocate your study time to each section of material by evaluating your score in each section. First, find the percent of the questions you answered correctly in each section by dividing the number you answered correctly by the number of questions in the section. Spend more time studying the material in those sections for which the percent you answered correctly is less than your total percent correct and less time studying the sections for which the percent you answered correctly is greater than your total percent correct. Next, look at how much each section is weighted on the AP® exam. Spend more time studying those sections that are given a higher weight.

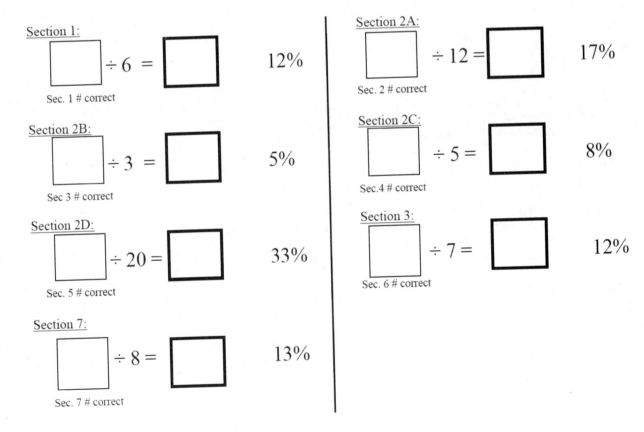

Section 1:

$$\boxed{} \div 6 = \boxed{} \qquad 12\%$$

Sec. 1 # correct

Section 2A:

$$\boxed{} \div 12 = \boxed{} \qquad 17\%$$

Sec. 2 # correct

Section 2B:

$$\boxed{} \div 3 = \boxed{} \qquad 5\%$$

Sec 3 # correct

Section 2C:

$$\boxed{} \div 5 = \boxed{} \qquad 8\%$$

Sec.4 # correct

Section 2D:

$$\boxed{} \div 20 = \boxed{} \qquad 33\%$$

Sec. 5 # correct

Section 3:

$$\boxed{} \div 7 = \boxed{} \qquad 12\%$$

Sec. 6 # correct

Section 7:

$$\boxed{} \div 8 = \boxed{} \qquad 13\%$$

Sec. 7 # correct

ANSWERS AND EXPLANATIONS

(Note that the section on the course outline is indicated in parentheses.)

1. e. – The first four choices are direct costs that must be paid. Forgone earnings represent the cost of the next best alternative to going to college (working). (I.)
2. b. – The additional cost of buying the third cookie is $0.50 ($2.25 - $1.75). (I.)
3. b. – Market economies allocate resources through the exchange of goods and services in markets. (I.)
4. c. – Point c is below the curve; therefore, the economy is not producing as much as is possible. (I.)
5. d. – Point d is beyond the curve and is therefore beyond the possibilities of the economy. (I.)
6. b. – A decrease in the labor force is a decrease in resources (labor) and will decrease the level of production possibilities. (I.)
7. b. – Cars and gasoline are complements. A decrease in the price of cars will lead to the purchase of more cars and, therefore, an increase in the demand for gasoline. (IIA.)
8. d. – Wages are the price of labor (an input into the production of textiles). An increase in price will lead to a decrease in the quantity of textile workers demanded and, therefore, a decrease in the supply of the textiles made by the workers. (IIA.)
9. d. – If the price of good X increases people will buy less X. If they then also buy less Y, it shows that X and Y go together (i.e. are complements). (IIA.)
10. c. – Both supply and demand will shift to the right. Shifts to the right always increase quantity. (IIA.)
11. b. – To prevent the price from going to equilibrium (and therefore have an effect on the market), the ceiling must be below equilibrium. (IIA.)
12. c. – A zero change in quantity demanded means that quantity never changes, regardless of the price. The percentage change in quantity – the numerator of the elasticity formula – is zero. Price elasticity of demand is zero which is perfectly inelastic. The demand curve is vertical. (IIA.)
13. b. – If elasticity of demand is less than 1, demand is inelastic. The quantity effect will be less than the price effect, so firms will increase total revenue by raising price. (IIA.)
14. a. – Income elasticity of demand is $(20/100)/(20,000/50,000) = .5$. The positive relationship tells us that the good is a normal good (she buys more as her income increases). (IIA.)
15. c. – A decrease in supply will raise the equilibrium price which will decrease consumer, producer, and total surplus. (IIA.)
16. c. – Consumer surplus is $\frac{1}{2} (1 \times 2) = 1$ and producer surplus is $\frac{1}{2} (1 \times 3) = 1.5$. Total surplus is consumer surplus plus producer surplus, or $1 + 1.5 = \$2.5$ m.
17. e. – Given the slopes of the supply and demand curves, the tax burden will be shared by consumers and producers (so a. and b. are not correct). The quantity sold in the market will decrease as a result of the tax, so government revenue will be less than $1 m. The tax will raise the price consumers pay and decrease the price producers receive so that total surplus decreases. Moving the market away from equilibrium creates a deadweight loss. (IIa.)
18. a. – The law of diminishing marginal utility. (IIB.)
19. e. – The additional utility from the first unit is 10 and the additional utility from the second unit is 8 for a total of $18. (IIB.)
20. a. – The marginal utility per dollar spent on goods A and B are equal (5), so the consumer is maximizing utility. (IIB.)
21. d. – The additional output from hiring the fourth worker is $32 - 26 = 6$. (IIC.)
22. d. – The average product $= TP/L = 18/2 = 9$. (IIC.)
23. c. – The law of diminishing (marginal) returns. (IIC.)
24. c. – At least 1 factor of production is fixed in the short run. (IIC.)
25. b. – The marginal product per dollar spent for labor is $50/10 = 5$ and $48/6 = 8$ for capital. The firm should hire more capital because the additional output it receives per dollar spent on capital is greater than the additional output it receives per dollar spent on labor. Hiring more capital means hiring less labor because the firm was already producing the desired level of output. (IIC.)
26. c. – Economic profit (which is zero in this case) includes both implicit and explicit costs. Accounting profit includes only explicit costs. Therefore, accounting profit must be positive since it excludes implicit costs. (IID.)

27. d. – $MC = MR$ is the rule for profit maximization. (IID.)
28. d. – For the average to be falling, the added units must be below the average (to pull it down). (IIC.)
29. b. – The firm is a price taker, so marginal revenue and demand are both equal to price. (IID.)
30. d. – Find MC as the change in TC in the table. $MC = MR = P = 8$ at an output of 5. (IID.)
31. a. – Profit equals total revenue minus total cost. Profit = (8×5) – 30 = 40 – 30 = $10. (IID.)
32. b. – Easy entry and exit will cause firms to enter when there are profits. This increases the number of firms, which increases supply and drives down price. (IID.)
33. e. – Perfectly competitive firms produce at minimum ATC in the long run. (IID.)
34. d. – Allocative efficiency occurs when resources are allocated so that the price equals marginal cost. (IID.)
35. d. – Quantity is found where $MC = MR$. Price is found on the demand curve at that quantity. (IID.)
36. c. – Price exceeds ATC, so the monopoly is earning a profit. Profit equals total revenue minus total cost. Profit = (14×100) – (10×100) = $1,400 - $1,000 = $400. OR, profit per unit is $14 - $10 = $4 on each of 100 units = $400. (IID.)
37. e. – Monopolies reduce quantity and increase price relative to perfectly competitive firms, creating deadweight loss. (IID.)
38. c. – Deadweight loss is the reduction in consumer surplus that does NOT go to the monopoly as increased profit due to the higher price from monopoly. (Note: there is no producer surplus when MC is constant.) This is the area of the triangle with a base of 8 – 3 = 5 and a height of 14 – 10 = 4. Deadweight loss equals ½ (5×4) = ½ (20) = $10. (IID.)
39. d. – Since price does not equal MC, the monopoly would not be allocatively efficient. When price equals ATC, the firm earns a normal profit. (IID.)
40. e. – A firm must have market power to engage in price discrimination. (IID.)
41. a. – The distinguishing characteristic of oligopoly is interdependent firms. (IID.)
42. a. - Firm 2 can earn either $1.5 m or $0.5 m if Firm 1 advertises. Its best strategy is to advertise and earn $1.5 m. (IID.)
43. c. - The best outcome for each firm and for the 2 firms combined is to advertise. (Each firm earns the maximum $1.5 m and the combined total of $3 m is the highest total for the market.) (IID.)
44. d. - Monopolistically competitive industries have many buyers and sellers. (IID.)
45. d. – Firms maximize profits, so $MC = MR$. In the long run they earn a normal profit, so $P = ATC$. The demand curve has a negative slope, so price will be above $MC = MR$. (IID.)
46. d. - The marginal revenue product curve is the individual firm's demand curve for labor. (III.)
47. e. - Online banking is a substitute for conducting a transaction with a bank teller, so more online banking will decrease the demand for tellers. (III.)
48. d. - The labor supply curve for an individual is described as "backward bending." It starts out at low wages with a positive slope and changes to a negative slope at a sufficiently high wage when the income effect begins to dominate the substitution effect. (III.)
49. d. – The profit-maximizing condition applied to factor markets is $MFC = MRP$. (III.)
50. a. - More opportunities will (and did) bring more women into the labor force, increasing the supply of labor. (III.)
51. a. - The requirements make it harder to become a mechanic, so the supply of mechanics will decrease. A decrease in supply will shift the supply curve to the left, raising wages and therefore the price of repairs. (III.)
52. d. - The marginal product per dollar spent on labor is higher (100/10 versus 100/12), so the firm should hire more labor, less capital. (III.)
53. d. - The other student's flu is spread to you, so that student's actions imposed a cost on you. (IV.)
54. c. - People can be prevented from viewing a cable TV broadcast. (IV.)
55. d. - Q_2 is the equilibrium quantity. At Q_2, marginal social cost is P_3 and price is P_1. $MEC = MSC - P_1$. (IV.)
56. c. - The market produces at equilibrium (Q_2), which is more than the efficient level of output (Q_1, where $MSC = P$). (IV.)
57. e. - To internalize the externality and move the market to the optimal quantity, the government must impose a tax equal to the MEC. (IV.)
58. e. - If I consume an apple, no one else can consume it. (IV.)

59. c. - Markets fail to produce enough of a public good. Therefore, the government must step in to provide it. (IV.)

60. b. - Marginal productivity theory applies to the division of income among factors. (IV.)

V. REVIEWING FOR THE AP® MICROECONOMICS EXAM

One of the best ways to prepare for the AP® exam is to work released free-response questions and to practice answering as many examples of multiple-choice questions as you can. As you begin, keep the list of key microeconomic formulas and graph review sheets handy and use them as study guides. With practice, you will discover that these formulas and graphs become planted in your memory. Make sure that you practice and review enough that you can recall and apply these formulas and draw and interpret graphs without the guides on the AP® exam.

The Formulas of Micro

There will be both multiple-choice and free-response questions on the AP® Microeconomics exam that require calculations. For example, you may be required to calculate one of several elasticities, costs, or profit. To answer calculation questions, you will need to remember and understand some important equations and formulas. The key microeconomics equations and formulas are listed below.

Marginal Analysis – Economics focuses on marginal analysis. Marginal analysis involves making a decision about incremental changes to the status quo. To make a decision "on the margin" (i.e. using marginal analysis), you compare the additional costs of an activity to the additional benefits. The optimal amount of an activity is found where marginal costs equal marginal benefits. In microeconomics, the solution is very often found at the quantity where $MC = MB$.

> Marginal cost = Marginal revenue
> $MC = MB$
> *For a firm, revenue is the benefit, so profit-maximizing output is found where $MC = MR$.
> *When hiring factors of production, we use terminology specific to the factor market, but the analysis is the same. A firm will hire a factor of production up to the point where $MFC = MRP$.

Elasticity – Elasticity is a general concept that measures the relative responsiveness of one variable to changes in another. You will need to be able to calculate (and interpret) several different elasticities. But remember, the formula for calculating any elasticity is always the same! Only the variables being evaluated are different.

$$\text{Elasticity} = \frac{\% \text{ change in dependent variable}}{\% \text{ change in independent variable}} = \frac{\left(\dfrac{\text{Change in dependent variable}}{\text{Average value of dependent variable}}\right)}{\left(\dfrac{\text{Change in independent variable}}{\text{Average value of independent variable}}\right)}$$

Price elasticity of demand: How does the quantity demanded of a good respond to a change in price?

percentage change in Q_d (dependent variable) in response to a percentage change in P (independent variable)

Price elasticity of supply: How does the quantity supplied of a good respond to changes in price?

percentage change in Q_s (dependent variable) in response to a percentage change in P (independent variable)

Income elasticity of demand: How does the quantity demanded of a good respond to changes in income?

percentage change in Q_d (dependent variable) in response to a change in income (independent variable)

Cross-price elasticity: How does the Q_d of one good respond to a change in the price of another?

percentage change in Q_d/one good (dependent variable) in response to a percentage change in P/another good (independent variable).

Consumer/Producer Surplus

Consumer surplus: The area above price, below the demand curve
Producer surplus: The area below price, above the demand curve

The area of a triangle $= \dfrac{1}{2}(base)(height)$ or $\dfrac{(base)(height)}{2}$

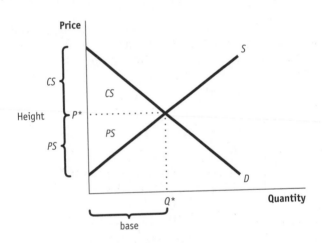

Utility maximization – Consumers maximize their utility by choosing the combination of goods where marginal utility per dollar spent is equal.

$$(MU_x/P_x) = (MU_y/P_y)$$

Measuring Production - Total product (Q) is the output produced using a given amount of a variable input (given the level of a fixed input).

Marginal Product (MP) is the additional output produced as a result of hiring additional units of a variable input.

MPL = change in TP/change in L

Average Product (AP) is the output produced per unit of the variable input used.

$APL = TP/L$

<u>Measuring Costs</u> - The "family" of short-run cost curves includes both fixed and variable costs. You will be expected to understand and calculate total, average, and marginal costs. You will need to understand the relationships between all of the different measures of cost. Remember, all of the costs in economics include both explicit and implicit costs!

$$TC = TFC + TVC$$

Average costs are "per unit" costs and are found by dividing TC by the number of units produced.

$ATC = TC/Q$	therefore	$TC = ATC \times Q$
$AVC = TVC/Q$	therefore	$TVC = AVC \times Q$
$AFC = TFC/Q$	therefore	$TFC = AFC \times Q$

Also, since $TC = TFC + TVC$, $ATC = AFC + AVC$

Marginal cost is the additional cost of producing one more.

MC = change in TC/change in Q

<u>Calculating Profit</u>

Profit = total revenue – total cost

$$\Pi = \underset{(P \times Q)}{TR} - \underset{(ATC \times Q)}{TC}$$

Normal profit is an economic profit equal to zero.

<u>Cost Minimization</u> – Cost-minimizing firms minimize their costs by choosing the combination of inputs (labor and capital) where marginal product per dollar spent is equal.

MPL/wage = MPC/rental rate

Microeconomics Graphs

To do well on the AP® Microeconomics exam you will need to be able to interpret graphs, use graphs to answer questions, and draw graphs as part of free-response questions. Use the following review sheets to help you learn and review the important Microeconomics graphs.

Production Possibilities Curve

The production possibilities curve illustrates trade-offs and opportunity costs incurred as a result of scarce factors of production.

The concave shape indicates that the opportunity cost of producing more consumer/capital goods is ever increasing

In the graph on top, an economy that is fully employing all of its available resources must sacrifice 2 units of capital goods in order to gain about 1 1/2 units of consumer goods.

The bottom graph illustrates the effect of an increase in available factors of production, the quality of those factors of production, increased technology, or increased productivity

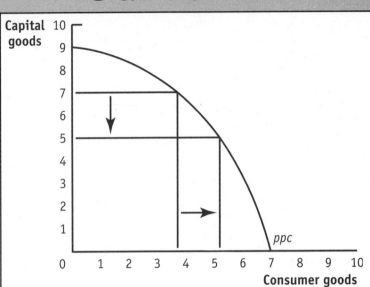

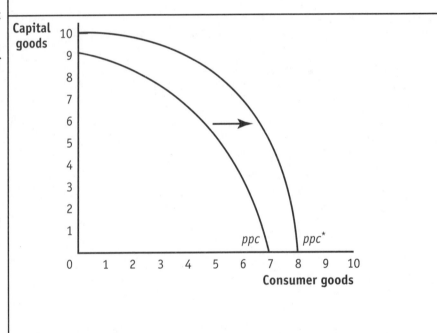

Supply and Demand

The supply & demand model illustrates producers' willingness and ability to produce a good or service (supply) combined with consumers' willingness and ability to consume a good or service (demand). The intersection of these two functions determines the equilibrium price and equilibrium quantity

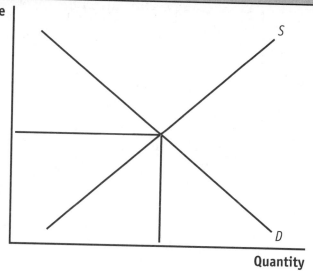

Changes in Demand
Δ in M.E.R.I.T. .:
ΔD .: ΔP & ΔQ
$\uparrow D$ right .: $P \uparrow$ & $Q \uparrow$
$\downarrow D$ left .: $P \downarrow$ & $Q \downarrow$

Changes in Supply
Δ in N.I.C.E.J.A.G.T. .:
ΔS .: ΔP & ΔQ
$\uparrow S$ right .: $P \downarrow$ & $Q \uparrow$
$\downarrow S$ left .: $P \uparrow$ & $Q \downarrow$

Demand Shifters
M.E.R.I.T.

M - market size
E - expected prices
R - related prices
    (complements & substitutes)
I - income
T - tastes

Supply Shifters
N.I.C.E.J.A.G.T.

as in, "Nice Jag, T!"

N - natural phenomenon
I - input prices
C - competition
E - expected prices
J - joint production prices
    (think beef and leather)
A - alternate production prices
    (think corn and wheat)
G - government taxes and subsidies
T - technology

Welfare Analysis

Total surplus is the sum of consumer and producer surplus. It represents the net gain to consumers and producers from trading in a market.

When a competitive market reaches equilibrium, total surplus is maximized. This is the most efficient outcome because there is no way to make some people better off without making other people worse off. Any alternative to the equilibrium outcome reduces total surplus and thus reduces efficiency.

For example, price controls, including price ceilings and floors, and quantity controls will lead to inefficiency. Imperfect competition will also result in a reduction in total surplus.

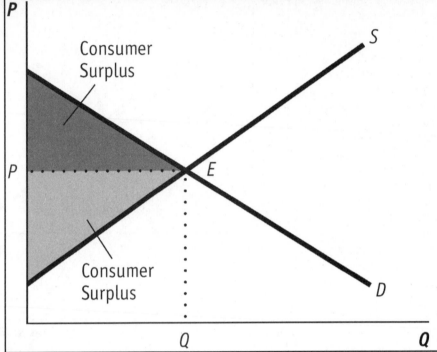

Taxes in a market will also lead to a reduction in total surplus.

An excise tax can be either a tax on sellers or a tax on buyers. If it is a tax on sellers, the supply curve shifts upward by the amount of the tax. If it is a tax on buyers, the demand curve shifts downward by the amount of the tax.

The burden of the tax is paid by both the buyers and the sellers, but not always in equal shares, depending on the elasticities of demand and supply.

Excise taxes have the benefit of generating tax revenue for the government.

Excise taxes typically reduce the number of transactions made between buyers and sellers, leading to a reduction in total surplus.

The loss in total surplus that is not offset by a gain in tax revenue is the deadweight loss resulting from a tax.

Production Function

A production function illustrates the way in which fixed and variable inputs are combined to produce output.

A fixed input is an input whose quantity cannot be easily changed for a period of time. Typical fixed inputs are land and capital.

A variable input is an input whose quantity can be easily changed at any time. Typical variable inputs are labor and raw materials.

A production function graph illustrates the level of output (total product) produced using different levels of the variable input. Fixed input(s) are held constant along a production function.

The marginal product of an input is the additional output produced by using one more unit of that input.

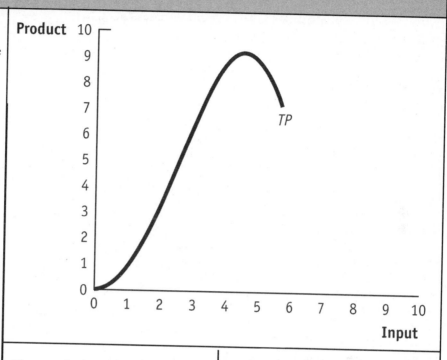

The marginal product equals the change in output resulting from a change in a variable input.

$$MP_L = \Delta TP / \Delta L$$

The marginal product is also the slope of the total product curve.

When more of a variable input (like labor) is added to a fixed input (like capital), the marginal product of the variable input eventually declines. This is shown on the graph as a decrease in the slope of the total product curve from left to right. This is referred to as the "principle of diminishing returns" to that input.

The average product of an input is the output produced *per unit* of the input used. Average product equals the total product divided by the units of input used.

$$AP_L = TP / L$$

The short run is a period of time too short to change the fixed input(s). The long run is a period of time long enough to vary all inputs.

In the long run, firms can increase the level of fixed inputs. An increase in fixed inputs will shift the production function upward.

Average and Marginal Cost Curves

In the short run, there are fixed inputs that create fixed costs. There are also variable inputs that create variable costs.

Total cost of production in the short run is the sum of fixed costs and variable costs.

$TC = VC + FC$.

Marginal cost of production is the additional cost of producing the next unit of output.

$MC = \Delta TC / \Delta Q$.

Marginal cost initially declines due to specialization, but eventually diminishing returns to production cause marginal cost to increase.

Average, or per unit, costs are found by dividing total costs by the number of units being produced.

$ATC = TC/Q$, $AVC = VC/Q$
$AFC = FC/Q$

AFC declines as more output is produced. FC is constant and we are dividing by more and more output.

The ATC and AVC curves have a U-shape.

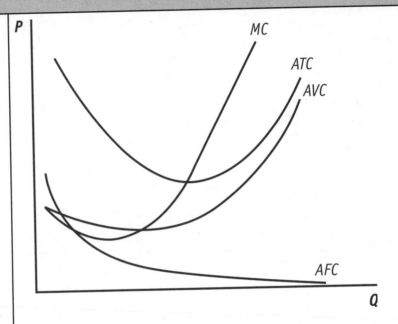

The AC curves have a U-shape because of two effects:

The spreading effect. The larger the output, the greater the quantity over which fixed cost is spread, leading to lower average fixed cost.

The diminishing returns effect. The larger the output, the greater the variable input required to produce additional units, leading to higher average variable cost.

At low levels of output, the spreading effect is very powerful. As output rises, diminishing returns becomes the dominant effect.

The marginal cost curve intersects both ATC and AVC, two U-shaped curves, at their respective minimum points.

MC must cross ATC and AVC at their minimums because if the cost of the marginal (next) unit of output is below the average, it will pull the average down.

If the cost of the marginal (next) unit of output is above the average, it will pull the average up.

Initially, ATC and AVC are falling, so MC must be below them. When ATC and AVC increase, MC must be above them.

Perfect Competition

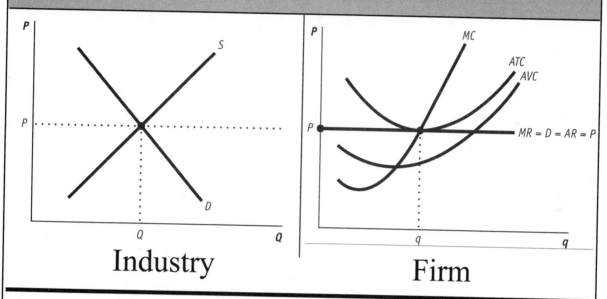

Industry

Firm

The industry and firm graphs for a perfectly competitive industry show the market price of the good and the market/firm level of output.

The market price of the good is determined in the market. Once the market price is determined by the intersection of the supply and demand curves, the perfectly competitive firm takes that price as given (firms are "price takers") and the firm's demand and marginal revenue curves are horizontal at the market price. Showing that the firm's price comes from the market is the purpose of asking for side-by-side graphs.

The firm maximizes profit by producing the level of output at which $MC = MR$. If $P > ATC$ at that level of output, the firm earns a profit. If $P < ATC$, the firm earns a loss. If $P = ATC$, the firm earns a normal profit.

In the long run, the firm will earn a normal profit due to the free entry and exit of firms in response to profits or losses. Note: we know the firm above is in the short run because there are fixed costs. Remember the shut-down rule – a firm continues to produce in the short run when $P > AVC$

Monopoly

Because the monopolist is the only producer in the market, the market demand is the same as the firm's demand. The demand is downward-sloping; therefore, the marginal revenue curve is below the demand curve, creating a gap between price and marginal revenue.

The monopolist maximizes profit at the output level at which $MR = MC$.

Price is found on the demand curve above the output level at which $MC = MR$.

Economic profit is a rectangle with area equal to $(P - ATC)(Q)$.

When compared to the perfectly competitive outcome, the monopolist produces less and charges a higher price. Unlike perfect competitors, monopolists can earn long-run economic profit.

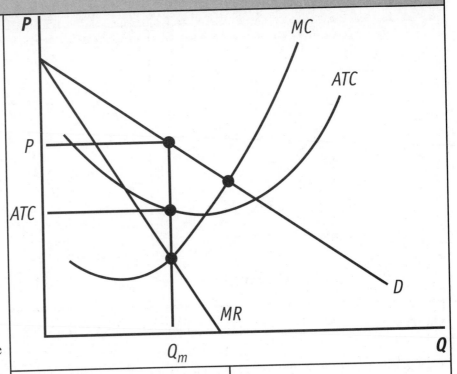

Since price exceeds average total cost on this graph, the firm is earning a profit. The profit per unit for this firm is equal to $(P - ATC)$. The total profit is equal to the profit per unit multiplied by the quantity, which is equal to the area of the rectangle, $(P - ATC)(Q)$.

If price is below average total cost, the firm earns a negative profit (a loss).

If price is equal to average total cost, the firm earns a normal profit.

In the short run, a monopoly firm can earn a profit, a loss, or a normal profit.

If a monopoly is earning a loss in the short run, it will use the shut-down rule to decide whether or not to continue to produce. If $P > AVC$, the firm will continue to produce at a loss in the short run. If $P < ATC$, the firm will shut down.

In the long run, due to barriers to entry, a monopoly can earn a profit or a normal profit.

Monopolistic Competition (Short-Run)

Many firms exist in a monopolistically competitive market, but not as many as in perfect competition.

The product is differentiated, so each firm has some ability to set their price.

A monopolistic competitor faces a downward-sloping (but relatively elastic) demand for its output. Because the firm's demand curve is downward-sloping, its marginal revenue curve is below it. $P > MC$, but not as much as with monopoly.

The firm maximizes profit by producing the level of output where $MC = MR$.

The firm will charge the price indicated by the demand curve above the profit-maximizing output.

There are no barriers to entry or exit.

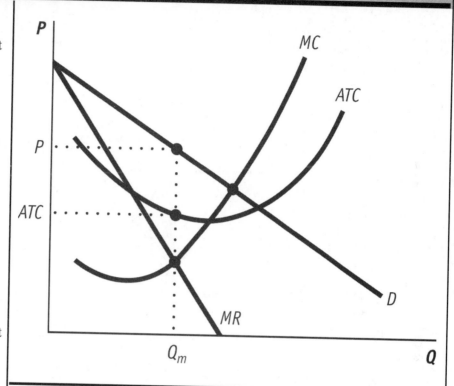

Because price exceeds average total cost on this graph, the firm is earning a profit. The profit per unit for this firm is equal to $(P - ATC)$. The total profit is equal to the area of the rectangle $(P - ATC)(Q)$.

If price is below average total cost, the firm earns a negative profit (a loss).

If price is equal to average total cost, the firm earns a normal profit.

In the long run, monopolistically competitive firms earn a normal profit because of easy entry and exit in the industry.

When firms earn a short-run profit, new firms enter the industry. This decreases demand for existing firms which reduces profit. Entry continues until profit disappears

When firms are operating at a loss in the short-run, firms exit the industry. As firms exit, demand increases for remaining firms which reduces losses. Exit continues until firms no longer operate at a loss.

Deadweight Loss

A monopoly reduces quantity and increases price compared to a competitive market.

The lower quantity and higher price in a monopoly market lead to a decrease in consumer surplus and an increase in producer surplus (in the form of profit). The loss of consumer surplus outweighs the gain to producer surplus resulting in a deadweight loss.

Deadweight loss occurs because output is reduced and $P > MC$, which causes mutually beneficial transactions to go unmade.

Deadweight loss from monopoly markets can be reduced through regulation, antitrust laws, or public ownership.

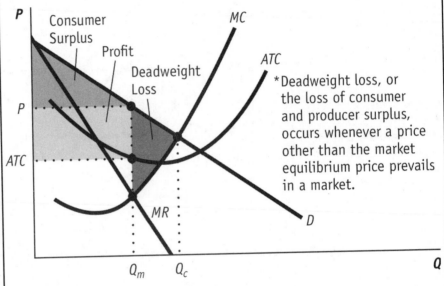

*Deadweight loss, or the loss of consumer and producer surplus, occurs whenever a price other than the market equilibrium price prevails in a market.

A natural monopoly exists when one large firm can produce the product at lower average costs than can several competing firms. The markets for utilities like electricity, natural gas and water are good examples.

In the case of a natural monopoly, there is increased productive efficiency (lower ATC) when one firm produces the entire industry output. However, left unregulated, a monopoly will lead to deadweight loss.

The government can try to regulate a natural monopoly to achieve the gains of productive efficiency (lower ATC) while preventing deadweight loss.

If the government regulates the natural monopoly to achieve allocative efficiency ($P = MC$), deadweight loss is eliminated but the firm will suffer losses. If the government regulates price such that normal profits are earned ($P = ATC$), then deadweight loss is not eliminated

Hiring with a Perfectly Competitive Factor Market

In a competitive factor market, firms can hire any quantity of the factor at the market price. Therefore, the marginal factor cost is constant at the market price. The *MFC* curve is the firm's supply curve for labor.

The benefit of hiring the next unit of a particular factor is the marginal product (*MP*) of that unit multiplied by the marginal revenue received from selling the product being produced. This is the marginal revenue product (*MRP*). The marginal revenue product curve is the firm's demand curve for labor.

The profit-maximizing hiring decision for ANY factor of production is to hire a factor until the *MRP* of the last unit hired is equal to the marginal cost of hiring it, shown on the graph as Q^*.

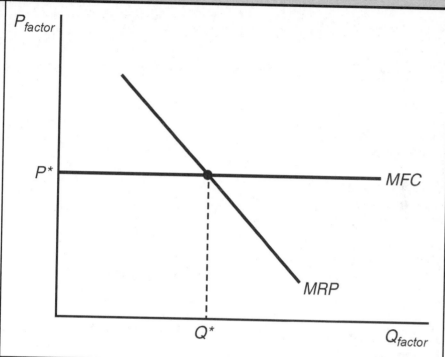

The profit-maximizing hiring decision is to hire units of a factor to the point at which marginal revenue product is equal to the market price of the factor.

For example, hiring workers, like other decisions in microeconomics, requires a comparison of the marginal benefit of the next worker (the MRP_L) to the marginal cost of the next worker. In perfectly competitive labor markets, each unit of labor can be hired at a constant wage *W*.

Hire a worker if: $MRP_L \geq W$

Don't hire a worker if: $MRP_L < W$

Stop hiring workers at the point at which: $MRP_L = W$.

The marginal revenue product curve is the demand curve for a factor. It will shift outward if:

A. the price of the output rises.

B. other factors become more available.

C. production technology improves.

Hiring with an Imperfectly Competitive Factor Market

When we assumed a perfectly competitive factor market, we assumed that many small firms could employ as much of a factor as they wish at the prevailing price. So the additional cost of hiring the next unit of a factor, or marginal factor cost (*MFC*), was constant. This meant that the supply of the factor was a horizontal line at the market price.

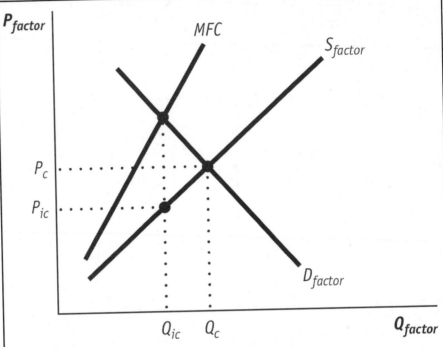

When there is one very large firm in the market it is called a monopsony. To hire more of a factor, a monopsony must increase the price it pays. This is because the factor supply curve is upward-sloping. The price of the factor must be increased for ALL units so the *MFC* rises as more of the factor is hired.

When a monopsony employer wants to hire one more unit of a factor, it must raise the price it pays. The price must also be increased for the factor units that came before. So when both the product market and the factor market are imperfectly competitive, the firm will still hire up to the point at which the *MRP* = *MFC*. However, the *MFC* curve will be upward-sloping and lie above the supply curve for the factor.

One thing we can see from the graph is that the factor is being paid less than its *MRP*. This is because a monopsony is the sole employer in the factor market. This monopsony power allows the employer to pay less for factors than if the factor market were perfectly competitive.

Positive Externality

When the production and consumption of a good provides benefits to third parties, that good is said to provide positive externalities to society.

The marginal private benefit (*MPB*) includes the benefits that go to consumers of a good – this is the market demand curve.

External benefits go to others (not the consumer). They are measured by the distance between the *MPB* (or *D*) curve and the *MSB* curve.

The sum of all private and external benefits is the total benefit received by society (*MSB*).

On an incremental basis, an additional unit of a good provides marginal social, marginal private, and marginal external benefits.

$MSB = MPB + MEB$

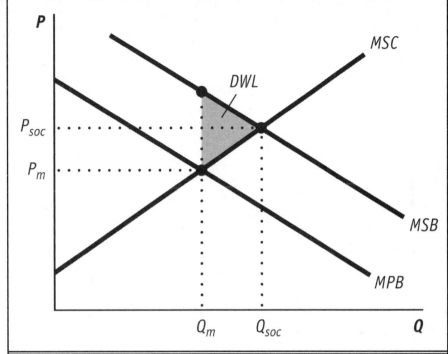

An unregulated private market will consider only private costs and benefits; Q_m and P_m are found where *MPB* equals *MPC* (which equals *MSC* in this case because there are no external costs).

The efficient price and quantity consider all costs and benefits; Q_{soc} and P_{soc} are found where $MSB = MSC$.

The unregulated market quantity (Q_m) is lower than the efficient quantity ($Qsoc$).

A subsidy (called a Pigouvian subsidy) equal to marginal external benefit internalizes the positive externality. Providing a subsidy equal to the external benefit of the good results in the exchange of the efficient level of output in the market, reducing deadweight loss in the market equal to the area shown in the graph.

Negative Externality

A negative externality exists when the production or consumption of a good imposes an uncompensated cost on society.

The marginal private cost (*MPC*) includes the costs of producing a good that are paid by producers– this is the market supply curve.

External costs fall on others (not the producer). They are measured by the distance between the *MPC* (or *S*) curve and the *MSC* curve.

The sum of all private and external costs is the total cost to society (*MSC*).

On an incremental basis, an additional unit of a good provides marginal social, marginal private, and marginal external costs.

$MSC = MPC + MEC$

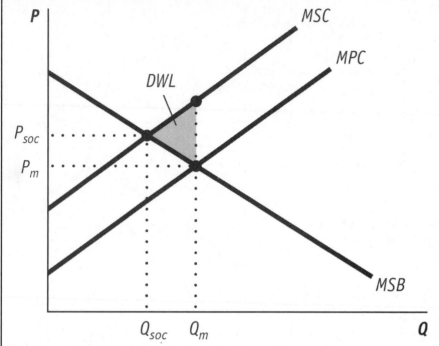

An unregulated private market will consider only private costs and benefits; Q_m and P_m are found where *MPB* (which equals *MSB* in this case because there are no external benefits) equals *MPC*.

The efficient price and quantity consider all costs and benefits; Q_{soc} and P_{soc} are found where $MSB = MSC$.

The unregulated market quantity (Q_m) is higher than the efficient quantity (Q_{soc}).

A tax (called a Pigouvian tax) equal to marginal external cost internalizes the negative externality. Forcing the market to pay the total cost of the good results in the exchange of the efficient level of output in the market, reducing deadweight loss in the market equal to the area shown in the graph.

The Coase Theorem states that, so long as property rights are clearly defined and transaction costs are minimal, the market will find a private solution to the problem of externalitites.

VII. TEST-TAKING TIPS

Once you have mastered all of the course material, you are ready to begin reviewing for the AP® exam. Below is a description of the types of questions you will find on the exam, as well as tips and suggestions for how to answer these types of questions.

The Multiple-Choice Section

When you are taking the multiple-choice section of the exam, be careful that you do not spend too much time on any one question. Remember that you have 70 minutes to answer 60 questions, so don't get stuck on any one question. Skip and return to a difficult question or make a guess if you have no idea how to answer it. Also, be very careful that you fill in the correct bubble for your answer (be especially careful if you do skip a question) and that each bubble is filled in neatly.

Unlike tests that you might take in a class, the AP® exams do not use all of the above, none of the above, or true/false type questions. Instead, the multiple-choice questions you will encounter will come in several different formats, e.g. define or classify, cause and effect, calculate an answer, and interpret a graph. The common types of questions are discussed below.

Define/Classify Format

This format asks you to simply identify or classify information. These are often the simplest questions and require that you have read and understood the material. Read through each question carefully and then analyze the answer choices. Some of the answer choices will contain 'correct' information in them, but they may not be relevant to the question being asked, so avoid the temptation to skim the question and look for the first 'true' thing you see. Make sure the answer matches the question being asked.

Question: Which of the following is true when the production of a good results in a positive externality?
  a. The government must produce the good.
  b. The private market will produce too much of the good.
  c. The private market price will be too high.*
  d. The government must prevent production of the good.
  e. Private firms will not be able to earn profits.

Cause-and-Effect Format

The cause-and-effect format questions are quite popular on the AP® Microeconomics exam and can be a real challenge unless you have a strategy. The strategy that works well for many successful students is to analyze a single column and see what distractors you can eliminate. For example, in the following question you are asked to determine which answer best describes what will happen to demand and equilibrium price and quantity in the market. If you know that the scenario presented will result in an increase in demand, then you can immediately eliminate answer choices a. and b. If you also know that an increase in demand will increase quantity, then you can eliminate choice c. and d. You have your answer and you did not even look at the other column.

Question: What is the effect on equilibrium price and quantity in the market for good Y if the price of a complement in consumption decreases?

Demand	Quantity	Price
a. decrease	increase	decrease
b. decrease	decrease	decrease
c. increase	decrease	decrease
d. increase	decrease	increase
e. increase	increase	increase*

Calculation

When answering calculation questions, pull out the relevant information from the question to use in your calculations. For example, in the following question income changes from 50 to 70 (you can drop the zeros to make it easier to calculate elasticity) and quantity demanded changes from 900 to 1,100. Write these numbers down where you will complete your calculations so you don't have to keep rereading the questions to find the numbers you need. Eliminate any answers you know cannot be correct before you complete your calculations. For example, when you read the following question, note that there is a positive relationship between income and the quantity purchased (quantity went up when income went up), which tells you that the income elasticity will be positive and allows you to exclude choices c. and d.

Question: Eric's income increases from $50,000 to $70,000 and his purchases of good X increase from 900 to 1,100. What is Eric's income elasticity of demand?

    a. 0.6*
    b. 1.67
    c. -0.6
    d. -1.67
    e. 0

Graphic Interpretation

AP® Economics exams will frequently ask you to refer to a graph to answer questions. These questions require you to understand what is shown on the graph provided. Pay close attention to the specific information provided on the graph – especially the labels on the axes of the graph - as you determine your answer.

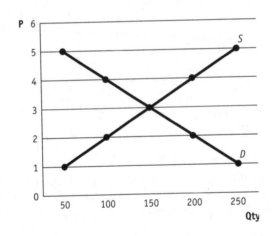

Question: In the preceding diagram, an increase in quantity demanded is best shown as a
    a. shift of the demand curve to the right.
    b. shift of the supply curve to the right.
    c. shift of the demand curve to the left.
    d. leftward movement along the demand curve.
    e. rightward movement along the demand curve*.

The Free-Response Section

The second section of the AP® Economics exams is made up of free-response questions. You will have 60 minutes to answer the free-response questions in the designated areas in your answer booklet. Make sure you use your time wisely by outlining your answers and using graphs, symbols, and abbreviations where applicable. Note: the readers who score your free-response questions will only see answers written in the designated area of your answer book, so do not write anything on the question sheet.

Remember that someone will eventually read and score the answers that you write. The easier it is to find and follow your answers, the easier it is to give you points! Practice writing clear, concise, organized answers. Clearly label the question number in the box on the top of each answer booklet page that you use. Denote which part of the question you are answering as you write your answer. Provide a clear, organized answer to each part of the question. Use the scoring guides provided for the practice tests that follow as an example of a clear, complete, concise, organized response and strive to use a similar format for your answer. But don't be concerned if you must answer questions out of order, cross out an answer and start again, include extraneous information, etc. Exam readers will do their best to award you the points that you deserve – it is just in your best interest to make that as easy as possible for them!

You should also make sure that you answer each part of each question to the best of your ability. Even if you are unsure of the correct answer, write something. You may actually know more than you think. Also, make sure that you answer each part of the question even when you think your answer on an earlier part may not be correct. Each part of a free-response question is scored independently, so an incorrect answer on one part of a question does not mean you can't receive points for a subsequent part.

The free-response section is divided into three separate questions. The first question is the longest and most comprehensive; you should allocate roughly half of your time, about 30 minutes, to answering it. The second and third free-response questions are shorter and typically test a particular area of the course outline. You should allocate roughly a quarter of the time available, or about 15 minutes, to each of the shorter questions. Allocate and monitor your time carefully so that you are able to provide at least a basic response to each question. Each question usually has parts that require a simple "coin-flip" response, e.g. yes/no or increase/decrease. Make sure you take the time to at least answer these parts of every question. Under no circumstances should you leave a free-response question unanswered. Omission is a guarantee of no points and therefore probably no 5.

In the free-response section, read each question carefully. Pay close attention to what each question is specifically asking. According to the experts, i.e. those who score your responses, one of the best ways to make sure you receive maximum points for your answer is to read the question and do *exactly* what it says. Following are examples of some of the phrases and terms used in free-response questions and the responses that should go with them.

'Draw a correctly labeled graph' - Draw the required diagram and *correctly label* the axes and curves on the graph!

Question: (i) Draw a correctly labeled supply and demand graph. On your graph, indicate consumer surplus.
Response:

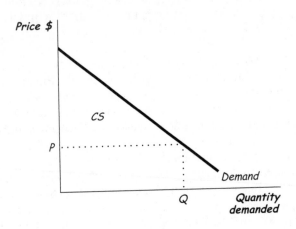

'Show' - This tells you to go back to a graph that you have previously drawn and clearly change that graph.

Question: (ii) Show the effect of an increase in price on the amount of consumer surplus shown in part (i).
Response:

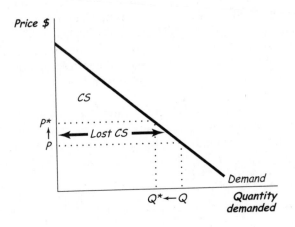

'Identify' - Make an assertion based on the information given in the question.

Question: Identify the effect of a decrease in supply on price.
Response: Price increases.

'Explain' - Go beyond the assertion and describe why the assertion you made happened.

Question: Identify the effect of a decrease in supply on price. Explain.
Response: When supply decreases, the supply curve shifts to the left and the new equilibrium price is higher.

'List' - Make a bulleted list of items.

Question: List three examples of entry barriers.
Response: patents
economies of scale
ownership of resources

'Define' - Write a definition.

Question: Define marginal product.
Response: Marginal product is the additional output produced as a result of hiring an additional unit of an input.

'Calculate' - Do some math and find a numerical answer!!!

Question: If fixed costs equal $1,000 and the average variable cost of producing 100 equals $5, what is the total cost of producing 100?
Response: $TC = TFC + TVC$. If AVC of producing 100 is $5, then TVC is $5 × 100 = $500, so $TC = 1,000 + 500 = $1,500$ <-- ANSWER!!!

VIII. PRACTICE TESTS

You should use the following sample tests to help you prepare for your AP® Microeconomics exam. Allow yourself 70 minutes to complete the multiple-choice section without using a calculator or any outside resources. There is no penalty for guessing, so attempt each question. After you have completed the multiple-choice section, give yourself 60 minutes to complete the free-response questions.

Answers and explanations along with scoring guidelines for the free-response section are available to your teacher on our website at bcs.worthpublishers.com/krugmanap2e.

Practice Test #1

Multiple-Choice Questions

1. Every economic issue involves, at its core, the existence of
   a. scarcity.
   b. costs.
   c. unlimited human wants.
   d. government policies.
   e. markets.

2. A student attending her first year of college pays $12,000 for tuition, books, and fees. If the student's next best alternative is to work and earn $20,000, what is her opportunity cost for the first year of college?
   a. zero, since the lost earnings are offset by the benefit of attending college
   b. $32,000
   c. $20,000
   d. $12,000
   e. $8,000

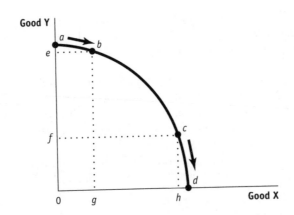

3. The preceding graph shows an economy's production possibilities curve for the production of goods X and Y. Assume that the economy is currently at point c. What is the opportunity cost of moving from point c to point d?
   a. 0g units of good Y
   b. 0f units of good Y
   c. 0h units of good X
   d. 0d units of good X
   e. 0f units of good X

4. Economic growth is shown using a production possibilities curve by which of the following?
   a. a leftward shift of the curve
   b. a rightward shift of the curve
   c. a rightward movement along the curve
   d. a leftward movement along the curve
   e. a movement from a point below the curve to a point on the curve

5. Which of the following enables a country to consume beyond its current production possibilities curve?

   a. trade with other countries, based on comparative advantage
   b. reducing unemployment, thus increasing output
   c. taking advantage of decreasing opportunity costs
   d. research and development leading to future advances in technology
   e. increases in productivity over time

6. Use the following table to answer this question. The table provides data for an economy's production possibilities curve.

Good X	Good Y
0	500
200	450
400	400
600	350

   If the economy is producing 400 units of Good X and 350 units of Good Y, which of the following must be true?

   a. The economy is engaging in trade.
   b. Production is efficient.
   c. There has been a technological advance.
   d. The economy is experiencing unemployment.
   e. Resources are being fully utilized.

7. According to the law of demand, an increase in the price of a product will do which of the following?
   a. decrease the demand for the product
   b. increase the demand for the product
   c. increase the demand for substitutes for the product
   d. increase the demand for complements to the product
   e. decrease the quantity of the product demanded

8. Which of the following will lead to a decrease in the price of a product?
   a. a decrease in income and an increase in wages
   b. an increase in population and an increase in input prices
   c. an increase in consumer preferences for the product and improvement in production technology
   d. a decrease in the price of a substitute product and an improvement in production technology
   e. a decrease in the price of a complement product and an increase in the price of an input

9. Assume that Good X is an inferior good. A family's consumption of Good X will
   a. increase when a family member wins the lottery.
   b. decrease when a family member gets a higher-paying job.
   c. never change as long as the family is meeting its minimum needs for the good.
   d. decrease when a family member loses a job.
   e. decrease when the price of a substitute good increases.

10. A leftward shift in the supply curve of oranges could be caused by an increase in which of the following?
    a. the price of oranges
    b. the wages of farm workers
    c. the demand for orange juice
    d. consumer incomes
    e. the number of orange groves

11. A government tax on the production of soda will result in which of the following in the market for soda?
    a. There will be a movement to the right along the supply curve.
    b. There will be a movement to the right along the demand curve.
    c. The supply curve will shift to the right.
    d. The supply curve will shift to the left.
    e. The demand curve will shift to the right.

12. There has just been a salmonella outbreak caused by the consumption of contaminated eggs. Which of the following changes in the egg market is most likely to occur as a result?
    a. The supply curve will shift to the right, increasing the price of eggs.
    b. The supply curve will shift to the right, decreasing the price of eggs.
    c. The demand curve will shift to the left, decreasing the price of eggs.
    d. The demand curve will shift to the right, increasing the price of eggs.
    e. Neither the supply nor the demand curve will shift; quantity will increase and price will decrease.

13. A competitive firm produces a product using labor and wood. The firm is initially in equilibrium. If the cost of wood suddenly decreases, which of the following will occur?
    a. The supply curve for the product will shift to the left.
    b. The firm's demand curve for wood will shift to the right.
    c. The firm will decrease the quantity supplied.
    d. The firm earns a profit in the long run.
    e. The firm's marginal costs will decrease at each level of output.

14. In a competitive market, which of the following changes in supply and demand will cause both the equilibrium price and quantity to increase?

Supply Curve	Demand Curve
a. decrease	decrease
b. decrease	no change
c. increase	increase
d. no change	increase
e. increase	decrease

Questions 15 and 16 refer to the following graph. *The market is currently in equilibrium.*

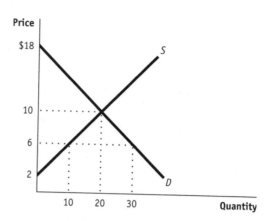

15. In a competitive equilibrium, what is the value of consumer surplus?
    a. $200
    b. $180
    c. $160
    d. $80
    e. $20

16. If a price floor is set at $6, price and quantity demanded will equal which of the following?

	Price	Quantity demanded
a.	$6	30
b.	$10	30
c.	$10	20
d.	$6	10
e.	$6	20

17. If a firm raises its prices by 5 percent and its total revenue increases by 5 percent, which of the following must be true of the price elasticity of demand for its product? It is
    a. less than zero.
    b. greater than zero.
    c. equal to zero.
    d. greater than one.
    e. unit elastic.

18. *Ceteris paribus*, the tax revenue generated from a tax will be greatest when the tax is imposed on a good with a more
    a. inelastic demand.
    b. elastic demand.
    c. elastic supply.
    d. elastic demand and supply.
    e. inelastic demand and elastic supply.

19. Which of the following must be true if total revenue increases when a firm decreases price?
    a. The supply is price elastic.
    b. The supply is income elastic.
    c. The supply is income inelastic.
    d. The demand is price elastic.
    e. The demand is price inelastic.

20. Assume a labor market has an effective minimum wage. If the supply of labor increases, which of the following will occur?
    a. Unemployment in that market will increase.
    b. Quantity of labor demanded will increase.
    c. Quantity of labor demanded will decrease.
    d. Market demand will increase.
    e. The market wage will decrease.

21. Which of the following decreases first as additional units of a product are consumed?
    a. total utility
    b. average utility
    c. marginal utility
    d. marginal product
    e. average product

22. The following table shows the total utility from consuming various quantities of pizza.

Slices of Pizza Consumed per Day	Total Utility
0	0
1	100
2	180
3	240
4	220
5	230

Which of the following statements is correct?
    a. The marginal utility from the first piece of pizza is 100 and the marginal utility from the second piece of pizza is 180.
    b. The marginal utility from the fourth slice of pizza is greater than the marginal utility from the fifth.
    c. Marginal utility increases at a constant rate.
    d. Diminishing marginal utility sets in with the consumption of the fifth slice of pizza.
    e. Marginal utility is greatest for the fourth slice of pizza.

23. Assume there are two goods, A and B. Consumer equilibrium occurs when which of the following is true?
    a. $TU_A/P_A = TU_B/P_B$
    b. $MU_A/P_A = MU_B/P_B$
    c. $TU_A = TU_B$
    d. $MU_A = MU_B$
    e. $(MU_A)(P_A) = (MU_B)(P_B)$

24. In the short run, a firm will shut down if price falls below
    a. *ATC.*
    b. *AVC.*
    c. *AFC.*
    d. *MC.*
    e. *TC.*

Refer to the following table to answer questions 25 and 26. The information is for a perfectly competitive firm.

Quantity	Average Variable Costs	Marginal Costs
0		
1	$55.00	$55.00
2	45.00	35.00
3	50.00	60.00
4	55.00	70.00
5	60.00	80.00
6	65.00	90.00

TFC = $200

25. The average total cost of producing 5 units of output is
    a. $60.00.
    b. $80.00.
    c. $100.00.
    d. $300.00.
    e. $400.00.

26. If the product price is $60, how many units of output will maximize profit?
    a. 0
    b. 1
    c. 3
    d. 5
    e. 6

27. Which of the following is true about the relationship between average cost and marginal cost? If average cost is rising, marginal cost is
    a. rising.
    b. falling.
    c. equal to average cost.
    d. above average cost.
    e. below average cost.

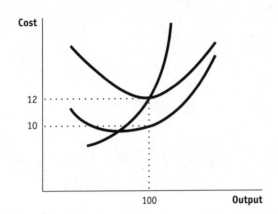

Cost

12

10

100 Output

Questions 28 and 29 refer to the preceding graph, which shows the cost curves for a perfectly competitive firm.

28. What is the fixed cost of producing an output of 100?
    a. $2
    b. $10
    c. $12
    d. $120
    e. $200

29. If marginal revenue is $10, which of the following statements is true? The firm will
    a. earn a normal profit.
    b. lose money in the short run.
    c. maximize profits by producing 100 units of output.
    d. maximize profits by producing less than 100 units of output.
    e. shut down in the long run.

30. Perfectly competitive firms are allocatively efficient because they produce at a level of output such that
    a. average cost is at a minimum.
    b. price equals marginal revenue.
    c. price equals marginal cost.
    d. price equals average total cost.
    e. the firm earns a normal profit.

31. Interdependence among firms is a distinguishing characteristic of what type of market structure?
    a. monopolistic competition
    b. perfect competition
    c. monopsony
    d. oligopoly
    e. monopoly

32. Which of the following makes it more difficult to maintain a collusive agreement?
    a. a small number of firms in the market
    b. complex products and pricing schemes
    c. many individual buyers
    d. agreement as to the division of profits between firms
    e. lawsuits to enforce agreements

33. Which of the following is true for a perfectly competitive firm in long-run equilibrium?
    a. Price equals marginal revenue.
    b. It is allocatively inefficient.
    c. Marginal cost is below average total cost.
    d. Average variable cost is at a minimum.
    e. It has no variable costs.

34. The supply curve for a perfectly competitive firm is
    a. its marginal cost curve.
    b. its average cost curve.
    c. the upward-sloping portion of its marginal cost curve.
    d. horizontal at the market price.
    e. its marginal cost curve to the right of where it crosses *AVC*.

35. Assume that a competitive industry is in long-run equilibrium. If the number of buyers in the market increases, what will happen to short-run price and output in the market and the number of firms in the industry in the long-run?

	Short-run price	Short-run industry output	Movement of firms
a.	Increase	Increase	Enter
b.	Increase	Decrease	Exit
c.	Decrease	Increase	Exit
d.	Decrease	Decrease	Enter
e.	Decrease	Decrease	Exit

36. In a perfectly competitive industry, the market price is $2. A firm produces at a level of output where average total cost is $3, marginal cost is $2, and average variable cost is $1. In the short run, the firm should
    a. decrease its price.
    b. increase its price.
    c. continue to produce, but decrease quantity.
    d. shut down.
    e. leave both price and output unchanged.

37. Assume a perfectly competitive firm is earning economic profits by producing and selling 500 units of output at a price of $10 per unit. If its marginal cost is $15, which of the following statements is correct?
    a. The firm is maximizing profits.
    b. The firm should increase production.
    c. The firm should decrease production.
    d. The firm should shut down in the long run but not the short run.
    e. The firm should shut down in the short run.

38. The typical firm in a monopolistically competitive industry earns zero profit in long-run equilibrium because
    a. advertising costs make monopolistic competition a high-cost market structure.
    b. the firms are price-takers.
    c. the industry has easy entry and exit.
    d. the firms in the industry do not engage in product differentiation.
    e. each firm sells a standardized product.

39. Compared with firms in perfectly competitive industries, firms in monopolistically competitive industries are inefficient because they
a. earn profits.
b. produce where price equals marginal cost.
c. charge lower prices.
d. don't produce at minimum average total cost.
e. waste resources by producing an excess amount of output.

Questions 40 and 41 refer to the following graph.

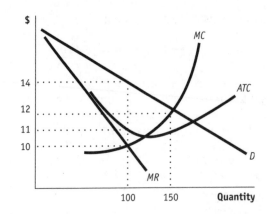

40. Which of the following statements about the firm shown above is correct?
a. Its profit-maximizing price is $10.
b. Its profit-maximizing output level is 100 units.
c. Its maximum profit is $200.
d. If it produces 150 units, it will earn no economic profits.
e. At the profit-maximizing level of output, its total cost is $1,000.

41. Compared to the outcome if the industry were perfectly competitive, a monopoly will produce _____ and charge _____.
a. 50 fewer, $2 more
b. 50 fewer, $2 less
c. 50 more, $3 more
d. 50 more, $4 more
e. the same output, $4

42. A natural monopoly occurs in an industry when
a. diseconomies of scale allow only one firm to exist in that market.
b. one firm controls an essential natural resource.
c. a single firm can produce the entire industry output.
d. average total cost is declining over the relevant output range.
e. above-normal profits persist in the industry.

43. A justification for government regulation of a monopoly is that the unregulated monopoly charges a price that
a. allows it to earn a normal profit.
b. is above marginal cost.
c. is above average total cost.
d. is less than the allocatively efficient price.
e. results in the sale of more than the efficient quantity.

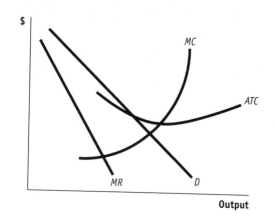

44. The preceding graph shows a firm's long-run cost and revenue curves. If the firm maximizes profit, it
a. will produce where demand is inelastic.
b. is operating at a loss.
c. can produce at any level of output.
d. will experience economies of scale.
e. produces the efficient level of output.

45. Which of the following is true at the profit-maximizing equilibrium of a single price monopolist?
a. $P = ATC$
b. $P > MC$
c. $MR > MC$
d. ATC will be minimized.
e. MC will be minimized.

46. Which of the following is true if a firm engages in price discrimination? The firm
a. is a price taker.
b. is not maximizing profits.
c. does not set $MC = MR$.
d. reduces consumer surplus.
e. improves efficiency in the market.

47. Which of the following is true for both a monopoly and a perfectly competitive firm?
a. $P = MC$
b. MC is declining at the profit-maximizing level of output.
c. $P = ATC$ in the long run.
d. $AVC = MC$ when AVC is at a minimum.
e. AVC decreases as production increases.

48. Which of the following statements is true for a monopoly but is *not* true for a perfectly competitive firm?
a. The firm's price is equal to marginal revenue.
b. The firm cannot affect the market price for its good.
c. It is easy for firms to enter the industry.
d. The demand for the firm's product is perfectly inelastic.
e. The firm must lower its price in order to sell more of its product.

49. The wage rate is $20 per hour and the last worker hired by the firm increased output by 100 units. Computers rent for $50 per hour and the last computer rented by the firm increased output by 200 units. If the firm is producing the desired level of output, what should the firm do to minimize costs?
    a. Hire more workers and rent more computers because the marginal revenue products of both workers and computers are greater than their respective prices.
    b. Hire more workers and reduce the number of computers rented because the marginal product per dollar spent is higher for workers.
    c. Lay off workers and rent more computers because computers produce more output per dollar of additional expenditure.
    d. Lay off workers and rent more computers because computers produce more output.
    e. Keep the same number of workers and computers because the marginal revenue products of both workers are positive.

50. Which of the following will shift the demand for high school teachers to the left?
    a. a decrease in the teenage population
    b. a decrease in teachers' wages
    c. an increase in the marginal productivity of teachers
    d. an increase in the value of a high school diploma
    e. development of educational technology used by teachers

51. Which of the following is most likely to increase the supply of nurses?
    a. an increase in nurses' salaries
    b. an increase in the average salary paid to doctors
    c. an increase in scholarships for nursing school
    d. the imposition of stricter requirements for nursing certification
    e. an increase in the demand for healthcare

52. An increase in which of the following will cause a shift in the demand curve for farmland?
    a. demand for agricultural products
    b. wages of farm workers
    c. supply of farm machinery
    d. supply of farmland
    c. rate of increase in "urban sprawl"

53. Good A is produced in a competitive market. If the price of good A increases, which of the following will occur in the market for workers who produce good A?

	Demand for labor	Number of workers hired	Wage
a.	Increase	Increase	Increase
b.	Increase	Increase	Decrease
c.	Increase	Decrease	Increase
d.	Decrease	Increase	Increase
e.	Decrease	Decrease	Decrease

Number of workers	Number of car washes produced per day
0	0
1	8
2	15
3	21
4	26
5	29
6	31
7	32

54. Given the production information in the preceding table, how many workers will be employed if the wage rate is $20.00 per day and the price of a car wash is $10?
   a. 0
   b. 1
   c. 2
   d. 4
   e. 6

55. In a market economy, public goods such as fire protection are provided by the government because
   a. private firms are less efficient at producing fire protection than local governments.
   b. the market will not provide fire protection.
   c. the market will not provide the efficient amount of fire protection.
   d. efficiency requires that those who benefit from fire protection pay taxes.
   e. fire protection does not have a high marginal benefit.

56. Private provision of a public good will lead to less than the efficient level of provision of the good due to the
   a. free-rider problem.
   b. problem of imperfect competition.
   c. higher costs of private firms.
   d. existence of positive externalities.
   e. overuse of these goods.

57. Assume the production of a good results in a negative externality. The government can increase efficiency in the market by
   a. providing the good itself.
   b. subsidizing producers.
   c. instituting a Pigouvian tax.
   d. enforcing antitrust laws.
   e. imposing a price ceiling.

58. Which of the following shows the distribution of income in an economy by plotting percentage of households on one axis and percentage of income on the other axis?

   a. Gini coefficient
   b. Lorenz curve
   c. Phillips curve
   d. Nash equilibrium
   e. Herfindahl index

Refer to the following graph to answer question 59.

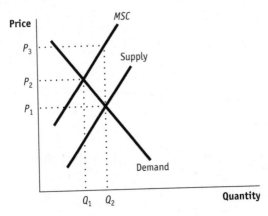

59. To achieve the optimal level of output of the good produced in this market, the government should impose a Pigouvian _____ equal to _____.

   a. tax; $(P_3 - P_2)$
   b. tax; $(P_3 - P_1)$
   c. tax; $(P_2 - P_1)$
   d. subsidy; $(P_3 - P_1)$
   e. subsidy; $(P_2 - P_1)$

60. Which of the following best states the goal of antitrust legislation?

   a. promoting product differentiation
   b. preventing economic profits
   c. eliminating negative externalities
   d. moving markets toward competitive outcomes
   e. restricting overuse of scarce resources

Free-Response Questions

1. Assume that there is only one firm supplying good X and that the firm charges a single price and maximizes its profits.

   a. Draw a correctly labeled graph showing each of the following if the firm is earning an economic profit.

   (i)   Monopoly output, labeled Q_m
   (ii)   Monopoly price, labeled P_m
   (iii)   The amount of the firm's profit

   b. Now use your graph to compare the monopoly outcome to the outcome if the market were perfectly competitive by showing each of the following on your graph:

   (i)   The level of output with competition, labeled Q_{pc}
   (ii)   The price with competition, labeled P_{pc}

   c. Identify the deadweight loss from monopoly on your graph. What happens to the value of each of the following with monopoly rather than competition in this market?

   (i)   Consumer surplus
   (ii)   Producer surplus

2. Assume the market for good X is a duopoly and each firm must decide whether or not to advertise its product.

    a. Construct the payoff matrix for the firm if the following describes the alternative outcomes they face:

        If a firm does not advertise, it adds zero to its current profit.
        If both firms advertise, sales increase and each firm will add $10,000 to its current profit.
        If one firm advertises and the other does not, the firm that advertises will add $15,000 to its profits.

    b. What is the dominant strategy for each firm?

        (i)   Firm 1
        (ii)   Firm 2

    c. Is there a Nash equilibrium in this situation? Explain.

3. Assume the market for unskilled labor in a large city is competitive.

    a. Draw a correctly labeled graph showing equilibrium price and quantity in the labor market.

    b. Assume the government enacts an effective minimum wage. On your graph, identify each of the following:

(i)   The minimum wage
(ii)   The quantity supplied (label this Q_s) and quantity demanded (label this Q_d) at the minimum wage

c. Use the quantities identified on your graph to identify the result of the minimum wage in this market.

d. What happens as the result of the minimum wage in the market if the supply of unskilled workers increases? Explain.

Practice Test #2

Multiple-Choice Questions

1. Eric has three choices for how to spend his Saturday afternoon. He could work at home and earn $40 or work at the library and earn $48. He chooses instead to spend the afternoon studying at the library. What is Eric's opportunity cost?
   a. $8
   b. $40
   c. $48
   d. $88
   e. staying home

2. You are dining out at an all-you-can-eat buffet. After two trips to the buffet, you decide not to eat any more. Which of the following must be true of the third serving of food?
   a. Marginal cost exceeds the marginal benefit.
   b. Marginal benefit is less than or equal to zero.
   c. Marginal cost is positive.
   d. Net marginal benefit is positive.
   e. Marginal benefit is increasing.

3. Which of the following statements is true of a market economy? Resources are primarily
   a. owned by the public.
   b. allocated through the price system.
   c. allocated through government agencies.
   d. controlled by large businesses.
   e. acquired from other countries.

4. Canada trades timber to the United States in exchange for trucks. If the two countries are trading based on comparative advantage, which of the following must be true?
   a. Canada has an absolute advantage in timber production, and the United States has an absolute advantage in truck production.
   b. The United States has an absolute advantage in timber production, and Canada has an absolute advantage in truck production.
   c. The United States has a comparative advantage in timber production.
   d. Canada has a comparative advantage in truck production.
   e. The United States has a lower opportunity cost of producing trucks.

5. If a market is in equilibrium, which of the following will cause both price and quantity to fall?
   a. an increase in demand
   b. an increase in supply
   c. a decrease in demand
   d. a decrease in supply
   e. a decrease in both demand and supply

6. Which of the following is the best example of a public good?
   a. an ocean fishery
   b. a cable television broadcast
   c. a bologna sandwich
   d. national defense
   e. an amusement park

7. If the government sets a price ceiling below equilibrium price in a market, which of the following would occur?
   a. A shortage would occur.
   b. A surplus would occur.
   c. The market would not be affected.
   d. Prices would rise.
   e. The quantity sold would increase.

8. Which of the following would shift the supply curve for a good to the left?
   a. an increase in price
   b. an advance in production technology
   c. a decrease in consumer income if the good were a normal good
   d. an increase in the cost of a production input
   e. an increase in the number of suppliers of the good

9. If the price of a good increases, total revenue for the sale of the good will
   a. decrease if demand is price elastic.
   b. increase if demand is price elastic.
   c. decrease if demand is price inelastic.
   d. increase if demand is unit elastic.
   e. decrease if demand is unit elastic.

10. Assume you can choose between two goods, X and Y. If you are currently spending all of your income and the marginal utility of X is 10 and the marginal utility of Y is 20, which of the following is true if the price of X is $5 and the price of Y is $10? To maximize your utility you should consume
   a. more X and less Y.
   b. more Y and less X.
   c. less X and less Y.
   d. more X and the same amount of Y.
   e. your current combination of X and Y.

11. Which of the following is most likely to create a positive externality?
   a. pollution
   b. a half-price coupon
   c. a flu shot
   d. cigarette smoking
   e. a concert ticket

12. Economics is best described as the study of how
   a. money circulates through the economy.
   b. scarce resources are allocated among unlimited wants.
   c. unlimited resources are allocated among scarce wants.
   d. businesses make profits.
   e. nations trade goods across international borders.

13. If the elasticity of demand for a good is greater than one, an excise tax imposed on its production will change price, quantity, and expenditures in the market in which of the following ways?

Price	Quantity	Expenditures
a. Decrease	Increase	Increase
b. Decrease	Increase	Decrease
c. Decrease	Decrease	Decrease
d. Increase	Increase	Decrease
e. Increase	Decrease	Decrease

14. An effective minimum wage will lead to which of the following?
    a. an increase in the quantity of labor demanded
    b. a decrease in the quantity of labor demanded
    c. a decrease in the quantity of labor supplied
    d. a shortage in the market
    e. an increase in income

15. If a 10% increase in income leads to a 20% decrease in the quantity of a good purchased, which of the following is true? The income elasticity of demand for the good is
    a. 0.5 and it is a normal good.
    b. 2 and it is a normal good.
    c. -0.5 and it is a normal good.
    d. -2 and it is an inferior good.
    e. -0.5 and it is an inferior good.

16. Which of the following is most likely to increase the demand for pencils? A decrease in
    a. the price of lead
    b. the price of pens
    c. the price of paper
    d. consumer income
    e. the price of pencils

Questions 17 – 19 refer to the following graph showing an economy that can produce cars or corn.

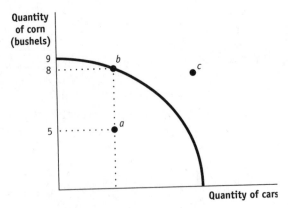

17. Which of the following points represents an efficient level of production?
    a. a
    b. b
    c. c
    d. a and b
    e. b and c

18. Which of the following must be true if the country produces at point c next year?
a. There is an advance in technology.
b. The economy experiences a decline in natural resources.
c. The economy begins to trade with other countries.
d. The rate of unemployment decreases.
e. The price level falls.

19. What is the opportunity cost of a movement from point a to point b?
a. 0 cars
b. 20 cars
c. 3 bushels of corn
d. 4 bushels of corn
e. 5 bushels of corn

20. The deadweight loss from monopoly is the result of the monopoly
a. earning a profit.
b. setting $MC = MR$.
c. earning long-run normal profits.
d. setting price above MC.
e. setting price above ATC.

21. Producer surplus will increase as a result of which of the following?
a. a decrease in price
b. an increase in demand
c. a decrease in demand
d. a movement toward competition in the market
e. an increase in input costs

22. In a perfectly competitive market, if the additional cost of producing an additional unit of output is constant, which of the following is true of the firm's supply curve? It will be
a. perfectly inelastic.
b. upward-sloping.
c. horizontal.
d. unit elastic.
e. equal to the price of the product.

23. Assume you received 20 units of utility from consuming your first donut and your total utility is 35 after consuming a second donut. If your donut consumption follows the law of diminishing marginal utility, your marginal utility from consuming a third donut will equal which of the following?
a. 10
b. 15
c. 20
d. 40
e. more than 35

24. When a firm is earning an accounting profit, which of the following is true?
a. $P = ATC$
b. $TR > TC$
c. $TR >$ total explicit costs
d. $TR >$ total implicit costs
e. $P > ATC$

25. If the cross-price elasticity of demand between two goods is +2, it means that the two goods are
    a. normal goods.
    b. inferior goods.
    c. complements.
    d. substitutes.
    e. elastic.

26. Which of the following is true of a firm's factors of production in the short run?
    a. All factors are fixed.
    b. Some factors are variable.
    c. At least one factor is fixed.
    d. All factors are variable.
    e. At least one factor is variable.

27. If the total product of capital is increasing at an increasing rate, which of the following is true?
    a. Marginal product of capital is rising.
    b. Marginal product of capital is at a minimum.
    c. Marginal product of capital is at a maximum.
    d. Marginal cost of capital is rising.
    e. Average product of capital is at its minimum.

28. For a perfectly competitive firm, the demand curve for its product is equal to the
    a. marginal cost curve starting where it equals AVC.
    b. market price of the product.
    c. marginal revenue product curve.
    d. marginal product curve.
    e. AVC curve at the profit-maximizing level of output.

29. In the long run, which of the following will be true for a perfectly competitive firm?
    a. $P > MR = MC = ATC$
    b. $P = MR = MC > ATC$
    c. $P > MR = MC > ATC$
    d. $P = MR = MC = ATC$
    e. $P = MR > MC > ATC$

30. In the long run, firms will enter an industry when which of the following is true?
    a. $MR > MC$
    b. $MR < ATC$
    c. $P > MC$
    d. $P > ATC$
    e. $P > AVC$

31. If firms in an oligopoly market collude, the market will move toward which of the following?
    a. allocative efficiency
    b. normal profits
    c. the Nash equilibrium
    d. the monopoly price and quantity
    e. the long-run equilibrium price in perfect competition

32. A firm is maximizing profit in a perfectly competitive market. Price is $12 and quantity is 10. Total variable costs are $50 and total fixed costs are $100. Which of the following is true? The firm should
   a. produce in the short run, with profits of $30.
   b. produce in the short run, with losses of $30.
   c. produce in the short run, with profits of $70.
   d. shut down in the short run, with losses of $30.
   e. shut down in the long run, with losses of $60.

33. Which of the following is true of a monopolistic market?
   a. There is allocative efficiency because $MC = MR$.
   b. The firm will earn an economic profit in the short run and the long run.
   c. Collusion leads to a price above marginal cost.
   d. Firms will enter the market in response to profits.
   e. Barriers to entry allow price to exceed marginal cost.

Questions 34 – 36 refer to the following graph.

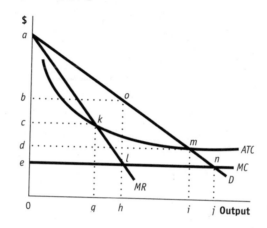

34. The profit-maximizing price and quantity are
   a. $0b$ and $0h$.
   b. $0c$ and $0g$.
   c. $0d$ and $0i$.
   d. $0e$ and $0j$.
   e. $0e$ and $0h$.

35. The deadweight loss created by this monopoly is equal to which of the following areas?
   a. *aen*
   b. *abo*
   c. *lno*
   d. *ebol*
   e. *ebom*

36. If this monopoly were regulated so that it earned a normal profit, which of the following would be true?
   a. Price would equal $0e$ and total revenue would equal $0enj$.
   b. Price would equal $0d$ and total revenue would equal $0dmi$.
   c. Price would equal $0c$ and total revenue would equal $0boh$.
   d. Price would equal $0e$ and total revenue would equal $0elh$.
   e. Price would equal $0e$ and total revenue would equal zero.

37. When the average product of labor is equal to the marginal product of labor, which of the following is true?
   a. MPL is at its maximum.
   b. ATC is at its minimum.
   c. TPL is at its maximum.
   d. MC is at its minimum.
   e. MC is equal to minimum AVC.

Questions 38 – 39 refer to the following graph.

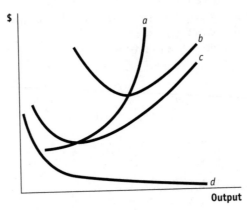

38. The curve labeled *a* represents which of the following?
   a. AFC
   b. AVC
   c. ATC
   d. MP
   e. MC

39. Which of the following is true about the curves depicted in the preceding graph?
   a. *d* will eventually decrease to zero.
   b. *c* and *b* will intersect when output is maximized.
   c. At any output level, the value of *a* is equal to the difference between *b* and *c*.
   d. *b* has a "U" shape due to economies of scale.
   e. *c* is the average variable cost curve.

40. Which of the following is true for monopolistically competitive firms? They
   a. produce a homogeneous product.
   b. will never earn a profit due to entry and exit.
   c. differentiate and advertise their products.
   d. eliminate excess capacity.
   e. often collude to raise their profits.

41. When a monopolistically competitive firm is in long-run equilibrium, which of the following is true?
   a. $P = ATC = MR = MC$
   b. $P = ATC > MR = MC$
   c. $P > ATC > MR = MC$
   d. $P > ATC > MR > MC$
   e. $P = ATC > MR > MC$

42. If firms are exiting a monopolistically competitive market, which of the following is true?
 a. Firms are not maximizing profits.
 b. The demand curve for remaining firms will shift to the right.
 c. Profits for existing firms will decrease.
 d. The supply curve for existing firms will shift to the right.
 e. The market price of the product will fall.

43. In a competitive market for construction workers, which of the following will decrease demand?
 a. an increase in the wage rate
 b. implementation of an effective minimum wage
 c. a decrease in the demand for new houses
 d. an increase in construction worker productivity
 e. government subsidies for construction worker training programs

44. Antitrust laws are used to do which of the following?
 a. make monopolies illegal
 b. prevent deadweight loss
 c. ensure productive efficiency
 d. prevent higher levels of output
 e. correct for negative externalities

45. Which of the following describes what would happen to the wage and employment in a labor market if it changed from perfect competition into a monopsony?

	Wage	*Employment*
a.	Decrease	Decrease
b.	Decrease	Increase
c.	Increase	Decrease
d.	Increase	Increase
e.	Decrease	No change

Questions 46 – 48 refer to the following table.

Units of labor	Total Product (# of cups per hour)
0	0
1	8
2	18
3	26
4	32
5	36
6	38
7	36

46. What is the marginal product of the fifth unit of labor?
    a. 68
    b. 36
    c. 32
    d. 4
    e. 2

47. If the product market is perfectly competitive and the price of the product is $5, what is the marginal revenue product of the third worker?
    a. $130
    b. $44
    c. $40
    d. $32
    e. $8

48. If the product market and the factor market are perfectly competitive and the product price and the wage are $5 and $10, respectively, how many workers will the firm hire?
    a. 0
    b. 1
    c. 2
    d. 4
    e. 6

49. Which of the following best describes an oligopoly?
    a. normal profits in the long run
    b. incentives for collusive behavior
    c. many small firms
    d. barriers to entry
    e. independence

50. Which of the following would lead to a decrease in the supply of unskilled workers?
    a. an effective minimum wage
    b. an increase in government worker training programs
    c. a decrease in the wage rate in the market for unskilled labor
    d. a high unemployment rate
    e. an increase in immigration

51. Suppose a firm is producing the profit-maximizing level of output and the *MP* of capital and labor are 10 and 20, respectively. If the rental rate for capital is $25 and the wage rate is $10, which of the following is true? To minimize costs, the firm should
    a. use more capital.
    b. hire more labor and use less capital.
    c. hire less labor and use more capital.
    d. hire less labor.
    e. continue using the current levels of capital and labor.

52. If more college graduates decide to go to law school, what will happen to the demand for the LSAT (Law School Admission Test) and to wages and employment in the market for lawyers?

Demand for LSAT	Wages	Employment
a. Increase	Increase	Increase
b. Increase	Decrease	Decrease
c. Decrease	Decrease	Increase
d. Decrease	Increase	Increase
e. Increase	Decrease	Increase

53. In a perfectly competitive labor market, firms hire labor up to the point where the wage is equal to which of the following?
   a. *MFC* of labor
   b. *MP* of labor
   c. *MRP* of labor
   d. *MR*
   e. *MP* of labor divided by the wage

54. If a person making $50,000 per year pays a 10% income tax and a person who makes $60,000 per year pays a 5% income tax, the tax system is which of the following?
   a. progressive
   b. proportional
   c. regressive
   d. excise
   e. confiscatory

55. Private provision of a public good will lead to less than the efficient level of provision of the good due to the
   a. free-rider problem.
   b. problem of imperfect competition.
   c. higher costs of private firms.
   d. existence of positive externalities.
   e. overuse of these goods.

56. Assume that production of a good results in a positive externality. The government can increase efficiency in the market by
   a. providing the good itself.
   b. subsidizing production of the good.
   c. instituting a Pigouvian tax.
   d. enforcing antitrust laws.
   e. imposing a price ceiling.

57. Which of the following is true when the production of a good results in negative externalities?
   a. The government must produce the good.
   b. The market will produce more than the optimal quantity of the good.
   c. The market price will be too high.
   d. The market will produce less than the optimal quantity of the good.
   e. The government should impose a Pigouvian subsidy.

58. A Lorenz curve that lies along the horizontal axis for all percentages of the population up to 99%, and then equals 100% when the percentage of the population is 100 indicates that
    a. income is equally distributed in the economy.
    b. income is concentrated in the hands of the middle quintile of income earners.
    c. all of a country's income goes to one person.
    d. all of a country's income is divided between two people.
    e. the average income in the country is equal to the highest income in the country.

Refer to the following graph to answer questions 59 and 60.

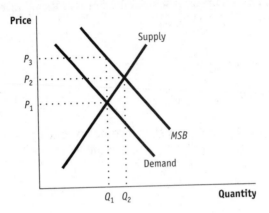

59. Production in this market creates which of the following?
    a. a negative externality
    b. a positive externality
    c. a public good
    d. external costs
    e. a shortage of the good

60. To achieve the optimal level of output of the good produced in this market, the government should impose a Pigouvian _____ equal to _____.
    a. tax, $(P_3 - P_2)$
    b. tax, $(P_3 - P_1)$
    c. tax, $(P_2 - P_1)$
    d. subsidy, $(P_3 - P_1)$
    e. subsidy, $(P_2 - P_1)$

Free-Response Questions

1. Assume that goods X and Y are complementary goods produced in perfectly competitive markets and that the two markets are in long-run equilibrium.

   a. Suppose the price of good X increases. Draw a correctly labeled graph of the market for good Y, showing each of the following:
      (i) the equilibrium price and quantity in the market for good Y before the increase in the price of good X (label these P_1 and Q_1)
      (ii) the equilibrium price and quantity in the market for good Y after the increase in the price of good X (label these P_2 and Q_2)

   b. Draw a correctly labeled graph of a representative firm producing good Y. On your graph, show each of the following:
      (i) the market price of good Y before and after the change described in part (a) (Label these P_1 and P_2.)
      (ii) the quantity produced by the firm before and after the change described in part (a) (Label these Q_1 and Q_2.)
      (iii) the profit or loss incurred by the firm after the change described in part (a). Is this area a profit or a loss?

   c. What will happen in the long run as a result of the decrease in demand for good X? Explain.

2. Assume that the market for unskilled labor in a city is perfectly competitive.
   a. Draw correctly labeled side-by-side graphs of the market for unskilled labor and a firm that hires unskilled labor. On your graphs, label each of the following:
      (i)   the supply and demand curves for labor
      (ii) the equilibrium wage
      (iii) the quantity of labor hired

   b. Suppose the productivity of unskilled workers increases. Show how this will affect the equilibrium wage and employment of unskilled workers.

3. A paper mill is located along the bank of a river. The mill dumps the pollution that results from paper production directly into the river. Draw a correctly labeled graph of the market for paper and show each of the following.
   a. The market equilibrium price and quantity (label these P_1 and Q_1).
   b. The marginal private cost, marginal social cost, and marginal external cost of paper production.

   c. Identify an appropriate policy to achieve the socially optimal level of paper production.